institute of f

Administration of Trusts

Nigel A Clayton
LL.B., LLM., (London)
of Lincoln's Inn, Barrister-at-Law
Lecturer in Law, City University

The Institute of Financial Services
c/o The Chartered Institute of Bankers
Emmanuel House
4–9 Burgate Lane
Canterbury
Kent CT1 2XJ
United Kingdom

Institute of Financial Services Publications are published by The Chartered Institute of Bankers, a non-profit making registered educational charity, and are distributed exclusively by Bankers Books Limited which is a wholly owned subsidiary of the Chartered Institute of Bankers.

Typeset by Digital Type

ISBN 0-85297-416-7

Contents

Introduction

Administration of Trusts

The Concept of the Course

This is a practical course written for students studying for banking and finance qualifications and also for practitioners in the financial services industry who are looking for a practical refresher. This study text is structured so that many will find it to be the most coherent way of learning the subject.

This book is the set text for the Administration of Trusts option of the ACIB-Degree link and for the compulsory subject in the Diploma of Trust and Estate Practice.

Each chapter or unit of the Study Text is divided into sections and contains:

- learning objectives

- an introduction, indicating how this subject area relates to others to which the reader may have cause to refer

- clear, concise topic-by-topic coverage

- examples and activities to reinforce learning, confirm understanding and stimulate thought

- usually, an exam-style question to try for practice.

Activities

Activities are provided throughout to enable you to check your progress as you work through the text. These come in a variety of forms; some test your ability to analyse material you have read, others see whether you have taken in the full significance of a piece of information. Some are meant to be discussed with colleagues, friends or fellow students.

Each of the main units consists of study notes designed to focus attention upon the key aspects of the subject matter. These notes are divided into convenient sections for study purposes.

At the end of each unit there are self-assessment questions. These comprise a number of short answer questions and a full specimen examination question. The answers to all these questions are to be found at the back of the book in the Appendix. Students should remain aware of the fact that the examination itself will comprise questions drawn from across the whole Chartered Institute of Bankers syllabus; the key sections of which for this subject are:

Classification of Trust

Trusts and Powers

Creation and Validity of Trusts

Constitution of Trusts

Trusts of Land

The Beneficiary Principle

Trusteeship

Duties of Trustees

Powers of Trustees

Breach of Trust

Variation of Trusts

Outline of the Law of Charities

Outline of Taxation Aspects of Trusts

Although the workbook is designed to stand alone, as with most topics, certain aspects of this subject are constantly changing. Therefore, it is of great importance that students should keep up to date with these key areas.

It is anticipated that the student will study this course for one academic year, reading through and studying approximately two units every three weeks. However, it should be noted that as topics vary in size and as knowledge tends not to fall into uniform chunks, some units in this workbook are unavoidably longer than others.

The masculine pronoun 'he' has been used in this Workbook to encompass both genders and to avoid the awkwardness of the constant repetition of 'he and/or she'.

Study Guide

In the next few pages, we offer some advice and ideas on studying, revising and approaching examinations.

Studying

As with any examination, there is no substitute for preparation based on an organised and disciplined study plan. You should devise an approach which will enable you to get right through this Study Text and still leave time for revision of this and any other subject you are taking at the same time. Many candidates find that about six weeks is the right period of time to leave for revision, enough time to get through the revision material, but not so long that it is no longer fresh in your mind by the time you reach the examination.

This means that you should plan how to get to the last chapter by, say, the end of March for a May sitting or the end of August for an October sitting. This includes not only reading the text, but making notes and attempting the bulk of the illustrative questions in the back of the text.

We offer the following as a starting point for approaching your study.

●   Plan time each week to study a part of this Study Text. Make sure that it is 'quality' study time: let everyone know that you are studying and the you should not be disturbed. If you are at home, unplug your telephone or switch the answerphone on; if you are in the office, put your telephone on 'divert'.

●   Set a clearly defined objective for each study period. You may simply wish to read through a chapter for the first time or perhaps you want to make some notes on a chapter you have already read a couple of times. Don't forget the illustrative questions.

●   Review your study plan. Use the study checklist a couple of pages on to see how well you are keeping up. Don't panic if you fall behind, but do think how you will make up for lost time.

●   Look for examples of what you have covered in the 'real' world. If you work for a financial organisation, this should be a good starting point. If you do not, then think about your experiences as an individual bank or building society customer or perhaps about your employer's position as a corporate customer of a bank. Keep an eye on the quality press for reports about banks and building societies and their activities.

Revising

- The period which you have earmarked for revision is a very important time. Now it is even more important that you plan time each week for study and that you set clear objectives for each revision session.

- Use time sensibly. How much revision time do you have? Remember that you still need to eat, sleep and fit in some leisure time.

- How will you split the available time between subjects? What are your weaker subjects? You will need to focus on some topics in more detail than others. You will also need to plan your revision around your learning style. By now, you should know whether, for example, early morning, early evening or late evening is best.

- Take regular breaks. Most people find they can absorb more this way than if they attempt to revise for long uninterrupted periods of time. Award yourself a five minute break every hour. Go for a stroll or make a cup of coffee, but do not turn the television on.

- Believe in yourself. Are you cultivating the right attitude of mind? There is absolutely no reason why you should not pass this exam if you adopt the correct approach. Be confident, you have passed exams before so you can pass this one.

The day of the exam

- Passing professional examinations is half about having the knowledge, and half about doing yourself full justice in the examination. You must have the right technique.

- Set at least one alarm (or get an alarm call) for a morning exam.

- Have something to eat but beware of eating too much; you may feel sleepy if your system is digesting a large meal.

- Don't forget pens, pencils, rulers, erasers and anything else you will need.

- Avoid discussion about the exam with other candidates outside the exam hall.

Tackling the examination paper

First, make sure that you satisfy the examiner's requirements

Read the instructions on the front of the exam paper carefully. Check that the exam format hasn't changed. It is surprising how often examiners' reports remark on the number of students who attempt too few - or too many - questions, or who attempt the wrong number of questions from different parts of the paper. Make sure that you are planning to answer the right number of questions.

Read all the questions on the exam paper before you start writing. Look at the weighting of marks to each part of the question. If part (a) offers only 4 marks and you can't answer the 12 marks part (b), then don't choose the question.

Don't produce irrelevant answers. Make sure you answer the question set, and not the question you would have preferred to have been set.

Produce an answer in the correct format. The examiner will state in the requirements the format in which the question should be answered, for example in a report or memorandum. If a question asks for a diagram or an example, give one. If a question does not specifically asks for a diagram or example, but it seems appropriate, give one.

Second, observe these simple rules to ensure that your script is pleasing to the examiner.

Present a tidy paper. You are a professional and it should always show in the presentation of your work. Candidates are penalised for poor presentation and so you should make sure that you write legibly, label diagrams clearly and lay out your work professionally. Markers of scripts each have dozens of papers to mark; a badly written scrawl is unlikely to receive the same attention as a neat and well laid out paper.

State the obvious. Many candidates look for complexity which is not required and consequently overlook the obvious. Make basic statements first. Plan your answer and ask yourself whether you have answered the main parts of the question.

Use examples. This will help to demonstrate to the examiner that you keep up-to-date with the subject. There are lots of useful examples scattered through this study text and you can read about others if you dip into the quality press or take notice of what is happening in your working environment.

Finally, make sure that you give yourself the opportunity to do yourself justice.

Select questions carefully. Read through the paper once, then quickly jot down any key points against each question in a second read through. Reject those questions against which you have jotted down very little. Select those where you could latch on to 'what the question is about' - but remember to check carefully that you have got the right end of the stick before putting pen to paper.

Plan your attack carefully. Consider the order in which you are going to tackle questions. It is a good idea to start with your best question to boost your morale and get some easy marks 'in the bag'.

Read the question carefully and plan your answer. Read through the question again very carefully when you come to answer it.

Gain the easy marks. Include the obvious if it answers the question and do not spend unnecessary time producing the perfect answer. As suggested above, there is nothing wrong with stating the obvious.

Avoid getting bogged down in small parts of questions. If you find a part of a question difficult, get on with the rest of the question. If you are having problems with something the chances are that everyone else is too.

Don't leave the exam early. Use your spare time checking and rechecking your script.

Don't worry if you feel you have performed badly in the exam. It is more likely that the other candidates will have found the exam difficult too. Don't forget that there is a competitive element in exams. As soon as you get up and leave the exam hall, forget the exam and think about the next - or , if it is the last one, celebrate!

Don't discuss an exam with other candidates. This is particularly the case if you still have other exams to sit. Put it out of your mind until the day of the results. Forget about exams and relax.

Preface

A person who acts as a trustee or who is involved in trust administration will need to know the rules of trust law that govern the position.

Such rules are in the process of change from a variety of sources. Equity which originally developed the trust to minimise the hardship caused by the application of common law rules has itself used principles at common law in the very important decision of *Tinsley* v *Milligan* (1994).

In addition, there is the issue of what effect certain restitutionary principles will have upon the development of trust law. In another landmark decision, *Westdeutsche Landesbank Girozentrale* v *Islington London Borough Council* (1996), the House of Lords placed considerable restrictions upon the effect and imposition of restitutionary rules where they would undermine or modify traditional principles of the law of trusts.

Law reform has also been important. The Trusts of Land and Appointment of Trustees Act 1996 has given new rights to beneficiaries to be consulted regarding certain decisions affecting the trust. Such rights would not and could not have been granted by the courts applying the doctrine of precedent.

The need to regulate charities and pensions has seen the introduction of two important pieces of legislation, the Charities Act 1993 and the Pensions Act 1995. These acts are not a complete code in themselves but add to existing law. This is seen as regards pension surpluses for which there is a developing body of case law, which is continuing to grow. Such acts of Parliament give a general backbone which the judges themselves could not develop because of their width and coverage of commercial matters. Further, the courts are not and cannot be regulators.

The role of the trust is changing, and there is an overlap with areas previously governed by common law, such as contract and the tort of negligence. Claims for breach of fiduciary duty, and liability as a constructive trustee are increasingly being used in general commercial situations. This has been recognised by Lord Browne-Wilkinson in *Target Holdings* v *Redferns* (1996). One effect is that detailed and precise rules have emerged for liability. These are much more than the imposition of liability where it is just and equitable to do so.

In particular, in *Target Holdings* v *Redferns* (1996), the House of Lords again looked to the common law to determine the position of liability in equity, - in the particular case, liability as a constructive trustee. It was established that the breach of trust must cause the loss. This confirms that causation questions at common law are now equally relevant in equity.

Sadly, commercial fraud is also on the increase, and much of the work of the Chancery division of the High Court is involved with seeking recovery of misapplied assets by way of tracing or the imposition of a constructive trust. This has also led to the emergence of a wide ranging body of case law in this area, including law relating to jurisdictional matters.

Since assets or funds are received, there is the issue of the exact role of restitution in recovering such assets, which has not currently been completely clarified. There have been calls for a simplification of the various claims in order to produce a clear and rational body of case law. This would obviously aid the recovery of such funds or assets

The possible expansion of the constructive trust to remedy inequitable and unconscionable conduct has been called for by Lord Browne-Wilkinson in Westdeutsche Landesbank Girozentrale v Islington London Borough Council (1996). This shows that there is an active and important role for the courts.

In some cases, the courts have been prepared to adapt precedents in order to produce a fair and just result. In *Midland Bank plc* v *Cooke* Waite L J recognised that in determining the respective shares of a couple in their home, he was making a decision which would affect a large number of individuals, since such disputes are a frequent occurence.

Developments in the law of trusts affecting the administration of trusts are coming about because of changing social and financial circumstances, judicial development, and law reform through specific legislation.

The aim of the author has been, where appropriate, to give the views of others writing in this field, since there are differing opinions not only about the scope of the particular rule, but also how that rule should be developed and applied in other cases.

Where a case or article, has been cited in the main text, this is to show the source or authority. It is not necessary for a student to read the case or article. However, a student who has a particular interest in the subject may wish to refer to one or more of the various text books mentioned in the main text and case list as an additional source of information.

The nature of the subject is that various areas interact. To aid understanding of the subject, cross references are included to previous chapters.

The recent, considerable developments in the law of trusts, have been considered. The law stated is at 31st August 1997.

Nigel A. Clayton
Department of Law, City University
31st August 1997

1

Introduction

Objectives

After studying the text and working through this Unit, students should understand:

- **the origin of trusts**

- **the Judicature Acts 1873–75 and their current enactment as part of the Supreme Court Act 1981**

- **the nature of equitable (beneficial) interests**

- **the bona fide purchaser for value without notice doctrine.**

1.1   Equity developed the concept of the trust: a trust is the separation of the legal interest from the equitable interest. The legal interest is the formal ownership; on the other hand, the equitable interest is the entitlement to benefits, often in the form of income or capital under the trust. This is dealt with in Unit 2. It is necessary to say a little about it at this stage, since both cases below are concerned with equitable interests.

1.2   There have been two important recent cases on the general development of equity. The first is *Tinsley* v *Milligan* (1994). The case involves two female lovers in Wales who bought a property, who lived together in that property and who used that property as part of their 'bed and breakfast' business. To minimise the detection of their joint fraud on the Department of Social Security (DSS), the property was put in the sole name of Tinsley. In other words, legal title was put into the sole name of Tinsley. This enabled Milligan to claim Social Security and other benefits from the DSS, on the basis that she was a tenant of Tinsley. This was not the actual position. Subsequently, the parties separated. Tinsley claimed possession of the property which she wished to sell. Milligan, who was still living in the property, claimed an equitable interest in the property, and wished to receive a share in the proceeds of its sale.

1.3   The case thus involved a dispute over Milligan's equitable interest under a presumed resulting trust. See further in Unit 3. Tinsley argued that Milligan was not entitled to such an interest because of 'illegality'. Both parties had conspired together to defraud the DSS, by putting the property into the sole name of Tinsley so that Milligan could claim greater benefits.

1.4   There was an important finding of fact: that monies used to purchase the property came from the parties' joint business earnings in running a bed and breakfast business at the property, and not from benefits received from the DSS.

1.5   In equity there is a general, vague principle known as a 'maxim' whereby a person who comes to equity must come with clean hands. That is to say, must act in a proper and legal way in relation to the particular facts before the court. This might have meant that Milligan would be unable to claim her equitable interest in the property by virtue of her contribution to the bed and breakfast business. For a detailed discussion of Presumed Resulting Trusts of Land see Unit 7.

1.6   The House of Lords, although adjudicating upon an equitable right, did not follow the equitable maxim, but instead a common law rule. It derived this from a common law contract case (see generally: Berg, 'Illegality and Equitable Interests' [1993] JBL 513).

1.7   The rule at common law is more rigid: can you plead (bring your case) without relying on the illegality? Since Milligan's interest derived from monies solely from the bed and breakfast business, and not from monies from the DSS, she was able to bring her case. This meant that Milligan could establish her equitable interest. On the particular facts, both had contributed to the purchase of the property in which they both lived and both ran as a bed and breakfast business. There was a general intention that each should have an equal share in the property. Once it was established that Milligan could claim her equitable interest, she was awarded a half share in the property, which meant that she was entitled to a half share in the proceeds of its sale.

1.8   What was interesting was that the House of Lords, in a very important decision, followed the common law rule rather than the equitable rule. The Judicature Acts 1873–1875 (enacted in the Supreme Court Act 1981) provide that, where there is a conflict between equity and common law, then the former should prevail. The House of Lords took the opposite view. Thus the common law rule of illegality took precedence over the equitable rules of illegality, and the Judicature Acts were not followed.

1.9   The House of Lords, in an important policy decision, decided that the common law was the better rule since it was more certain. It was a better, clearer and more specific rule.

1.10   The flexible approach in equity was modified by the common law. Equity adopted the common law rule as its own rule. The rule of common law as regards illegality became the rule of equity.

1.11 The normal, and historical, approach has been for equity to modify the common law. Instead, the House of Lords decided that the common law rules should modify the approach in equity.

1.12 The case which follows on from *Tinsley* v *Milligan* is *Tribe* v *Tribe* (1995). Here, a father transferred shares into his son's name to defraud his creditors. In equity, the relationship of parent and child is regarded as a close one (that is, where the parties are not 'strangers', see Unit 2), so that the presumption of gift applies. The starting point was that the father intended to make a gift to his son. The father did not want to do this, but merely to defraud his creditors. The question was whether this 'illegality' would stop the father from being allowed to bring evidence that he intended a trust.

1.13 Subsequently the father decided to abandon his attempts to defraud his creditors. The illegality had not been carried out. So the father was able to bring evidence that he did not intend to make a gift to his son and that he intended to retain his equitable interest in the shares. The result was that the son only obtained the legal title in the shares. The father had not parted with his equitable interest. So no gift of shares had been made to the son. The Court of Appeal held that the father could succeed in his claim in equity for the equitable interest in the shares.

1.14 The Chancellors, who administered the system of equity and the equity court, were originally clerics. They were influenced by their own conscience and believed in the importance of doing what was fair and just. They therefore adopted wide discretion in interpreting the law. This influenced the development of equity. Later in its development, lawyers who were not clerics were appointed as Chancellors. They relied upon precedent and, as a result, the system became more rigid in its interpretation.

1.15 Equity developed the trust, that is the separation of legal and equitable interests which we have seen in *Tinsley* v *Milligan*. In particular equity developed the concept of the equitable interest.

1.16 In addition, equity developed certain additional remedies such as specific performance and injunction which were not available at the common law courts. These equitable remedies would be used to assist with certain rights which were available before the common law courts such as in contract and tort. Equity would therefore compel the performance of a contract. At common law, all that would be available would be the remedy of damages for loss caused by a breach of that contract.

1.17 Similarly, equity would assist the common law by granting the equitable remedy of injunction. Thus, if a defendant was making a noise on his land, then equity would stop the defendant from making that noise. If the defendant continued to make a noise in breach of court order then the defendant could be committed to prison. This was therefore a very effective remedy, and certainly more effective than the common law which would only award damages.

1.18 Additionally, equity developed the important procedural device of the subpoena whereby a defendant could be compelled to attend court. This was a significant procedural weakness in the common law which was mitigated by equity.

1.19 The equitable remedies were said to be discretionary whereas the common law rules, in theory, were more rigid. The court will generally grant specific performance or an injunction in the circumstances described above. However, equity is discretionary and may not always grant its remedies of specific performance or injunction.

1.20 If we take a situation involving land, equity regards each piece of land as unique. If Albert agrees to sell land to Bob, then equity will generally compel Albert, by the remedy of specific performance, to carry out his obligation. Equity will regard damages as inadequate in this situation. Bob has had his rights infringed, and in addition, will be regarded as not having received adequate compensation in the form of damages.

1.21 In one leading case, *Patel* v *Ali* (1984) Suriya Ali and her husband sold their house in Kingsbury to the Patels. There were certain delays and the property was not transferred to the plaintiffs (the Patels). In the meantime the circumstances of Suriya Ali changed considerably and disastrously:

● First, her husband was made bankrupt.

● Second, Suriya developed cancer of one of her legs and it had to be amputated.

1.22 Suriya had three young children to look after and was dependent upon the assistance of her neighbours. Goulding J in the High Court was of the opinion that hardship suffered by a plaintiff, but which had not been caused by that plaintiff, was a ground whereby specific performance could be refused.

1.23 The judge reasoned that Suriya Ali was being asked to do something that she had not bargained for, namely to transfer the property four years after the contract had been made when her circumstances had worsened, and worsened in a way which could not be forseen. In such exceptional circumstances the court would not grant specific performance although it would normally do so in the context of the sale of land. The plaintiffs were of course entitled to damages for the loss that they had suffered.

1.24 It is suggested that this case does demonstrate that equity still has discretion, and that its rules may be exercised in a way which promotes justice. This was the reason for the growth of equity in the first place.

1.25   This historical development mentioned in paragraph 1.14 is still seen today. There are current cases, however, where the courts follow established precedents and appear to have limited discretion.

1.26   Such a rigid approach was taken by the Court of Appeal in *Burns v Burns* (1984). This was a case involving two cohabitees where one sought to argue a resulting trust. This principle will be dealt with in Units 3 and 7.

1.27   The female cohabitee moved in with the male cohabitee and took his surname. They lived together for a number of years. Ms Burns stayed at home in order to look after their children until she resumed work. Mr Burns was comparatively well-off and did not need any financial assistance from his female partner. Furthermore, there was no common intention that she should have an interest. Applying the rules of equity she was not entitled to any interest in the home in which they lived.

1.28   Fox LJ accepted that the result was an unfair one. However, there was no discretion in the principles. He was of the view that the courts could not, in this case, modify the precedents so as to produce a fair result. Any injustice that she suffered was a matter for Parliament to remedy by specific legislation. The judge considered that it was not appropriate for the courts to modify the position by changing the principles that had been previously developed.

1.29   A similar view was put forward in the Court of Appeal in *Re Diplock* (1948). It was stated in this case that the court could no longer invent a jurisdiction to deal with a particular matter, where none existed previously, even if this would achieve justice.

1.30   An important point is that the female cohabitee was seeking to establish an equitable interest. Such an interest is a property right. Had she been able to establish such an interest she would be entitled to a share in the property, and also to a share in the net proceeds in the event that the property was sold.

1.31   In *Tinsley v Milligan* (1994) Lord Browne-Wilkinson makes the point that such an interest is effectively a property right (a right in rem). In his view, the equitable interest is the same type of interest as a legal interest. His Lordship felt it important to emphasise that both of these rights were of the same nature.

1.32   This view added force to his judgment (discussed earlier in this chapter) that it was appropriate to apply a common law rule of illegality when a person was seeking to establish an equitable interest. The reason was that since legal and equitable rights were similar, it made common sense to have one rule which applied to both.

1.33   His Lordship did accept the historical approach in equity that an equitable interest could be defeated by a bona fide purchaser for value without notice (a good faith buyer who purchases the property without any actual or constructive notice of any defect in its title). This doctrine will be discussed in more detail in Unit 7 (Trusts of Land).

1.34   Similarly, a beneficiary of a trust who seeks to trace his or her property into the hands of a third party will lose his or her right to trace if that third party is a bona fide purchaser for value: *Re Diplock* (1948). This will be dealt with in Unit 12.

Evaluation of Introduction

1.35   It is suggested that *Tinsley* v *Milligan* (1994) does mark the beginning of an important role reversal. Historically equity developed to mitigate the injustices of the common law. As equity has evolved and become more rigid and precedent based, this has meant that it cannot always achieve its historical ambition of remedying injustice. In *Tinsley* v *Milligan* (1994) the House of Lords was prepared to look to another source of law, the common law, to stop the injustice which would be perpetrated by the equitable rule as it then stood.

1.36   The maxim in equity that 'he who comes to equity must come with clean hands' would probably have meant that Milligan's counterclaim for an equitable interest would have failed on the basis of the joint plot to defraud the DSS.

1.37   Lord Goff, in his dissenting judgment, placed considerable emphasis upon this maxim as it stood prior to its interpretation in *Tinsley* v *Milligan* (1994). This is pointed out by Pearce and Stevens in their excellent book: *The Law of Trusts and Equitable Obligations* (1995) in Chapter 1 'Historical Introduction'.

1.38   The House of Lords might have reasoned that because both Tinsley and Milligan had dirty hands of broadly equal dirtyness, both dirty hands could be ignored on the basis that they would cancel each other out and Milligan could therefore bring her claim. Although the maxim could have been interpreted in this way before *Tinsley* v *Milligan* (1994) Lord Goff was not prepared to do so.

1.39   Lord Goff's approach was simply that Milligan's hands were dirty because of her participation in the fraud on the DSS, so she could not successfully bring a claim to establish her equitable interest. It was sufficient that the fraud on the DSS was in general terms relevant to her claim. She was claiming an interest in a property, and title to that property had been changed so as to enable a fraud to be perpetrated on the DSS.

1.40   Lord Browne-Wilkinson (Lord Jauncey and Lord Lowry agreeing) adopted the more rigid rule based on the *Bowmakers* case (1945) that Milligan could plead her claim for an equitable interest in the home since it had been acquired with her own monies and not those monies obtained from the DSS.

1.41 It is suggested that the application of this rule produced a fair and just result. In that sense, it is suggested that this case is a true case of equity.

1.42 Nevertheless, the approach of Lord Browne-Wilkinson has not received widespread approval.

1.43 There is a detailed discussion of *Tinsley* v *Milligan* (1994) by Nelson Enonchong in his article 'Illegality: The Fading Flame of Public Policy' (1994) Oxford J Legal Stud 295. The author, a leading writer in this field, describes the various judgments. He confirms that the majority view was that a plaintiff is able to bring a claim if that claim can be established without relying on his or her own illegality.

1.44 The author also makes the point that this test does not require the courts to engage in any further analysis. In particular the courts do not have to investigate the reasons why the property was put into one person's sole name.

1.45 He thus regards the majority view as being rigid, technical, and omitting to look at the substance of the matter. It is suggested that this is a forceful criticism of the majority judgments.

1.46 Nelson Enonchong develops his criticism by making the point that once a plaintiff is able to bring a claim on the basis that he or she does not rely on any illegality then it does not matter how immoral he or she has been, or how serious the illegality is.

1.47 In a further article by Nelson Enonchong, 'Title Claims and Illegal Transactions' (1995) Vol III LQR 135, additional criticisms of *Tinsley* v *Milligan* (1994) are put forward.

1.48 He makes the point in substance that the plaintiff's claim is for a share under a resulting trust. He points out that the establishment of a resulting trust depends upon showing the common intention (agreement) that there should be such a trust. He argues that in *Tinsley* v *Milligan* (1994), Milligan's claim was based on that agreement, and that part of that agreement was the objective of defrauding the DSS, This supports his earlier criticisms. Again, it is suggested that there is force in these criticisms.

1.49 There has been further discussion about *Tinsley* v *Milligan* (1994) by Derek Davies: 'Presumptions and Illegality', in *Trends in Contemporary Trust Law*, 1996 (ed. Oakley). This author looks at the Australian decision of *Nelson* v *Nelson* (1995) which also involved putting property into the names of others for 'illegal' reasons. In this particular case, it was in order to obtain a subsidised loan. His criticism is that there is no discretion in the rule formulated by the majority in *Tinsley* v *Milligan* (1994).

1.50 Derek Davies suggests that the whole of the facts be looked at to determine whether a plaintiff is able to bring a claim despite the illegality. A similar approach is adopted by Enonchong in his LQR article (referred to above).

1.51 If we apply this to *Tinsley* v *Milligan* (1994) then his approach can be seen. First, one has to evaluate the seriousness of the illegality. In *Tinsley* v *Milligan* (1994), Milligan did own up to the fraud and it was established that virtually none of the improperly obtained monies from the DSS was used to purchase the property in which she claimed to own an equitable interest.

1.52 Second, that the parties were also engaged in a joint business venture and had a clear common understanding that the business profits, and the property in which they lived, were to be shared. Tinsley disputed Milligan's entitlement only on the basis of the illegality, and not on the basis that there was no agreement between the parties.

1.53 Third, whether the particular transaction is directly affected by any statute, and the remedies proposed by the statute if any. In *Tinsley* v *Milligan* (1994) the criminality of the conduct was not considered, nor were any provisions of the Social Security legislation. The House of Lords determined the effect of the illegality upon Milligan's claim in accordance with precedent. However, the precedent it followed was that at common law.

1.54. In a slightly wider, but very important context, it has been suggested by Derek Davies in his chapter 'Presumptions and Illegality', that the position be viewed in a wider restitutionary context. This means that a claimant would be entitled to bring a claim for the equitable interest despite the illegality, if to deny the claim would unduly enrich the other party. The exact basis upon which the English courts would determine whether, and the extent to which, there has been any 'unjust enrichment' still has to be worked out.

1.55 In a recent casenote by Francis Rose entitled 'Confining Illegality' (1996) 112 LQR 545, the case of *Taylor* v *Bhail* (1996) is discussed. Although the case is not about a claim for an equitable interest, it does concern a contractual claim affected by illegality. In this case Millett LJ recognised that a plaintiff whose claim was barred on the basis of illegality could suffer injustice. Furthermore, the defendant might be 'unjustly enriched' at the expense of the plaintiff in such a situation. The concept of 'unjust enrichment' will be further discussed in Units 7, 12 and 16. Consideration will be given to the extent to which this concept is affecting equity and trusts in its various areas.

1.56 It may be that equity is searching for new principles or a formula at the present time. Lord Browne-Wilkinson sought to use a rule of common law and adopt it as part of the rule in equity so as to produce a better result. It may be that this rule is currently too rigid. It shows that judges are prepared to reach out to other rules to improve equity.

1.57 It may be that as an alternative, equity will instead use certain rules from restitution in order to augment itself. The extent to which such rules will be used and their impact upon traditional equitable rules is not known at the present time. Nevertheless, this is an important role reversal. Instead of equity coming into play so as to modify and improve the common law, rules of common law and restitutionary formulae are being used to modify equity.

1.58 *Tinsley* v *Milligan* (1994) was a case concerning a claim to a resulting trust. Resulting trusts will be discussed in more detail in Units 3 and 7. Such a trust is imposed by a court. Constructive trusts are also imposed by a court. This type of trust will also be discussed in more detail in Units 3, 7 and 16.

1.59 Express trusts, in contrast, are trusts which are expressly set up and are deliberately intended to be created. Often this will be by a formal written document. It is necessary for there to be an intention on the part of the settlor to set this trust up. In addition the necessary formal requirements must be satisfied. These formal requirements will be examined in Units 2 and 5.

1.60 *Tinsley* v *Milligan* (1994) was an example of a situation where the parties had an intention to set up a trust. Their intention was not formally recorded in their agreement since the property was put into one name in order to assist with the fraud on the DSS In this case the court had to decide whether Milligan would obtain an equitable interest despite the lack of her name on the title deeds which would have asserted her interest.

1.61 In contrast, the aim behind an express trust is formally to create a trust which is expressed and does not need the involvement of a court. The express trust in contrast is administered by trustees. Express trusts will be examined in the next chapter.

Summary

Now you have studied the text and worked through this Unit, you should understand:

☐ **the origin of trusts**

☐ **the Judicature Acts 1873–75 and their current enactment as part of the Supreme Court Act 1981**

☐ **the nature of equitable (beneficial) interests**

☐ **the bona fide purchaser for value without notice doctrine.**

Self-assessment questions

1   What were the facts of *Tinsley* v *Milligan?*

2   What was the decision in *Tinsley* v *Milligan?*

3   What was the importance of *Tinsley* v *Milligan?*

4   What are the major criticisms that have been raised against the majority decision in *Tinsley* v *Milligan?* Do you think such criticisms are justified?

5   Artania is a fictitious country which has the same system of equity and trusts as in England. It has legislation which provides that ex-servicemen or their wives are entitled to subsidised loans provided that they do not already own a property. Jane, the widow of a former pilot in the state airforce, decides that she will take full advantage of this opportunity. She already owns her own home, a bungalow called 'Bleak Cottage'. She agrees with her son Larry, aged 15, and daughter Kay, aged 17, to transfer her bungalow into their joint names so that she will be able to obtain a subsidised loan in order to purchase another property, a flat, in which all three will participate in renovating. The intention is that Kay and Larry will live in this flat, but Jane will continue to live in the bungalow. In order that the plan will not be detected by the authorities, the flat is purchased and put into the sole name of Jane. The aim is that each will own a one third share in this flat and receive a third of the profit on any resale. Jane falls out with Kay and Larry. Kay and Larry decide to sell 'Bleak Cottage' and seek a half share in the proceeds of sale. Jane seeks to sell the flat and claims that she is entitled to 100% of the proceeds.

Advise the various parties as to their respective rights, if any.

(The answers are given in the Appendix)

Caselist for Unit 1 Introduction

Tinsley v *Milligan* [1994] 1 AC 340.

Berg, 'Illegality and Equitable Interests' [1993] JBL 513.

Supreme Court Act 1981.

Tribe v *Tribe* [1995] 3 WLR 913.

Patel v *Ali* [1984] Ch 283.

Burns v *Burns* [1984] Ch 317.

Re Diplock, Diplock v *Wintle* [1948] Ch 465.

Pearce and Stevens, *The Law of Trusts and Equitable Obligations*, Butterworths, (1995).

Nelson Enonchong, 'Illegality: The Fading Flame of Public Policy' (1994) Oxford J Legal Stud 295.

Nelson Enonchong, 'Title Claims and Ilegal Transactions' (1995) III LQR 135.

Derek Davies, 'Presumptions and Illegality', Chapter 2 of *Trends in Contemporary Trust Law* (ed. Anthony Oakley), Clarendon Press, Oxford (1996).

Francis Rose, 'Confining Illegality' (1996) 112 LQR 545.

2

Basic Concepts

Objectives

After studying the text and working through this Unit, students should be able to:

- **understand the basic terminology of trust law**

- **describe the parties involved in the creation of a trust**

- **consider the methods of creating a trust**

- **describe ways in which an existing equitable interest will become a trust**

- **understand the termination of a trust.**

1 Parties to a trust

1.1 There are three parties involved in a trust, the settlor, the trustee and the beneficiary. Usually the settlor has the particular property involved, say a painting, and wishes it to be held on trust. At this point the settlor owns both the legal and equitable title in the painting; the two are joined together at this point. The legal title is the technical title, in the sense of being the formal title. It will also often be associated with possession, or rights to possession. On the other hand, the equitable title is the right to the fruits of the tree. The beneficiary, the person who will have the equitable title, has the right to benefit from the trust, in terms of income and capital. In the case of the painting, if the trustees sold it, the income would be held on trust for the beneficiary.

1.2 The settlor normally agrees in advance with the trustee or trustees that they are willing to be the trustees. They will only ever obtain the legal title.

1.3 Another clear and established rule in equity is known as the presumption of trust. This applies to transactions between everyone – regarded as 'strangers' in equity – except parent and child, and husband and wife. This presumption is that one does not intend to make gifts to others. So, when property is transferred to them, only the legal title, not the equitable title, is transferred. (This presumption was discussed in Unit 1, Introduction.) The result of applying the presumption of trust is that equitable title remains with the transferor (the person making the transfer). In the case of the settlor and trustee, the presumption of trust operates, so the settlor transfers legal and not equitable title.

1.4 As indicated above, the beneficiary is to obtain the equitable interest. The trustee, who obtains the legal title, will hold the property transferred to him – in our example the painting – on trust for the beneficiary.

1.5 At the point when the painting is transferred to the trustees, the trust is 'constituted', i.e. completely and irrevocably set up. It is clear that a trust is intended and who the beneficiary is. It is also clear what property is being held on trust. Once the trust is set up, the settlor drops out: he has passed his legal title to the trustee. Furthermore, the equitable interest is now owned by the beneficiary, for whom the trustee holds it.

1.6 If the trust is not carried out properly, the beneficiary can sue the trustee (i.e. bring a personal claim against him for breach of trust). See Unit 12.

2 Ways of creating a trust

2.1 The first method is where the settlor declares himself trustee for the intended beneficiary. The settlor must use words indicating that he is to be the trustee for the intended beneficiary, and that the latter is to obtain an equitable interest. Words such as 'I hereby declare myself trustee for you of [a particular painting]' would be sufficient. Less formal language may also be sufficient, *Paul* v *Constance* (1977).

2.2 The second way of creating a trust is by transferring the property to be held in trust to the trustee, and thus 'constituting' it. The settlor must previously have agreed with the trustees that they will act. As soon as the trustee receives the property, the legal title will move to the trustee. At that same moment, the equitable title will move to the beneficiary, and the trust will have come into existence.

2.3 For both methods, the 'three certainties' discussed in Unit 5 must be satisfied.

3 Trusts of an equitable interest

3.1   We now turn to the situation where the beneficiary of an existing trust is to change and the benefits be transferred. The trustee holds property on trust for the existing beneficiary, whom we will call B1, and it is intended (by B1) that there will be a new beneficiary, B2. What happens is that the trustee declares himself trustee for B2. If sufficient words of declaration of trust are used, see above, then B1 will drop out and the original trustee will now hold on trust for B2.

3.2   Note that in this situation, the original beneficiary had an equitable interest held in trust. Section 53(1)(c) of the Law of Property Act 1925 requires that separate and already existing equitable interests be disposed of in writing (this is discussed in Unit 5). The declaration of trust must be in writing. One leading authority confirms this, see Brian Green, 'Grey, Oughtred and Vandervell – A Contextual Reappraisal' (1984) 47 MLR 385.

4 Termination of a trust

4.1   One situation in which a trust will come to an end is where all the income and capital have been distributed to the various beneficiaries by the trustee.

4.2   Equity will not allow a trust to fail for lack of a trustee. The courts of equity have certain jurisdiction to appoint new trustees where necessary. In addition, there are certain statutory powers under the Trustee Act 1925 (discussed in Unit 9).

4.3   A well-recognised situation in which a trust will be terminated is through use of the rule in *Saunders* v *Vautier* (1841). Consider a situation where a trustee holds on trust for one beneficiary. If there are no express or implied terms in the trust to the contrary, then the beneficiary, if of full age and sufficient capacity, has the right to call for the legal title. By merging the legal title with the beneficiary's own equitable title, the beneficiary will have everything himself. The trust will be ended when the beneficary calls for the legal title in this way. The trustee is obliged to transfer the legal title to the beneficiary.

4.4   The *Saunders* v *Vautier* rule also extends to the situation where there is more than one beneficiary. However, the beneficiaries must collectively be a complete, closed, total, ascertained and mentally competent group, who are together entitled to the whole of the equitable interest. There must be no unborn, unascertained or unascertainable beneficiaries.

5 Evaluation of Unit 2

5.1   Some additional cases are discussed in the leading casebooks: in particular *Maudsley and Burn's Trusts and Trustees Cases and Materials* (ed. E.H. Burn) 1996. In one of them, *Milroy* v *Lord* (1862), the court confirmed that there were two ways of setting up a trust. On the particular facts of this case the settlor had not transferred the legal title of the shares to the trustees. In addition, the settlor had not declared himself trustee.

5.2   The settlor had intended to make a gift of the shares, but had not carried this out. The court confirmed that it could not perfect an imperfect gift by creating a trust. This will be discussed in more detail in Unit 6.

5.3   Another case discussed in this casebook is that of *Jones* v *Lock* (1865). One question for the court to decide was whether a declaration of trust had been made in relation to a cheque, when words 'Look you here, I give this to baby...' had been used. It was held that these were words of gift not trust. The gift failed, owing to the death of the drawer before the proceeds of the cheque could be cashed in favour of the baby. This death revoked the payment order under the cheque.

5.4   The court regarded those words as words of gift and not as a declaration of trust. The result was that the gift failed.

5.5   In a third case *Richards* v *Delbridge* (1874) mentioned in this casebook, the issue again revolved around the question of whether a declaration of trust had been created. Delbridge wrote 'This deed and all thereto belonging I give to [Richards] from this time forth, with all stock in trade.'

5.6   Again, the court regarded these words as words of gift. Further, Delbridge did not intend to make himself a trustee and had not used words of declaration of trust.

5.7   *Paul* v *Constance* (1977) which has been considered above in paragraph 2.1 probably marks the most relaxed approach of the courts to holding that a declaration of trust had been made. The statement by Dennis Albert Constance to Doreen Grace Paul (with whom he lived) that the monies in his account were 'as much yours as mine' could be seen to be words of gift. In particular, that half of those monies were to become the property of Doreen Grace Paul.

5.8   To analyse these words as words of gift might have presented the courts with problems. First, if it was a gift to take place at the time the words were spoken, then it might have presented difficulties with the operation of the account. In particular, when the account was set up it was in the name of Mr Constance only and Doreen Grace Paul was (after discussions with the bank manager) to be allowed to use the account.

5.9 Second, if the gift to Doreen Grace Paul was to take place on the death of Mr Constance then this would be invalid as contravening the provisions of the Wills Act 1837 which requires dispositions that take effect on death to be in a form (including writing) prescribed by that act. This act will be briefly considered when dealing with secret trusts in Unit 16.

5.10 The case may be seen as a 'true' equity case in which the courts could achieve justice by holding that a declaration of trust had been validly created. This would give effect to the wishes of Mr Constance. We have seen in Unit 1 that achieving justice is an important aspect in equity. Where the precedents allow this, the courts will follow an approach which produces a fair result.

5.11 It was important in the reasoning of Scarman LJ in the Court of Appeal that Mr Constance was not trained in the subtleties of equity. In such circumstances one could not expect him to use the language of a lawyer, nor formal words indicating that he intended a trust to be created.

5.12 Conversely, in *Swain* v *The Law Society* (1983) the House of Lords stated that a lawyer or someone acting on legal advice would be expected to use appropriate language if they were intending to create a trust.

5.13 In terms of ending a trust, the leading authority of *Saunders* v *Vautier* (1841) enables the beneficiaries to end a trust. This important case in equity has been discussed in paragraphs 4.3 and 4.4 above. This jurisdiction to end a trust has been developed by recent statute law. The Trusts of Land and Appointment of Trustees Act 1996 is discussed in Units 7, 8 and 9.

5.14 A settlor may expressly exclude the operation of this case by putting an express clause into a trust that the beneficiaries shall not be able to end the trust by collectively calling for the legal title. An example of this would be a clause which did not allow a beneficiary to obtain a share (interest in) of capital until he or she had attained a certain age.

5.15 Often this will be done impliedly. Where a settlor sets up a trust to carry out a purpose, then it is arguable that the beneficiaries cannot divide up the trust funds and stop that purpose being carried out. In such a situation a court would have to decide whether the trust is for a purpose or whether it is to benefit individuals. Where it is for individuals, they are entitled to divide up the trust fund for themselves, *Re Bowes* (1896).

5.16 However, it must be the trustee who controls the running of the trust. It is for a trustee to decide whether another trustee shall be appointed. If the beneficiaries disagree with the action taken by the trustee acting properly within the terms of the trust, their course of action is to end the trust under the rule in *Saunders* v *Vautier* (1841). They are not entitled to dictate to the trustee how the trustee shall exercise the powers and discretions contained in the terms of the trust, *Re Brockbank* (1948).

5.17 The Trusts of Land and Appointment of Trustees Act 1996 gives considerable new powers to beneficiaries. It is suggested that the judges would not and could not develop the rule in *Saunders v Vautier* (1841) so as to create these powers. They would regard such development as a matter to be left to Parliament. Indeed, the Trusts of Land and Appointment of Trustees Act 1996 came about as a result of detailed proposals by the Law Commission in their report *Transfer of Land, Trusts of Land* (Law Commission No. 181) which was put before Parliament in 1989.

5.18 Under section 19 of the Trusts of Land and Appointment of Trustees Act 1996, the decision of *Re Brockbank* is reversed. The beneficiaries, if the whole class is ascertained and they are all of competent capacity, are able collectively to do the following: First, they are able by written direction to remove a trustee. Second, they may appoint a new trustee, by their written direction, in place of the removed trustee.

5.19 Similarly, by section 20 of the Trusts of Land and Appointment of Trustees Act 1996, the beneficiaries, as a collective group, are able, by written direction, to remove a mentally incapacitated trustee and appoint a replacement.

5.20 In exercising their rights under sections 19 and 20 the complete group of beneficiaries must continue in their wish for the removal of a trustee and for the appointment of another replacement trustee: section 21(1) of the Trusts of Land and Appointment of Trustees Act 1996.

5.21 Where trustees partition land they shall obtain the consent of each of the affected beneficiaries: section 7(3) of the Trusts of Land and Appointment of Trustees Act 1996.

5.22 In exercising their powers, trustees of a trust of land shall consult with the beneficiaries, and shall give effect to the majority wish of the beneficiaries where that wish is consistent with the general interest of the trust: section 11(1) of the Trusts of Land and Appointment of Trustees Act 1996.

5.23 An important new power is given to trustees by section 9(1) of the Trusts of Land and Appointment of Trustees Act 1996. This enables trustees to delegate their functions to beneficiaries who are of full age and mental capacity and who have an interest in the land.

5.24 This delegation is done by power of attorney. It is also done by the trustees jointly as a collective unit: section 9(3) of the Trusts of Land and Appointment of Trustees Act 1996.

5.25 Where a beneficiary, who previously had an equitable interest in the land and to whom a power has been delegated, no longer retains an equitable interest in the land then that power will be revoked: section 9(3) Trusts of Land and Appointment of Trustees Act 1996.

5.26   The extent of delegation is discussed by Chris Whitehouse and Nicholas Hassall, two expert solicitors in this field, in their book *The Trusts of Land and Appointment of Trustees Act 1996*, which covers the whole of the act in considerable detail. They make the point that this includes the trustees' power of sale under section 6 of the act. They also make the point that the trustees may delegate their functions as regards one piece of land but not another, where several pieces of land are held in trust.

5.27   If the trustees fail to exercise reasonable care in delegating their duties to beneficiaries, then the trustees will be jointly and severally (collectively and individually) liable for any loss caused to the trust: section 9(8) Trusts of Land and Appointment of Trustees Act 1996.

5.28   William Goodhart QC in his article 'Trust Law for the Twenty-first Century' (1996) TruLI, and also published in Unit 11 in *Trends in Contemporary Trust Law* (ed. A.J. Oakley) 1996, regards the Trusts of Land and Appointment of Trustees Act 1996 as commendable and meritorious. He does, however, make certain criticisims of the act.

5.29   In particular, he criticises section 9(3) of the act (discussed above) as being too wide. He suggests that liability should be imposed upon the trustees only where they have not adequately considered whether a beneficiary has the necessary competence to have had powers delegated to him or her. A trustee's liability for delegation of his or her duties will be considered in Unit 12.

5.30   It will be apparent that the Trusts of Land and Appointment of Trustees Act 1996 is of considerable importance. It extends the scope of equity to allow for considerable involvement and decision making by beneficiaries. The *Saunders* v *Vautier* (1841) decision could not and did not allow for such involvement. The equitable doctrine did not allow for consultation between trustee and beneficiaries. Trustees were required to make the decisions and not the beneficiaries.

5.31   *Re Brockbank* (1948) denied the beneficiaries the power to choose and appoint a new trustee. The court simply concluded that in such a situation the beneficiaries would have to end the trust. As a consequence of sections 19 to 22 of the Trusts of Land and Appointment of Trustees Act 1996, this has been reversed, and beneficiaries now do have that choice.

5.32   It is suggested that equity has been improved by this legislation. In this situation, not by adopting any rule of common law, nor by using the concept of 'unjust enrichment'. Statute law has improved equity in a way which the judges could not. The result is that equity now fits in with the demands and needs of the present and the future. The right to be consulted and the right to choose are important rights which have now been extended to beneficiaries.

Summary

Now you have studied the text and worked through this Unit, you should understand:

☐ **the basic terminology of trust law**

☐ **who is involved in the creation of a trust**

☐ **the ways of creating a trust**

☐ **the ways an existing equitable interest will become a trust**

☐ **how a trust is terminated.**

Self-assessment questions

1 Distinguish an equitable interest from a legal interest.

2 What rights does a settlor have after a trust has been created?

3 What are the two ways in which a trust can be created?

4 How may a trust of an already existing interest be created?

5 When will an existing trust be terminated?

6 'If it is intended to take effect by transfer, the Court will not hold the intended transfer to operate as a declaration of trust, for then every imperfect instrument would be made effectual by being converted into a perfect trust.' Turner L J in *Milroy* v *Lord* (1862).

   Discuss, with reference to decided cases.

7 Jack and Jill are 'emotional cohabitees' who are living together. Jack is well-off and when Jill moved in with him said to her 'I'll be responsible for the mortgage, and I don't need any financial assistance from you'. After their second child, when they were in the park together Jack said to Jill 'The house is for you and me equally, and you should have no worries about looking after the children'. A week later Jack is killed in an accident at work.

   Advise Jill as to her entitlement, if any, to the home in which they lived.

8 Consider the extent to which the rule in *Saunders* v *Vautier* and its application in subsequent cases has been developed by the Trusts of Land and Appointment of Trustees Act 1996.

(The answers are given in the Appendix)

Caselist for Unit 2 Basic Concepts

Paul v *Constance* [1977] 1 WLR 527.

Brian Green, 'Grey, Oughtred and Vandervell – A Contextual Reappraisal' (1984) 47 MLR 385.

Saunders v *Vautier* (1841) 4 Beav 115.

Maudsley and Burn's Trusts and Trustees Cases and Materials, 5th edition (ed. E.H. Burn) Butterworths (1996).

Milroy v *Lord* (1862) 4 De GF and J 264.

Jones v *Lock* (1865) 1 Ch App 25.

Richards v *Delbridge* (1874) LR 18 Eq 11.

Swain v *The Law Society* [1983] 1 AC 598.

Re Bowes, Earl Strathmore v *Vane* [1896] 1 Ch 507.

Re Brockbank, Ward v *Bates* [1948] Ch 206.

The Trusts of Land and Appointment of Trustees Act 1996.

Chris Whitehouse and Nicholas Hassall, *The Trusts of Land and Appointment of Trustees Act 1996: A Practical Guide*, Butterworths (1996).

William Goodhart QC, 'Trust Law for the Twenty-first Century' (1996) TruLI, and Chapter 11 in *Trends in Contemporary Trust Law* (ed. A.J. Oakley), Clarendon Press, Oxford (1996).

3

Classification of Trusts

Objectives

After studying the text and working through this Unit, students should be able to:

- appreciate the reasons for classifying trusts

- understand public and private trusts

- understand express trusts and executed and executory trusts

- understand resulting trusts and constructive trusts.

1 Reasons for classifying trusts

1.1 Here we are following the classification put forward by the courts. Equity developed the concept of trusts. The variety of trusts follows the various situations that arise and the need to recognise and deal with these situations.

The Express Trust

1.2 The express trust is one where the terms have been expressed in an actual document, or in a clear statement.

1.3 Trusts may be divided into two categories. First, those based upon intention; second, those which arise through the operation of law. This distinction was put forward by Megarry J in *Re Vandervell's Trusts (No. 2)*(1974).

Resulting Trusts

1.4 Express trusts are based upon intention. Resulting trusts are of two kinds, one being called presumed resulting trusts, the other automatic resulting trusts. Presumed resulting trusts are also based upon intention, being the parties' implied intention. They have a general intention, but have not properly formalised the situation.

1.5   Automatic resulting trusts are those which arise through the operation of law. They arise automatically, for they are imposed irrespective of intention, indeed often contrary to the intention of the parties. Some particular illustrations of the circumstances in which automatic trusts arise will be described below.

1.6   The presumed resulting trust would come into existence (based upon the parties' intentions) where the parties had both contributed to the purchase price of, say, a property. There is an implied understanding that both are to have an equitable interest in the property. This type of presumed resulting trust will be dealt with in detail in Unit 7.

1.7   On the other hand, the automatic resulting trust comes about irrespective of intention. In some circumstances, the parties may not have thought about what will happen to the equitable interest. Where the parties are 'strangers' (i.e. in all cases except where parent and child or husband and wife are concerned), then equity will presume a trust relationship.

1.8   So, if Albert and Bob are 'strangers', and Albert transfers certain property to Bob, it will be assumed in equity that Albert did not intend to make a gift to Bob. In such a situation, only the legal title will move to Bob, and Albert will retain the equitable title. The automatic resulting trust will ensure that the equitable interest in the property does not go to Bob. The equitable interest (a conceptual creature) will either not move at all, or insofar as it tries to move with the legal interest, it will be unable to do so. It will 'result back' to Albert.

Quistclose Trust – an example of an Automatic Resulting Trust

1.9   Where one person transfers property or funds to another for a specific purpose, then this will create a trust relationship between the two parties. The recipient will be obliged to carry out the purpose.

1.10   In the leading case of *Barclays Bank Ltd* v *Quistclose Investments Ltd* (1970), it was decided by the House of Lords that there could be an express trust to carry out a purpose. Such a trust was of a transient nature. Where property had been transferred to another for a special purpose, the trust would end when that purpose had been completed.

1.11   This ruling has been applied in other cases and has generated much academic writing, in particular:

- Sir Peter Millett QC (as he then was): 'The Quistclose Trust: Who can enforce it?' (1985) 101 LQR 269.

- Charles Rickett: 'Different Views on the Scope of the *Quistclose* Analysis: English and Antipodean Insights' (1991) 107 LQR 608.

- Michael Bridge: 'The *Quistclose* Trust in a World of Secure Transactions' (1992) 12 Oxford J Legal Stud 333. In this article the author, a leading expert on security law, suggests that such a trust might be 'registered'. In that way, he argues, third parties could be protected on the register. The difficulty is that the *Quistclose* trust might arise where parties did not realise it and so would not register this interest. This approach has not been developed and is not part of English law at the present time.

1.12   In the *Quistclose* case, R (Rolls Razor Ltd) was provided with funds, by means of a loan from Q, in order to be able to pay a dividend. Barclays Bank, banker for R, was told of the position by letter. This letter informed the bank of the loan. It also informed the bank as to the reasons why R was being lent funds by Q. A new and separate account was set up. The funds from Q were put into this account by means of a cheque. R went into liquidation after having received these funds, but before the dividend was paid.

1.13   The House of Lords decided that Q had provided these funds for a particular purpose, so that R could pay this dividend to its shareholders. The consequence was that an express trust was created in favour of Q.

1.14   R had gone into liquidation. This meant that the funds provided by Q could not, and would not, be used for the purpose for which Q had lent them.

1.15   The consequence of this was that a resulting trust was created in favour of Q. The House of Lords decided that where funds had been provided for a special and specific purpose which could not be carried out, then a resulting trust would arise. Such a trust would be in favour of Q, which had provided the funds.

1.16   R was in overdraft in its trading account operated with Barclays Bank. The consequence was that Barclays Bank was not permitted to combine and set off the credit (surplus) of Q's trust account against the debit (overdraft) of R's trading account. The reason is that set-off is not allowed where the bank accounts are owned by different persons.

1.17   In some situations, the creation of this type of resulting trust will have important effects in an insolvency situation. Two cases which involved the *Quistclose* type of trust in an insolvency situation will be discussed below. Where a *Quistclose* trust is established, the beneficiary will have a proprietary remedy and take ahead of all the other creditors.

1.18   In *Re EVTR* (1987) Mr Barber was on friendly terms with a company called EVTR. He decided to give financial assistance to it. He drew a cheque in favour of EVTR for £60,000. It was cleared into a clients' account of a firm of solicitors acting for EVTR. Mr Barber did this in order to enable EVTR to lease a particular piece of new 'state of the art' equipment. However, this equipment was not easily or readily available. Instead, some temporary and alternative equipment was supplied to EVTR. In the meantime, EVTR went into receivership.

1.19   The Court of Appeal reversed the decision in 1986 of Michael Wheeler QC sitting as a deputy judge of the High Court. The Court of Appeal was unanimously of the view that Mr Barber had provided funds for a special purpose, to enable EVTR to hire this particular equipment. This had the consequence that those funds were impressed with an express trust. Furthermore, this purpose had not been carried out as this new equipment had not been supplied to EVTR. The receivers therefore held the sum of £60,000 on a resulting trust for Mr Barber.

1.20   In the view of the Court of Appeal, the purpose would have been carried out only when the particular special equipment had been supplied. In its opinion, to do otherwise would be to blow the final whistle at half time.

1.21   In *Carreras Rothmans Ltd* v *Freeman Mathews Treasure Ltd (in liquidation) and Another* (1985), Freeman Mathews (FM) was hired by Carreras Rothmans Ltd (CR) to conduct the advertising of certain products manufactured by CR. In carrying out this work, FM would act as principal, and be reimbursed on a regular basis by CR as part of its annual fee.

1.22   FM had financial problems. CR and FM reached an informal agreement whereby a special, separate account was set up at the bank where FM operated its trading account. This new separate account was to be used to receive the yearly fee from CR, and was specially created to ensure that the various creditors of FM would be paid for their advertising work which had benefited CR.

1.23   Shortly after this arrangement had been made between CR and FM, CR transferred funds into this new account. A few days after these funds had been transferred, FM went into voluntary liquidation. This liquidation was at the same time that cheques drawn on this account in favour of the various third parties were sent to them.

1.24   In the High Court, Peter Gibson J held that CR had provided those funds for a particular purpose so that the third parties would be paid. On the liquidation of FM they could not be paid. The result was that they would be held on a resulting trust for CR.

Constructive Trusts

1.25   The other types of trusts that arise through the operation of law are constructive trusts. These are remedial devices, i.e. imposed as remedies by the courts: *Chase Manhatten Bank NA* v *Israel-British Bank (London) Ltd*

(1981). Such a trust is generally imposed to remedy inequitable, unconscionable, improper or unjust conduct. It is also imposed irrespective of intention. If a thief steals my property, equity will impose a constructive trust against the thief. Although the thief may have possession of my property, equity will seek to protect me by ensuring automatically that my equitable interest in that property remains with me. This situation will be discussed at the end of this chapter in the evaluation.

1.26 In *Attorney-General of Hong Kong* v *Reid* (1994), Reid, who was in charge of criminal prosecutions in Hong Kong, accepted various bribes and purchased several properties in New Zealand with them. The Privy Council used the general principle (maxim of equity) that 'Equity regards as done that which ought to be done'. As soon as Reid received the bribe, he held it on a constructive trust for the Hong Kong authorities. It followed that the properties in New Zealand were held on a constructive trust for the Hong Kong authorities. The article by Sir Peter Millett (writing in a non judicial capacity) 'Bribes and Secret Commissions' [1993] RLR 7, was influential in assisting the court to reach its conclusion. This is an example of a constructive trust being used or created as a remedy against Reid's conduct.

1.27 Reid was not insolvent, so there was in fact no need for the court to impose a constructive trust so to ensure that the Hong Kong authorities would take ahead of any other creditors. Anthony Oakley, in his article: 'Proprietary Claims and their Priority on Insolvency' (1995) 54 CLJ 377, makes the point that the imposition of a constructive trust does worsen the position of the other creditors. In his view, this consequence is not desirable. To minimise this, he considers that the trust should only be used to recover actual or indentifiable property of the owner or that for which it is exchanged.

1.28 This view is followed in the article '*Lister and Co* v *Stubbs*: Who Profits?' by David Cowan, Rod Edmunds and John Lowry. The authors of this article are critical of the proprietary remedy awarded in this case for similar reasons to that put forward by Anthony Oakley. Keith Uff, 'The Remedies of the Defrauded Principal After *Attorney-General for Hong Kong* v *Reid*' in *Corporate and Commercial Law: Modern Developments* (ed. David Feldman and Frank Meisel) 1996, Chapter 13, suggests that rights be given, but that these should be less than full proprietary rights. The value of the bribe might be awarded. This would be a personal remedy as opposed to a proprietary one. This will be discussed in Unit 12. Simon Gardner, 'Two Maxims of Equity' (1995) CLJ 60 is critical of a proprietary remedy being awarded in this case since the Hong Kong authorities here had no proprietary right.

1.29 Another common situation concerns cohabitees. The position of husband and wife is regulated under matrimonial legislation so that disputes in equity are rare. Say we have a situation where Charles and Dawn are cohabitees living together in a property. Charles informally agrees with Dawn that she is to have a share in the property. If Charles seeks to act contrary to that agreement, then the courts of equity will impose a constructive trust in favour of Dawn.

1.30   Charles would act contrary to the agreement if he sought to sell the property without telling Dawn, or sought to deny that Dawn had an equitable interest. She obtains the share in the property she was promised by way of constructive trust.

1.31   *Grant* v *Edwards* develops the idea of a constructive trust, which will come into existence if two factors are shown. First, where there is an informal agreement between the parties (Charles agreed with Dawn that she is to acquire an equitable interest in the property); second, where acts of detriment in reliance on that agreement are done. If Dawn helps in Charles' business, that would certainly be sufficient. See Unit 7.

1.32   Certain statutory provisions recognise a distinction between the various types of trust. Examples include the Law of Property Act 1925 section 53(2), and the Law of Property (Miscellaneous Provisions) Act 1989 – both discussed in Unit 5 – and also the Companies Act 1989 section 360.

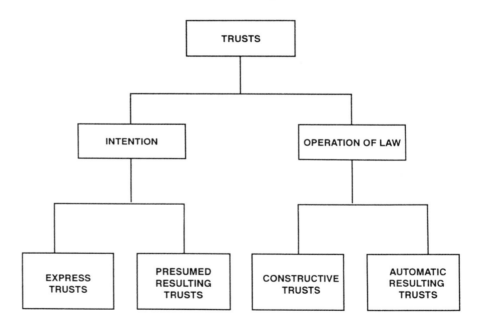

2 Private and Charitable (Public) Trusts

2.1   A private trust is one made for the benefit of individuals. It is normally made expressly and so is an example of an express trust. Apart from certain exceptional categories of purpose trusts and charitable trusts, an express private trust must be for identified individuals. A purpose trust is one phrased in terms of a purpose, such as a field for use by the Muppet Cricket

Club. As there are ascertainable individuals (beneficiaries) who use the field, the trust would be valid. This will be discussed in more detail in Unit 8.

2.2   There are four categories of charitable trust:

● for the relief of poverty

● for the advancement of education

● for the advancement of religion

● for other purposes beneficial to the community.

A charitable trust will be for the benefit of individuals, organisations or for wider purposes falling within one of the above categories. Such trusts are also normally made expressly, so they too are examples of express trusts. Charitable trusts will be dealt with in Unit 14.

3 Executed/Executory trusts

3.1   These may be subdivided into trusts which have already been carried out (i.e. executed), and those to be carried out in future (i.e. executory). As Unit 6 makes clear, until legal title is transferred into the hands of the trustee, the trust is not constituted (set up). With an executed trust, the trust will necessarily be constituted.

3.2   The position regarding the constitution of trusts will be examined in more detail in Unit 6.

4 Evaluation of Unit 3

4.1   The scope of a resulting trust was considered in detail in *Westdeutsche Landesbank Girozentrale* v *Islington London Borough Council* (1996). The case concerned a 'swap' contract (swapping rates of interest) which was entered into between the plaintiff bank and the defendant council. In earlier litigation, the swap contract had been ruled to be ultra vires (outside the powers of the council) and void. The plaintiff bank had transferred certain monies to the defendant authority. In this case, the plaintiff bank sought recovery of these funds together with compound interest. In order to obtain compound interest a trust had to be shown to exist.

4.2   The House of Lords considered the article by Peter Birks, 'Restitution and Resulting Trusts' in *Equity: Contemporary Legal Developments* (ed. Stephen Goldstein) 1992. In this article he argued that a resulting trust should be imposed in the above case because it involved either a total failure of consideration (no benefit had been received by the bank) or a mistaken payment situation (the parties believed their contract to be valid when it was void). Peter Birks argued that if this approach were taken, so that a resulting trust was imposed in this type of situation, it would make the law of trusts and restitution more consistent.

4.3 The resulting trust analysis of Peter Birks was rejected for the following reasons put forward by Lord Goff. First, by the time the local authority realised the position, it would have mixed the funds from the bank with its other funds. At this point in time, there would therefore be no separate fund to which the trust could attach.

4.4 Second, on these facts there was a mistake of law rather than a mistake of fact. A resulting trust could not arise where there was a mistake of law.

4.5 Lord Browne-Wilkinson considered that the imposition of a resulting trust on the facts of this case would be fundamentally inconsistent with the law of trusts as previously developed and would produce considerable uncertainty in commercial transactions.

4.6 In particular, the conscience of a recipient was a crucial factor. No trust could be imposed against such a recipient until he or she was aware of the situation. It followed that it was essential to have identifiable trust property. This point was broadly the same as Lord Goff's discussed above.

4.7 Applying those principles to the facts, there could be no trust in existence before the local authority's bank account went into overdraft. At no time before this date were there defined trust funds in existence which affected the conscience of the local authority.

4.8 Lord Browne-Wilkinson confirmed the two situations when a resulting trust arises. First, where one person transfers property or monies to another where the two are strangers. This creates a presumption of trust, and has been discussed in the previous chapter (Unit 2). Second, where one person transfers property to another but it is unclear, or becomes unclear, what is to happen to the equitable ownership.

4.9 The *Quistclose* trust, discussed above in paragraphs 1.9 to 1.24, was given by Lord Browne-Wilkinson as an example of this. His Lordship regarded such a trust as being an automatic resulting trust.

4.10 Another example given by Lord Browne-Wilkinson was the situation where funds are given to an unincorporated association for a purpose which cannot be carried out. This is a similar situation to that of the *Quistclose* trust, but its application is in the context of unincorporated associations. This will be discussed in Unit 8.

4.11 Lord Browne-Wilkinson subsequently went on to consider the circumstances in which a constructive trust will arise. He distinguished between the institutional constructive trust and the remedial constructive trust.

4.12 The institutional constructive trust will be further considered in Unit 7. Lord Browne-Wilkinson confirmed that such a constructive trust arises by operation of law. In particular it arises from the time that the circumstances happen that create it. So, if Charles seeks to sell the home in which he and Dawn live, where they have jointly contributed to the purchase of such a home, then a constructive trust will arise at that point. The court merely declares that such a trust has previously arisen.

4.13 Lord Browne-Wilkinson went on to deal with the remedial constructive trust. He considered that such a trust could be imposed at the discretion of the court. Such a remedy will be imposed where a thief steals property. The conscience of the thief is affected in such a situation. Because of this a constructive trust could be imposed against the thief.

4.14 Lord Browne-Wilkinson confirmed that such a trust would be a constructive trust and not a resulting trust.

4.15 His Lordship (unlike Lord Goff who declined to review this case) specifically dealt with the decision of *Chase Manhattan Bank NA v Israel-British Bank (London) Ltd* (1981) which was discussed in paragraph 1.25. Lord Browne-Wilkinson regarded this case as correct.

4.16 The plaintiff American bank had made a double payment to the defendant British bank. Because the defendant bank knew within two days of both payments that an error had been made, Lord Browne-Wilkinson was of the view that the conscience of the defendant bank was affected.

4.17 In Lord Browne-Wilkinson's opinion conscience was a crucial determining test in equity which justified the imposition of a constructive trust. The importance of conscience in equity has been put forward by The Hon. Sir Anthony Mason: 'The Place of Equity and Equitable Remedies in The Contemporary Common Law World' (1994) 110 LQR 238. The judge makes clear, in his conclusion, that this doctrine will enable the courts effectively to adapt equitable principle to the changing conditions in our society.

4.18 Lord Browne-Wilkinson regarded the imposition of this type of constructive trust, rather than a resulting trust, as the way forward. Furthermore, he was of the opinion that this type of constructive trust would be a suitable basis for developing proprietary (restitutionary) remedies. See generally, Anthony Oakley, 'The Liberalising Nature of Remedies for Breach of Trust', in *Trends in Contemporary Trust Law* (ed. A.J. Oakley) 1996, Clarendon Press, Oxford, Chapter 10.

4.19 Lord Browne-Wilkinson gave two reasons for this: first, the court would have discretion under such a restitutionary constructive trust to decide upon an appropriate remedy on the particular facts; second, the court could take account of the position of innocent third parties, and decide whether the defence of 'change of position' applied. This defence will be considered in Unit 12. The constructive trust will be considered in Unit 16.

4.20   This case and the issues arising from it are discussed in a very informative and interesting article by Peter Birks: 'Trusts Raised to Reverse Unjust Enrichment: The *Westdeutsche* Case' (1996) 4 RLR 3.

4.21   We have seen the importance of this case to both resulting and constructive trusts. If either trust is established, protection will be given to a beneficiary in an insolvency situation. The *Quistclose* trust has often been used to protect a provider of funds, where the recipient company has gone into liquidation or receivership. Similarly, the imposition of a constructive trust in *Attorney General of Hong Kong* v *Reid* (1994) would have protected the authorities in Hong Kong should Reid have been insolvent. In the event this did not materialise. Both these trusts have been criticised because they create a proprietary right ranking ahead of the creditors of the company.

4.22   Similarly, the creation of an express trust will also protect the beneficiaries. This is exactly what happened in *Re Kayford* (1975) where the company, which was concerned about its financial situation, set up a special trust account at its bank, so that mail order buyers would be protected.

4.23   It is unclear whether the *Re Kayford* result would be affected by the provisions of the Insolvency Act 1986. This act renders voidable two specific transactions: first, transactions at undervalue, where the company is transferring value or does not give full value; and second, preferences, the desire to prefer a particular creditor or guarantor at the expense of other creditors of the company. There is some discussion of this in Unit 14 'Commerce, Credit and the Trust' in Graham Moffat, *Trusts Law Text and Materials*, 1994.

4.24   However, there has been no specific case analogous to *Re Kayford* (1975) after 1986 where the effect of these provisions of the Insolvency Act has been specifically considered. In the absence of such a case it is sensible to look at *Re M.C. Bacon Ltd* (1990) which is a leading case on both transactions at undervalue and preferences.

4.25   Millett J, as he then was, would regard a transaction as being a preference only if there was a deliberate and positive desire by the company to improve that particular creditor's position through that transaction. If such a transaction was commercially necessary then although a company agreed to such a transaction, it did not follow that the company desired it.

4.26   In relation to a transaction at undervalue, the transaction must be one which is capable of being valued in money or money's worth. The court regarded the creation of security over the company's assets as not depleting or reducing them. It is possible that such an approach might be extended to the creation of a trust over a bank account set up by the company.

4.27 For a general discussion of the role of trusts, and particularly fiduciary relationships in a commercial setting, see *Commercial Aspects of Trusts and Fiduciary Obligations* (ed. Ewan Mckendrick) Clarendon Press, Oxford, (1992).

Summary

Now you have studied the text and worked through this Unit, you should understand:

☐ **how trusts are classified**

☐ **public and private trusts**

☐ **express trusts, and executed and executory trusts**

☐ **resulting trusts, and constructive trusts.**

Self-assessment questions

1 What is an express trust?

2 Distinguish between a presumed resulting trust and an automatic resulting trust.

3 What is a constructive trust?

4 What is a private trust?

5 What is a charitable trust?

6 What is a *Quistclose* trust and when will it arise?

7 A branch of Barks and Fencers faces financial difficulties. As part of its closing down sale, it allows various 'licensees' to sell their goods at the store, in addition to products sold by Barks and Fencers. The licensees agree to pay to Barks and Fencers a commission for each sale. In addition the monies that the licensees receive is paid into tills belonging to the store. It is then put into the Barks and Fencers account, which is in surplus, at the Sloppy Bank Plc. The Sloppy Bank Plc seek to set off this account against another Barks and Fencers account, at the Sloppy Bank Plc, which is in overdraft.

Advise Barks and Fencers.

8   Consider the similarities and differences between the following types of trust:

   a) express trusts;

   b) resulting trusts;

   c) constructive trusts.

9   Consider the importance of *Westdeutsche Landesbank Girozentrale v Islington London Borough Council* (1996) to the general classification of the types of trust.

Exam-style question

a) Describe the differences between a charitable trust and a private trust.

b) Gerald died recently. One of the bequests in his will is of a sum of money to his trustees 'for such charitable and deserving causes as they may choose'.

   Discuss the validity of this bequest.

[Spring 1995]

(The answers are given in the Appendix)

Caselist for Unit 3 Classification of Trusts

Re Vandervell's Trust (No. 2) [1974] Ch 269.

Barclays Bank Ltd v *Quistclose Investments Ltd* [1970] AC 567.

Sir Peter Millett, 'The *Quistclose* Trust: Who can enforce it? (1985) 101 LQR 269.

Charles Rickett, 'Different Views on the Scope of the *Quistclose* Analysis: English and Antipodean Insights' (1991) 107 LQR 608.

Michael Bridge, 'The *Quistclose* Trust in a World of Secure Transactions' (1992) 12 Oxford J Legal Stud 333.

Re EVTR, Gilbert v *Barber* [1987] BCLC 646.

Carreras Rothmans Ltd v *Freeman Mathews Treasure Ltd (in liquidation) and Another* [1985] Ch 207.

Chase Manhatten Bank NA v *Israel-British Bank (London) Ltd* [1981] Ch 105.

Attorney-General of Hong Kong v *Reid* [1994] 1 AC 324.

Sir Peter Millet, 'Bribes and Secret Commissions' (1993) RLR 7.

Anthony Oakley, 'Proprietary Claims and their Priority on Insolvency' (1995) 54 CLJ 377.

Keith Uff, 'The Remedies of the Defrauded Principal After *Attorney-General For Hong Kong* v *Reid*' in *Corporate and Commercial Law: Modern Developments* (ed. David Feldman and Frank Meisel), Lloyd's of London Press, London, Chapter 13 (1996).

David Cowan, Rod Edmunds, and John Lowry, '*Lister and Co v Stubbs*: Who Profits?' [1996] JBL 22.

Simon Gardner, 'Two Maxims of Equity' (1995) CLJ 60.

Grant v *Edwards* [1986] Ch 638.

Law of Property Act 1925

Law of Property (Miscellaneous Provisions) Act 1989.

Westdeutsche Landesbank Girozentrale v *Islington London Borough Council* [1996] 2 WLR 802.

Peter Birks, 'Restitution and Resulting Trusts' in *Equity and Contemporary Legal Developments* (ed. Stephen Goldstein) (1992).

Anthony Oakley, 'The Liberalising Nature of Remedies for Breach of Trust' *Trends in Contemporary Trust Law* (ed. A.J. Oakley) Clarendon Press, Oxford, Chapter 10, (1996).

Peter Birks QC, 'Trusts Raised to Reverse Unjust Enrichment: The *Westdeutsche* Case' (1996) RLR 3.

The Hon. Sir Anthony Mason, 'The Place of Equity and Equitable Remedies in the Contemporary Common Law World' (1994) 110 LQR 238.

Re Kayford [1975] 1 WLR 279.

Graham Moffat, 'Commerce, credit and the trust' in *Trusts Law Text and Materials*, Chapter 14, Butterworths, London (1994).

Re M.C. Bacon [1990] 3 WLR 646.

Commercial Aspects of Trusts and Fiduciary Obligations (ed. Ewan Mckendrick), Clarendon Press, Oxford (1992).

4

Trusts and Powers

Objectives

After studying the text and working through this Unit, students should be able to:

- **identify the nature of trusts and powers**

- **understand fixed and discretionary trusts**

- **understand powers of appointment**

- **understand gifts in default of appointment.**

1 Trusts and powers, their basic nature

1.1   A trust may be defined as where the trustee owns only the legal interest in some property; the equitable interest in it is held by the trustee on trust for the beneficiary. This has been discussed in Unit 2.

1.2   On the other hand, a power is where a person owns both the legal and equitable interest in some property. That person is the absolute owner, and is free to do whatever he wishes with the property. In such a situation he may, at his absolute discretion, transfer part or all of that property to another person.

1.3   Such a power is known as a 'bare power'. Thus, if I give some property or money to Albert 'with power to appoint [give] amongst his children and grandchildren', this would create a bare power.

1.4   In an important House of Lords decision, *McPhail v Doulton* (1971), Lord Wilberforce made an important distinction between a trust and a power put into a trust. The particular clause the court was asked to interpret used the word 'shall'. It was a word that was imperative; this one word was the reason Lord Wilberforce concluded that a trust had been created. The trustee must distribute amongst the various beneficiaries.

2 Fixed and discretionary trusts

2.1 In a 'fixed' trust, the particular share of each beneficiary is exactly quantified, i.e. a half share for Albert. With a discretionary trust, no particular beneficiary can point to any particular interest that he has. So, if a trust was created whereby 'the trustees shall distribute amongst my relatives and dependants', this would create a discretionary trust.

2.2 As we have seen, a discretionary trust must be carried out. In particular, a trustee has a duty to:

- select from the whole class of beneficiaries, and

- distribute the income and/or capital amongst the chosen beneficiaries in accordance with the terms of the trust.

2.3 With a fixed trust, the interest that the beneficiary has is clearly identified. However, with a discretionary trust, although the trustee has to carry out his duties, the particular beneficiary does not know how much he will receive. The beneficiaries of the trust own (collectively) the equitable interest in the trust. Individually, however, their shares are not identified.

2.4 So, if we use the example above, where 'the trustees shall distribute amongst my relatives and dependants', no relative or dependant could point to or identify any particular share.

3 Discretionary trusts

3.1 This is a particular trust and the requirements of 'the three certainties' must still be satisfied, as they are essential to create a valid trust. First, there must be a clear intention to create a trust; second, it must be certain who are the beneficiaries (objects) of the trust; and third, it must be certain what property is to be held under that trust. See Unit 5.

3.2 The particular certainty of importance in this context is that of objects. The class of beneficiaries may be widely drawn, so that no particular beneficiary has an identifiable interest. There was a wide clause of this type in *McPhail* v *Doulton* (1971). In this case the class of beneficiaries included the employees of a certain company and their relatives and dependants.

3.3   The width of the class of beneficiaries causes problems in terms of the trust satisfying the three certainties; in particular with the certainty of objects, and if this is not satisfied the trust will be invalid.

3.4   To try and resolve these problems, Lord Wilberforce, in *McPhail v Doulton* (1971), put forward a test for certainty of objects, which had to be satisfied for a discretionary trust to be valid. His test was: can a trustee tell with certainty, in relation to any hypothetical individual who presents himself before the trustee, whether he is a member of the class? This means that the class of each group of beneficiaries must be defined so that it has a clear meaning. This test of Lord Wilberforce has been confirmed in *Pearson v I.R.C.* (1980).

3.5   The House of Lords did not apply this test to the particular facts in *McPhail v Doulton* (1971). There were doubts about how to apply it. Subsequently, when this test was applied by the Court of Appeal in *Re Baden Deed Trusts (No. 2)* (1973), the test was satisfied. The Court of Appeal could tell of any individual whether he was:

● an employee

● a relative

● a dependant.

All the classes of beneficiary were sufficiently certain (clear), and the discretionary trust was held by the Court of Appeal to be valid.

3.6   In addition, the group of beneficiaries must form a distinct group: *McPhail v Doulton* (1971). They must also be 'administratively workable'; that is, it must be practical to administer the trust bearing in mind the size of the class and the funds that are available for distribution: *McPhail v Doulton* (1971).

4 Powers of appointment

4.1   We may classify these in two ways: a power given to an individual (which has been considered above); and a fiduciary power (a power put into a trust). Fiduciary powers will be examined below.

4.2   With a fiduciary power there is a duty to consider whether to distribute income or capital, though the person or trustee who has the power is not under a duty actually to distribute: *Turner v Turner* (1984). As we shall see below, this is the reason why powers normally have a gift in default. If there is no distribution then another class will take (i.e. to class A but in default to class B).

4.3   In the particular facts of *Turner v Turner* (1984) the trustees just signed the documents given to them without any independent consideration. It was held that they had not exercised their duty to consider what action to take.

4.4   However, there is no duty for trustees of a pension trust to give reasons to the beneficiaries as to why they have exercised their discretion in the way they have: *Wilson and another* v *Law Debenture Trust Corp Plc* (1995).

4.5   Lord Wilberforce makes the point in *McPhail* v *Doulton* (1971) that there is very little difference between a trust with a power to accumulate the income, and a power with a trust to distribute the income. He was making the point that clauses could include both powers and trusts and make the distinction between the two very difficult. That was precisely why he wanted the same test of certainty of objects for both trusts and powers.

4.6   Finally, one should conclude this part of this section by emphasising the point that there is a range of powers given to trustees quite independently of the duty to distribute. These powers and this whole area is considered in depth by R. Pearce and J. Stevens in Chapters 14, 15, and 17 of *The Law of Trusts and Equitable Obligations* (1996).

Fiduciary powers

4.7   Following the discussion above about the bare power a person can hold as an individual, we now consider the position where the same power is given to a trustee to exercise it under a trust.

4.8   This changes the position, since it is now a trustee who is to exercise the power.

4.9   The trustee must also consider whether and how he ought to exercise that power: *Mettoy Pensions Trustees Ltd* v *Evans* (1991).

4.10   The recent discussion in the case law is not so much about distribution of income or capital, but rather the rights of employees of a company to the surplus funds in their pension trust where the trustees of that trust have been given a power.

4.11   Millett J, as he then was, in *Re Courage Group's Pension Schemes* (1987) made a clear distinction between the contractual position and that under the law of trusts.

4.12   As a matter of contract, an employer (company A) could require an employee to contribute to the pension scheme, even though it was in surplus. That employer (company A) has to make payments to the employees in accordance with the terms of the scheme.

4.13   As a matter of trust law, because there was a fiduciary power under the scheme, the employees had the right to continued entitlement to any surplus. Another company (company B) could not simply purchase the share capital of the employer company (company A) and then dissipate the surplus.

4.14 This approach was developed in *Mettoy Pensions Trustees Ltd* v *Evans* (1991), which concerned a company administering a pension scheme trust. The trustees had a fiduciary power in relation to that trust.

4.15 Warner J adopted the same approach of Millett J in *Re Courage Group's Pension Schemes* (1987). On the insolvency of the company (Mettoy) the surplus in its pension scheme trust was held by Warner J not to be available for the general creditors of the company. This surplus was only available for distribution amongst the employees.

4.16 The approach of Warner J was followed by Sir Donald Nicholls V-C in *Thrells Ltd* v *Lomas* (1993), which again concerned a company (Thrells Ltd) that went into liquidation, with a deficiency of £2m. The question was what was to happen to the pension surplus of just over half a million pounds.

4.17 Sir Donald Nicholls considered, as a matter of equity, that the employees were entitled to share in this surplus. The fiduciary power given to the trustee (the company Thrells Ltd) in the Thrells pension trust fund could only be exercised in favour of the employees of the company. The surplus in this pension could not be paid over to the company to satisfy the creditors of the company.

4.18 In *Imperial Group Trust* v *Imperial Ltd* (1991), Sir Nicholas Browne-Wilkinson confirmed that powers held by trustees of a pension fund must be exercised in good faith. This meant that the trustees had to preserve the employees' rights under the trust.

4.19 The judge viewed this as being a contractual duty arising out of employment. However, this did not deny those employees the right to bring claims for breach of trust duties owing to them. There is further discussion about pensions, pension surpluses and the Pensions Act 1995 in Units 9, 10 and 11.

4.20 The above cases, regarding surplus pension funds, are discussed by David Hayton in Hayton and Marshall, *Commentary and Cases on the Law of Trusts and Equitable Remedies* (ed. D.J. Hayton) 10th edition, (1996), Chapter 9. In addition this chapter contains a number of useful sections of the Pension Act 1995.

4.21 The above cases are also discussed by Sir Robert Walker, 'Some Trust Principles in the Pensions Context' in *Trends in Contemporary Trust Law* (ed. A.J. Oakley) (1996), Chapter 5.

5 Gifts in default

5.1 Where a power over some property is granted to an individual, known as a bare power, it will normally be granted with 'a gift in default'. This means that if the donee of the power does not exercise the power, as he is free to do, the property will be taken by some other person or persons.

5.2   This principle may be be looked at in reverse. If a clause in a document contains 'a gift in default', this suggests that the clause has created a power. The reason is that, if a discretionary trust were created (where the trustee was obliged to exercise his discretion and distribute income and/or capital), there would be no need for a gift in default: *Re Leek* (1967).

6 Evaluation of Unit 4

6.1   There are still problems that remain after the decision in *McPhail* v *Doulton* (1971). In some cases the trust could be avoided on the basis that the class is conceptually uncertain. In *Re Barlow's Will Trusts* (1979), Browne-Wilkinson J considered that the term 'friends' would not satisfy the test put forward by Lord Wilberforce.

6.2   Nevertheless the judge was able to put forward a conceptual meaning to this term. Friendship meant a long-standing association in a social context where the parties meet on a frequent basis when able to do so.

6.3   This case does show that the courts are able to resolve difficulties of uncertainty. However, subsequent to *McPhail* v *Doulton* (1971) the Court of Appeal, in *R* v *District Auditor, ex parte West Yorkshire Metropolitan County Council* (1985), considered that a trust for inhabitants of the County of West Yorkshire could be rendered invalid on the basis of lack of certainty as to who was an inhabitant.

6.4   In particular, Lloyd L J was of the view that such a trust would fail for administrative unworkability. This idea had first been put forward by Lord Wilberforce in *McPhail* v *Doulton* (1971). Lord Wilberforce considered that administratively unworkable meant that the words used in the trust did not form a class.

6.5   Applying what Lord Wilberforce had said, Lloyd L J was of the view that since the potential class of beneficiaries could be greater than two and a halfm, the trust was administratively unworkable.

6.6   It is suggested that although the trustees had over £400,000 to spend in a relatively short space of time, it might have been possible to distribute. In particular, there were sufficient funds available to advertise and introduce some form of administration of the trust.

6.7   Another reason has also been put forward by which a trust could be rendered invalid. In *Re Manisty's Settlement* (1974), Templeman J considered that the class of objects could be capricious because it showed no sensible intention on the settlor's part.

6.8   This is similar to administrative unworkability but it is not the same test. It may be that because of a lack of sensible intention, nothing like a class of beneficiaries is formed.

6.9   There is another difficulty as a result of the test in *McPhail v Doulton* (1971). The test for certainty of objects is essentially a test for individuals to satisfy. This may not help the trustee decide how to distribute trust funds amongst the various beneficiaries. This criticism of the test established by Lord Wilberforce was put forward by Stamp LJ in *Re Baden's Deed Trusts (No. 2)* (1973).

6.10   His objection was that the whole class of beneficiaries had to be drawn up in order for an effective distribution of funds to be made. In the opinion of Stamp LJ, Lord Wilberforce had failed to concentrate on this aspect. Although the other two judges in the Court of Appeal in *Re Baden's Deed Trusts (No. 2)* (1973) did not take this view, Stamp LJ's approach does stress the need for the trustees to be able to distribute effectively.

6.11   Having established that the trust was valid, the trustees then had to decide how to administer the trust. Because they had genuine doubts about this, they sought the directions of the court. This was (and is) a sensible course of action for them to take. In deciding how this trust should be administered, the case went originally before the High Court and subsequently to the Court of Appeal.

6.12   In the Court of Appeal in *Re Baden's Deed Trusts (No. 2)* (1973) there were differing views put forward by the various judges.

6.13   Sachs LJ emphasised the importance of conceptual certainty. Provided the class used in the trust had a clear meaning (i.e. was conceptually certain), this was sufficient.

6.14   The reason was that once the class was conceptually certain, it could be decided whether any individual was a member of the class. This meant that the test put forward by Lord Wilberforce in the House of Lords would be satisfied in such a situation.

6.15   Applying his test to the facts, the classes of 'employees', 'relatives' and 'dependants' were all conceptually certain. It followed that since each of the classes of beneficiary was valid, the whole trust was valid.

6.16   Megaw LJ looked at the position differently. In his view, Lord Wilberforce in *McPhail v Doulton* (1971) wanted to abandon the complete list test. He did this so that it was no longer necessary for the trustees to have to draw up a complete list of objects. On the other hand, Megaw LJ recognised that

Lord Wilberforce did not want validity to be too easily established. It would not be sufficient if the trustees could tell that only one (just one) individual fell within the class of objects.

6.17 Megaw LJ put forward his own test in the light of his view of what Lord Wilberforce was trying to do. His test was that the court had to be able to tell whether a substantial number of objects fell within the class.

6.18 Again, provided the class was conceptually certain, it followed that the trustees would be able to tell whether a substantial number of objects fell within the class. In the opinion of Megaw LJ it did not matter that a substantial number of other persons fell outside the class.

6.19 It followed (as Sachs LJ had concluded) that since 'employees', 'relatives' and 'dependants' were conceptually certain, all the classes of beneficiaries were valid, and the trust was valid. The trustees could therefore be left to administer the trust.

6.20 *Re Hay's Settlement's Trust* (1982) confirms that the trustees do not have to compile a complete list of objects. Megarry V-C was of the view that, in terms of distribution of the trust funds, what the trustees have to do is to make a general survey of the potential objects, i.e. are there some, several, hundreds, or thousands of objects.

6.21 The trustees then have to proceed to look at the individual needs of particular beneficiaries. It is not necessary to compare one beneficiary against another.

6.22 In *Re Beatty (dec'd)* (1990), it was accepted by Hoffmann J that one could put words into a trust which made it clear that the settlor did not intend to create a discretionary trust. In such a situation, despite the use of the word 'shall', only a power was created.

6.23 This confirms the decision in *McPhail v Doulton* (1971) and also decides that its principle may be avoided. However, although a power is created, because it is put into a trust, the trustees still have duties in relation to it. It is these duties that will now be examined.

6.24 Graham Moffat, 'Creating the Trust II' in *Trusts Law Text and Materials* (1994) Chapter 5, makes the point that both a discretionary trust and also a power given to trustees involve the trustees in the exercise of discretion. However, in the case of a power with a gift in default, the trustees do not have to exercise that power.

6.25 In such a situation those entitled in default will take the property held in trust. Moffatt compares that with the duties imposed upon the trustees under a discretionary trust. In this second situation, the trustees must distribute in accordance with the terms and discretions given to them under the trust. If the trustees fail to do this, the court can order them to do so, or even take over the running of the trust.

6.26 Lord Wilberforce was clearly of the opinion in *McPhail* v *Doulton* (1971) that the court could step in where there was a failure on the part of the trustees under a discretionary trust. The court could appoint new trustees, or the court could administer the trust on the basis of proposals put forward by the trustees.

6.27 If a trustee is in genuine doubt as to how to administer such a trust then the trustee is able to seek the directions of the court. The court will consider sensible proposals put forward by the trustees. Lord Wilberforce confirmed that the courts had power to do this in *McPhail* v *Doulton* (1971).

6.28 This power was considered in *Marley* v *Mutual Security Merchant Bank* (1991). The defendant bank was the administrator of the estate of Bob Marley, an international singer and composer. The defendant bank wished to sell all the copyrights of various Bob Marley compositions.

6.29 The beneficiaries did not wish the sale to go ahead. As a result, the defendant bank sought the approval of the court. The Privy Council confirmed that it had the jurisdiction to approve such a sale, provided it was given full and complete information.

6.30 On the facts, the court felt that the defendant bank should discuss its sale of the copyrights with other buyers. In particular, it should show that it had explored all possible avenues in trying to achieve the maximum sale price. The court would therefore not sanction the sale of the copyrights until this had been done.

6.31 This is an important case. It shows that the courts will strive to validate a trust if they are able to. Further, if they are able to assist the trustees in carrying out their duties, or even exercise the court's discretion in place of the trustees, they are willing to do so.

6.32 Nearly two centuries ago, the court made clear that express trusts must be sufficiently certain, otherwise they will be held invalid: *Morice* v *Bishop of Durham* (1805). The reason for this is that the court must be able to administer the trust if the trustees request it to do so.

6.33 In addition, the courts must be able to tell if there has been a breach of trust. The courts can do these two things only if the trust is certain.

6.34 The *Marley* case does not change this approach. The courts are relying on expert evidence as to the correct sale price. They are then able to exercise their judgment in the same way that trustees do.

6.35 This is why trusts are invalidated for reasons of 'conceptual uncertainty'. If the class is unclear it will be impossible for the trustees to carry out their duties, and impossible for the courts to tell whether the trust is being administered properly.

6.36 In contrast, the sale price of a trust's key asset will undoubtedly affect the amount that each beneficiary will receive. However, the court can tell whether the sale price is a correct one in the light of expert evidence. The courts can consider whether the procedural steps taken by the trustees are adequate, as the court did in the *Marley* case.

6.37 Another way, which also assists in resolving uncertainty, is to appoint an expert to determine difficult questions. The expert is used to bring his or her knowledge to the particular difficulty: *Re Tuck's Settlement Trusts* (1978).

Summary

Now you have studied the text and worked through this Unit, you should understand:

- ☐ **the nature of trusts and powers**

- ☐ **fixed and discretionary trusts**

- ☐ **powers of appointment**

- ☐ **gifts in default of appointment.**

Self-assessment questions

1 What is a bare power?

2 How might one distinguish between a discretionary trust and a power put into a trust?

3 What is the distinction between a fixed trust and a discretionary trust?

4 Describe the duties of a trustee under a discretionary trust.

5   What is a fiduciary power?

6   What problems remain for the law of trusts after the decision of the House of Lords in *McPhail* v *Doulton* (1971)?

7   John is a former fighter pilot in the Royal Air Force. By his will, which he drafts himself, he leaves his estate 'to my trustees Bill and Ben to distribute income and capital for heterosexual pilots serving in the RAF and their relatives and dependants as they should select, but if this part shall fail, then to my relatives and good friends as my trustees consider deserving'.

John has recently died. Advise Bill and Ben.

Exam-style question

George died in 1985, having appointed your bank as executor and trustee of his will. Under the terms of the will, his son Adrian is to receive the income for life from the residuary estate. Adrian was 20 when his father died and, under the further terms of the will, he is given a power of appointment over the trust after his own death in favour of his own issue in such proportions and in such a manner as he may by deed or will decide.

In default of the exercise of this power, the capital will pass to a named charity.

a) Adrian has explained to you that his wife has recently given birth to a son, Henry. He has made a brief will leaving all his estate to Henry. Discuss whether Henry will also receive George's residuary estate.

b) Adrian asks whether he could leave a life interest in George's residuary estate to Henry with its capital eventually passing to Henry's children. Discuss whether this would be a valid way of exercising the power.

c) Adrian indicates that, when Henry is 18, he has it in mind to appoint the capital to him by deed, and then share the capital with him immediately so as to frustrate his late father's intention that Adrian should never be able to obtain any capital. Discuss whether he could do this.

[Spring 1996]

(The answers are given in the Appendix)

Caselist for Unit 4 Trusts and Powers

McPhail v *Doulton* [1971] AC 424.

Re Baden's Deeds (No. 2) [1972] Ch 607 (High Court); [1973] Ch 9 (Court of Appeal).

Turner v *Turner* [1984] Ch 100.

Wilson and another v *Law Debenture Trust Corp Plc* [1995] 2 All ER 337.

Pearce and Stevens, *The Law of Trusts and Equitable Obligations*, Butterworths, London (1995), Chapters 14, 15, and 17.

Mettoy Pension Trustees v *Evans* [1990] 1 WLR 1587.

Re Courage Group's Pension Schemes, Ryan and Others v *Imperial Brewing and Leisure Ltd* [1987] 1 WLR 495.

Thrells Ltd v *Lomas and Another* [1993] 1 WLR 456.

Imperial Group Pension Trust Ltd and Others v *Imperial Tobacco Ltd and Others* [1991] 1 WLR 589.

Hayton and Marshall, *Commentary and Cases on the Law of Trusts and Equitable Remedies* (ed. D.J. Hayton) Sweet and Maxwell, London (1996).

Sir Robert Walker, 'Some Trust Principles in the Pensions Context' in *Trends in Contemporary Trust Law* (ed. A.J. Oakley) Clarendon Press, Oxford (1996).

Re Leek, Darween v *Leek* [1967] Ch 1061 (High Court); [1969] 1 Ch 563 (Court of Appeal).

Re Barlow's Will Trust [1979] 1 WLR 278.

R v *District Auditor, ex parte West Yorkshire Metropolitan County Council* [1986] RVR 24.

Re Manisty's Settlement [1974] Ch 17.

Re Hay's Settlement Trust [1982] 1 WLR 202.

Re Beatty (dec'd), Hinves and Others v *Brooke and Others* [1990] 1 WLR 1503.

Graham Moffat, *Trusts Law Text and Materials*, Butterworths, London (1994), Chapter 5.

Marley v *Mutual Security Merchant Bank and Trust Co Ltd* [1991] 3 All ER 198.

Morice v *Bishop of Durham* (1805) 10 Ves 522.

Re Tuck's Settlement Trusts [1978] Ch 49.

5

Validity of Trusts

1 Capacity to act as a trustee

1.1 The settlor has the power to transfer the property into trust. First, the property must be owned by the settlor. Second, the settlor must have the necessary capacity. This means that the settlor must not be a minor (under 18) and must not be mentally incapable.

1.2 Similar rules apply to the capacity to act as an express trustee. (See Unit 9 on the appointment and removal of trustees.) There are now new rules on the removal of mentally incapable trustees of land by virtue of the Trusts of Land and Appointment of Trustees Act 1996 whereby trustees of land may be removed by direction of the beneficiaries.

1.3 This situation (removal of a mentally incapable trustee) should not arise in relation to minors since they are not able to hold an estate of land by section 1(6) of the Law of Property Act 1925. For this reason a minor should not be appointed as a trustee of land in the first place.

1.4 It is established that a minor can become a resulting or constructive trustee. In *Re Vinogradoff* (1935) the presumption of resulting trust applied to certain shares transferred by a grandmother to her grandchild. On the death of the grandmother the grandchild held the shares on resulting trust for the grandmother's estate.

1.5   However, the resulting or constructive trust is used in this context to protect the beneficiary. It is a temporary measure in contrast to an express trust, the trustee of which has continuing duties.

2 Formal requirements

Land

2.1   There are particular sections of importance in relation to land. Section 53(1)(a) of the Law of Property Act 1925 provides that no interest in land may be created or disposed of except in writing. Also, section 53(1)(b) of the same act provides that a declaration of trust of land must be manifested and proved by some writing. The section does not specify the amount of writing that is required.

2.2   The first provision, (53)(1)(a), is regarded as the general section, and the second, (53)(1)(b), as that dealing with trusts.

2.3   There is a further statute of importance. This is the Law of Property (Miscellaneous Provisions) Act 1989. Section 2(1) provides that a contract for the sale or other disposition of an interest in land can be made only in writing. In this regard, 'disposition' is construed narrowly, so as to be something analogous with a sale: *Spiro* v *Glencrown Properties Ltd* (1991). This act also applies to the variation of a contract for the sale of land: *McCausland* v *Duncan Lawrie Ltd and another* (1996).

3 Personalty

3.1   There are no particular sections dealing with personal property, such as shares, paintings, etc. However, where such property is held on trust, or there is a separate equitable interest in relation to it, the provisions of section 53(1)(c) of the Law of Property Act, discussed below, will apply.

4 Subsisting equitable interests

4.1   Section 53(1)(c) catches 'dispositions' of separate equitable interests. A separate equitable interest is one in which the equitable interest has been separated from the legal interest. The classic situation is where there is an existing trust. To transfer (dispose) a separated equitable interest to another, the disposition must be in writing: see section 53(1)(c) of the Law of Property Act 1925, *Grey* v *I.R.C.* (1960). In this case it was held by the House of Lords that 'disposition' meant its ordinary, natural meaning.

4.2 There is a particularly important qualification to section 53(1)(c). For this qualification to apply, a number of elements must be satisfied. First, the owner of the equitable interest must wish to make a gift to another; second, there must be a clear intention to that effect; and third, the legal interest is transferred to that person. In such a situation the equitable interest will 'move' to that recipient without the need for writing: *Vandervell* v *I.R.C.* (1967). This exception was created judicially.

4.3 Where a beneficiary seeks to create a sub-trust by assigning his equitable interest to another, because there is a separated interest, there are potential problems with section 53(1)(c); this was discussed in Unit 3.

5 Resulting and constructive trusts

5.1 Section 53(2) of the Law of Property Act 1925 provides that the other provisions in section 53 (described above) will not affect the creation or operation of resulting or constructive trusts.

5.2 This has been a problematic section. The following type of situation arises. Albert makes an oral contract with Bob to sell the separate equitable interest in those shares which he (Albert) has. Were it not for section 53(2), such a transaction would infringe section 53(1)(c), which provides that dispositions (the contract here being a disposition) of separated equitable interests must be in writing. The issue is whether the transaction is saved by section 53(2).

5.3 Take the situation where the seller has both the legal and the equitable interest in the shares. When a sale is made in equity, the equitable interest passes to the buyer. The legal interest remains with the seller. Because the buyer has the equitable interest, he is able to obtain the equitable remedy of specific performance.

5.4 The remedy of specific performance was not available at common law. Under it, the buyer can compel performance of the contract. The buyer contracted to receive both the legal and the equitable interest in the shares. Hence the buyer is able to compel the seller to transfer the legal title to him. Equity regards as done that which ought to be done: *Attorney-General of Hong Kong* v *Reid* (1994).

5.5 The situation that arises is one of split legal and equitable ownership under a constructive trust: *Oughtred* v *I.R.C.* (1960). It is of a temporary nature, until the seller transfers his legal title and performs his side of the contract.

5.6 The scope and effect of section 53(2) in this situation was considered by the House of Lords in *Oughtred* v *I.R.C.* (1960). A majority of their Lordships was able to deal with the case without making a final decision on whether the oral contract (and therefore the lack of writing) is saved by the constructive trust falling within section 53(2). One of their Lordships (who dissented on a different point), Viscount Radcliffe, was of the clear view that the oral contract would still create a constructive trust, and would be saved by section 53(2) from what would otherwise be invalidity.

5.7 Recent cases have sought to clarify the position. One involved oral contracts to transfer equitable interests in shares held in trust. The Court of Appeal (although a lower court than the House of Lords) was clearly of the view that such an oral agreement (contract) created a constructive trust and was saved by section 53(2). Therefore the oral agreement, to dispose of the shares which were held in trust, was valid: *Neville and Another* v *Wilson and Others* (1996).

5.8 The opposite approach was taken by the High Court in *United Bank of Kuwait Plc* v *Sahib* (1995). However this was a case not directly in point, and it was not necessary for the judge to come to a conclusion on it. When the case reached the Court of Appeal, it did not deal with the effect of section 53(2) at all: *United Bank of Kuwait Plc* v *Sahib* (1996).

5.9 There is also a similar saving provision for resulting and constructive trusts in the Law of Property (Miscellaneous Provisions) Act 1989. This is provided by section 2(5)(c) of that act.

6 Will trusts

6.1 A trust may be made during the settlor's life (called in technical language 'inter vivos'), or by will to take effect on the settlor's death. Their formalities require writing, so they necessarily comply with sections 53(1)(b) and (c).

6.2 Both sections will regard a will as satisfying the necessary formality. A will is able to declare a trust of land since section 53(1)(b) expressly says so. Similarly, one may dispose of a subsisting (separated) equitable interest in personal property – whether in a trust or otherwise – by will, since section 53(1)(c) expressly says so. In addition, section 55 of the Law of Property Act 1925 provides that nothing in section 53 shall invalidate a 'disposition' made in a will.

7 Evaluation of the rules relating to formalities

7.1 The Court of Appeal in *Neville* v *Wilson* (1996) looked with some care at the previous decision of the House of Lords in *Oughtred* v *I.R.C.* (1960).

7.2 The Court of Appeal gave particular weight to Lord Radcliffe's reasoning in the previous House of Lords decision. An oral agreement by A to transfer shares in a private company to B gives B the right of specific performance to compel A to transfer the shares as agreed.

7.3   Because the shares are those of a private company, they cannot be readily bought on the stock exchange. Damages (at common law) are therefore inadequate, and the remedy (in equity) of specific performance is available.

7.4   Since specific performance is available to B, it follows that B has obtained the equitable interest in those shares. B is seeking specific performance so that the legal title in those shares, which continues to be held by A, must be transferred to B.

7.5   As a consequence, a constructive trust is created in favour of B. This is a constructive trust so as to ensure that the agreement will be carried into effect, by requiring A to transfer the legal title to B as agreed, and to protect B in the meantime.

7.6   This was the view of Lord Radcliffe and Lord Cohen (the two minority judgments) in the House of Lords in *Oughtred* v *I.R.C.* (1960). It was these judgments that Nourse LJ followed in the Court of Appeal in *Neville* v *Wilson* (1996).

7.7   The majority of their Lordships in *Oughtred* v *I.R.C.* (1960) took a different view. In the view of Lord Denning, Lord Jenkins and Lord Keith (the three majority judgments) writing was still required.

7.8   Without writing there could not be a binding agreement. If there was no agreement then specific performance could not be available in order to compel the seller to carry out the agreement. If specific performance was not available then a constructive trust could not be imposed to protect the buyer.

7.9   If there was no constructive trust then writing would be required. The constructive trust is the exception provided by section 53(2) of the Law of Property Act 1925 and allows equitable interests to be disposed of without writing as required by section 53(1)(c) of the Law of Property Act 1925.

7.10   In the opinion of Nourse LJ, the minority judgments were the correct approach. He did not find the views of the majority convincing. He thought that there was nothing in the words of section 53(2) which required the original agreement to be in writing. He thought that to require this was restrictive and overtechnical.

7.11   An important factor was that *Oughtred* v *I.R.C.* (1960) involved a sophisticated scheme to avoid stamp duty. This was not the position in *Neville* v *Wilson* (1996), and accounts for the approach in the Court of Appeal.

7.12   Simon Gardiner in his chapter on 'Formalities' in *An Introduction to the Law of Trusts* (1990) makes the point that the reason why non written arragements are made is to avoid stamp duty, and that *Oughtred* v *I.R.C.*

(1960) was a deliberate and sophisticated attempt at avoidance. The House of Lords was not prepared to allow this to happen. Their Lordship's reasoning and decision must be viewed in this light.

7.13 This policy approach was not required in *Neville* v *Wilson* (1996) which was not a case concerning stamp duty avoidance. The Court of Appeal could therefore adopt a different approach. Broadly, the Court of Appeal was prepared to adopt a flexible approach to the interpretation of section 53(2). The House of Lords was not prepared to do this in *Oughtred* v *I.R.C.* (1960) since this would have led to the avoidance of stamp duty.

7.14 As Parker and Mellows point out in Chapter 14, 'The Taxation of a Trust' in *The Modern Law of Trusts* (ed. A.J. Oakley) (1994), ad valorem stamp duty was ended by section 82 of the Finance Act 1985. This has rendered the sophisticated tax avoidance devices unnecessary.

7.15 Richard Nolan in his casenote of *Neville* v *Wilson* (1996) – 'The Triumph of Technicality' (1996) CLJ 436. is of the view that both *Oughtred* v *I.R.C.* (1960) and *Neville* v *Wilson* (1996) should have been decided in the same fashion. As we have seen, they were decided differently.

7.16 In his view, the fact that the objective in *Oughtred* v *I.R.C.* (1960) was to avoid tax should be ignored. Hence, in principle the outcome should be the same when dealing with a case such as *Neville* v *Wilson* (1996) which did not involve a scheme to avoid tax.

7.17 Richard Nolan also makes the other interesting point that the constructive trust which is created (discussed previously) arises where the seller has both the legal and the equitable interest in the property. As we have seen, by virtue of the contract the equitable interest moves to the buyer. Richard Nolan indicates that the constructive trust in *Neville* v *Wilson* was extended to the situation where the seller had only an equitable interest in the shares.

7.18 This point was not discussed in the case, though it is a matter of importance.

8 The Three Certainties

8.1 In order to create a valid express trust, 'the three certainties' are required:

- Certainty of intention. In general terms, words must be used indicating an intention to create a trust.

- Certainty of object. It must be clear for whom such a trust is intended.

- Certainty of subject matter. It must also be established, with clarity, what property is to be held on the express trust.

8.2   A starting point in relation to certainty of intention is the equitable maxim (general statement) that 'equity looks to the intention not the form'. In this context the words used are important. However, the courts look at the words used in the light of all the circumstances.

8.3   If the word 'trust' is used then this will be a very strong factor pointing to a trust: *Re Kayford* (1975) (discussed previously in Unit 3). The director of a mail order company wanted to protect his customers, who had purchased goods by mail order, in the event of the insolvency of his company. A trust was expressly set up to achieve this objective. The monies from his customers were paid into a 'customers' trust deposit account'. The company went into insolvency. The High Court held that an express trust had been created. The result was that the intention of the director was carried out and the customers were protected.

8.4   The courts have to decide whether the settlor has the intention to impose a binding obligation (a trust) as opposed to using mere words of expectation (which are not intended to be binding). *Re Snowden* (1979) is a case involving the use of words of expectation.

8.5   A testatrix wished her brother Bert 'to look after the division for her'. The High Court was of the view that the testatrix had no need to bind her brother Bert formally or legally. She had not made up her mind as to how to distribute her estate. She trusted him to carry out her general wishes which she had not specifically formulated.

8.6   In reaching this conclusion the court looked at the particular words used and the cirumstances as well.

8.7   This is the approach in the modern cases. By looking at all the circumstances the courts are being flexible and are seeking to ascertain the true intentions of the purported settlor.

8.8   In *Paul v Constance* (1977) (discussed previously in Unit 2) the Court of Appeal looked not only at the words used by Dennis Constance, but also at the relationship he had with Doreen Grace Paul with whom he lived.

8.9   Although particular attention was paid to the words used by Dennis Constance to Doreen Grace Paul in relation to the bank account, other factors were taken into consideration.

8.10   In deciding that she had a half share in relation to his bank account, particular importance was placed on the conversation between Dennis Constance and the bank manager. Dennis Constance had indicated that he wanted Doreen Grace Paul to be able to operate the account even though it was put into his name (legal title in his name).

8.11   It was also relevant, in the view of the court, that the parties joint bingo winnings had been put into this account and that on one occasion funds had been withdrawn for their joint benefit.

8.12   It is clear that the courts wanted to give effect to the intention of Dennis Constance to benefit his partner Doreen Grace Paul, even though he did not manifest this intention clearly.

8.13   The courts have frequently dealt with cases of this type, and are aware that the parties do not know about the concept of trusts. They therefore try to give effect to what they perceive to be the wishes of the parties in the light of all the relevant evidence.

8.14   Certainty of object has been dealt with in Unit 4 in the context of the distinction between discretionary trusts and powers. It was seen that the House of Lords in *McPhail* v *Doulton* (1971) has developed a flexible test (now the same test) for both discretionary trusts and powers. This test (to recap) is as follows: can it be said with certainty that any given individual is a member of the class?

8.15   The courts did not want to invalidate such trusts. Indeed, their general objective is to produce a solution that will lead to validity whenever possible. This is what *McPhail* v *Doulton* (1971) achieved. As was evident in Unit 4, this flexible test for establishing validity produced difficulties in terms of the trustees knowing to whom and how much to distribute.

8.16   The courts were responding to the fact that a large number of trusts were being created where the trustee had considerable discretion, and where it was difficult to point to a particular beneficiary having a particular interest.

8.17   As a total group, the beneficiaries would have the equitable interest, but no individual beneficiary could say what his or her share was. This was the whole idea behind the discretionary trust. This structure had tax advantages at that time.

8.18   In contrast, for a fixed trust (e.g. to A and B equally), the rule relating to certainty of objects is rigid. For this type of trust, a complete list of objects must be ascertained. This is necessarily so, in order to be able to distribute as required.

8.19   There have been some important cases in relation to certainty of subject matter. One case concerned a declaration of trust by the defendant, Moss, in favour of the plaintiff, Hunter. In this declaration of trust, the defendant declared himself trustee for the plaintiff of 5% of the share capital of a company, Moss Electrical Ltd. Subsequently, the defendant sought to argue that there was not sufficient certainty as to the trust property and therefore the declaration of trust was invalid.

8.20 The Court of Appeal concluded that:

- the defendant, as the legal and equitable owner of those shares, could make a valid oral declaration of trust of them

- the defendant's declaration of trust had made it clear which shares were the subject of the declaration of trust, by identifying the particular company

- since all the shares were identical (they were sufficiently identifiable), then a transfer of any of those 50 shares would be sufficient.

8.21 It was held unanimously that there was a valid declaration of trust by the defendant. The plaintiff would be awarded monetary compensation to the value of those shares which had not been transferred to the plaintiff: *Hunter v Moss* (1994).

8.22 This third certainty has caused problems in recent cases where it has been sought to establish an express trust in an insolvency situation. The beneficiary of an express trust (the person who is to benefit under the trust) will have a proprietary right, so that if such a trust can be established, then it will rank ahead of all the creditors of the company. It is clearly advantageous to assert such a trust.

8.23 In one case, *Re Goldcorp Exchange Ltd (in receivership)* (1994), a number of people had bought gold bullion from Goldcorp Exchange Ltd. The company went into receivership after the Bank of New Zealand had appointed itself as the receiver under a 'debenture'. The bank would then take all the assets of the company. However, if a trust over the gold bullion (the main asset of the company) could be established, then the beneficiaries of that trust would be entitled to it ahead of the bank. The people who had bought the gold bullion sought to argue that it was held on trust for them. Their argument was rejected by the Privy Council since the gold bullion had all been stored together, and no individual buyer had been allocated any particular part of it.

8.24 In contrast, where stocks of wine were segregated for the benefit of individual customers, it was held that the wine had been sufficiently identified to satisfy the 'certainty of subject matter' requirement: *Re Staplton Fletcher Ltd* (1994). This meant that there was a trust in existence, and the particular customers that had ordered but not received any bottles of wine had a proprietary interest by way of a trust in the particular bottles that they had ordered.

8.25 In conclusion 'the three certainties' are all necessary in order to create a valid express trust.

8.26 It is essential that the courts know, or are able to determine that a trust was intended. If some other obligation, or no obligation, is shown, then a valid trust cannot be created.

8.27 The courts also have to know who are the intended beneficiaries. If the courts cannot tell, then neither can the trustees. Furthermore, the courts will not be able to determine whether the trustees are acting properly should one or more of the beneficiaries allege maladministration.

8.28 The trustees also have to know what property they are to distribute. It is necessary that they know the property that is to comprise the trust.

8.29 The three certainties have developed in separate ways. When the judges decide one certainty they look at the cases in that area and do not review the other cases. In that sense their decisions are compartmentalised.

8.30 There are also different reasons for the growth and discussion of each of these certainties.

8.31 The courts have responded to the large number of cohabitation relationships where informal language has been used to describe the position between the parties. On occasion the courts have had to determine whether an express trust was intended. As we have seen, the courts have adopted a flexible approach in determinining whether there is sufficient certainty of intention. In Unit 7 we will look at this situation in the context of resulting and constructive trusts of land. It will be seen that the courts have to consider informal discussions in this context as well.

8.32 As regards certainty of intention, the courts have had to apply and develop the rules to trusts where the trustees have considerable discretion and where one may not be able to point to a particular interest of any beneficiary. Such trusts have been created for tax reasons. On occasion, trust or tax issues have required a response from the courts. As we have seen, the courts have adopted a flexible approach in the test for certainty of objects in order to determine the validity of discretionary trusts.

8.33 The prevailing poor economic climate has seen a large number of liquidations and receiverships. If a trust can be established the beneficiaries will rank ahead of other (contractual) ordinary creditors. This has lead to a number of contested claims. The courts have adopted the standard and strict approach that it must be certain what property is to be held on trust.

8.34 There are excellent chapters on formalities and the three certainties in the following:

● Graham Moffat, *Trusts Law Text and Materials*, London (1994), Chapter 4.

● R. Pearce and J. Stevens, *The Law of Trusts and Equitable Obligations*, London (1995), Chapter 26.

9 Rules against perpetuities and accumulations

9.1 The rules relating to perpetuities and acccumulations may be divided into two main categories. First, those rules that affect trusts with individual beneficiaries, and second, those rules that affect valid purpose trusts with no individual beneficiaries.

9.2 At common law, the property left to the beneficiary must be transferred to the beneficiary within a particular period of time or the trust will be invalid. This period is the maximum of any living person's life-span plus 21 years.

9.3 The position at common law was modified by section 1 of the Perpetuities and Accumulations Act 1964, which enables a settlor to substitute for the above period a fixed period of 80 years. If a substituted period is not put in the trust, the common law period above continues to apply.

9.4 These rules apply with necessary modification to a discretionary trust (discretionary trusts being previously considered in Unit 4). Those beneficiaries who receive income or capital within the period of any living person's life-span plus 21 years will receive a valid distribution.

9.5 If distributions of income or capital are made after this period of time then these distributions will be void: section 4(3) of the Perpetuities and Accumulations Act 1964.

9.6 These sections, together with other important sections of the act, are quoted in full by David Hayton in *Hayton and Marshall, Commentary and Cases on the Law of Trusts and Equitable Remedies* (ed. D.J. Hayton), (1996), Chapter 3.

9.7 Professor Hayton makes the point that any surplus funds that have not been distributed by the expiry of the perpetuity period (any living person's life-span plus 21 years) will then be held on resulting trust for the settlor or the settlor's estate.

9.8 A purpose trust (a trust for purposes and not individual beneficiaries) cannot last for longer than any living person's life-span plus 21 years. This period for a purpose trust is the period provided at common law. It has not been modified by the Perpetuities and Accumulations Act 1964. Section 1 of that act applies only to a trust with beneficiaries. This is provided expressly by section 15(4) of the Perpetuities and Accumulations Act 1964.

Summary

Now you have studied the text and worked through this Unit, you should understand:

☐ **the formal requirements of being a trustee**

☐ **the requirements relating to land, personalty, subsisting equitable interests, resulting and constructive trusts, will trusts, and the three certainties**

☐ **the rules against perpetuities and accumulations.**

Self-assessment questions

1   To what extent is a written document or statement (writing) required when dealing with land?

2   Explain the scope and effect of section 53(1)(c) of the Law of Property Act 1925.

3   Explain the scope and effect of section 53(2) of the Law of Property Act 1925.

4   What are 'the three certainties'?

5   How have recent cases applied and developed the requirement of certainty of subject matter in relation to trusts?

6   Bert, by a will made in 1950, leaves his estate on trust to his three children, Adam, Charles and Eve, in equal shares as to both income and capital. Each child will be entitled to the whole of his or her share of capital on attaining the age of 25. There is a proviso in the will that: 'if any of my children shall marry a black or protestant partner, then his or her interest shall go to the others'.

Bert has recently died. Adam, Charles and Eve are all in their teens and the only children of Bert. They seek your advice as to the validity of this trust.

Exam-style questions

In the following cases, discuss whether a trust has been validly created.

1   George died recently, having by his properly executed brief will, left his residuary estate 'to my dear wife Anne, trusting that she will dispose of whatever she does not want between such of my relatives and friends as she shall select'.

2   Jane orally declared herself a trustee of her house, 'Everglades', for her son, Simon. She later wrote a letter to him to let him know what she had done.

[Spring 1995]

(The answers are given in the Appendix)

Caselist for Unit 5 Validity of Trusts

The Law of Property Act 1925, section 1(6).

The Trusts of Land and Appointment of Trustees Act 1996.

Re Vinogradoff [1935] WN 68.

Law of Property Act 1925, sections 53(1)(a), 53(1)(b), 53(1)(c), 53(2), 55.

Spiro v *Glencrown Properties Ltd* [1991] Ch 537.

McCausland and another v *Duncan Lawrie Ltd and another* [1996] 4 All ER 995.

Grey v *I.R.C.* [1960] AC 1.

Vandervell v *I.R.C.* [1967] 2 AC 291.

Attorney-General of Hong Kong v *Reid* [1994] 1 AC 324.

Oughtred v *I.R.C.* [1960] 2 AC 206.

Neville and Another v *Wilson and Others* [1996] 3 All ER 171.

United Bank of Kuwait Plc v *Sahib* [1995] 2 WLR 94 (High Court); [1996] 3 WLR 372 (Court of Appeal).

Law of Property (Miscellaneous Provisions) Act 1989, sections 2(1), 2(5)(c).

Simon Gardner, *An Introduction to the Law of Trusts*, Clarendon Press, Oxford (1990), Chapter 5.

Parker and Mellows, 'The Taxation of a Trust' in *The Modern Law of Trusts* (ed. A.J. Oakley), Sweet and Maxwell, London (1994), Chapter 14.

The Finance Act 1985, section 82.

Richard Nolan, 'The Triumph of Technicality' (1996) CLJ 436.

Graham Moffat, *Trusts Law Text and Materials*, Butterworths, London (1994), Chapter 4.

R. Pearce and J. Stevens, *The Law of Trusts and Equitable Obligations*, Butterworths, London (1995), Chapter 26.

Re Kayford [1975] 1 WLR 279.

Re Snowden, Smith v *Spowage* [1979] Ch 528.

Paul v *Constance* [1977] 1 WLR 527.

McPhail v *Doulton* [1971] AC 424.

Hunter v *Moss* [1994] 1 WLR 452.

Re Goldcorp Exchange Ltd (in receivership) [1995] 1 AC 74.

Re Staplton Fletcher Ltd [1994] 1 WLR 1181.

David Hayton, 'The Essentials of a Trust' in *Hayton and Marshall Commentary and Cases on the Law of Trusts and Equitable Remedies* (ed. D.J. Hayton), Sweet and Maxwell, London (1996), Chapter 3.

The Perpetuities and Accumulations Act 1964, sections 1(1), 3(3), 15(4).

6

Constitution of Trusts

Objectives

After studying the text and working through this Unit, students should be able to:

- understand the difference between completely and incompletely constituted trusts

- understand about imperfect gifts.

1 Completely and incompletely constituted trusts

1.1 We have already seen in Unit 2 that there are two basic ways of creating a trust. First by a declaration of trust, and second by transferring property to trustees. A valid declaration of trust takes effect immediately; but the second method requires that property be transferred before the trust is constituted.

1.2 If the settlor (donor) fails to transfer the property, he cannot be compelled to do so. The intended beneficiary will have no rights against the settlor, since the beneficiary will be a 'volunteer', that is, he or she will have given no consideration (value) to the settlor for the promise by the settlor. Normally, the beneficiary is not in a contractual relationship with the settlor, and therefore has not given consideration to him.

1.3 The intended trustee also has no rights against the settlor that will assist the intended beneficiary. Even if the intended trustee can successfully sue the settlor, the former can recover damages only for his own loss. The trustee is unable to recover any damages for the loss suffered by the intended beneficiary.

1.4 Equity developed certain 'maxims' during the course of its development. These are generalised statements of important principle. (One of these concerning illegality was looked at in the Introduction in Unit 1: 'he who comes to equity must come with clean hands'.)

1.5   Another maxim was 'equity regards as done that which ought to be done'. However, this has not been used much in this area of equity. Instead, two more specific maxims have been used. The first is 'equity will not assist a volunteer', and the second is 'equity will not perfect an imperfect gift'.

1.6   The intended beneficiary is a volunteer, see paragraph 1.2 above, and the first of the specific maxims means that the beneficiary cannot sue the settlor (donor) for breach of his promise if the settlor fails to transfer the property.

1.7   This approach, that equity will not assist a volunteer, is a strict one. As the authorities stand, this is the position. The bulk of case law concerns the proposed creation of 'family' or 'marriage' trusts (settlements) where the purported settlor promised to settle property on trust and then changed his or her mind and did not transfer the property to the proposed trustees. In such a situation, there is no trust.

1.8   The trust is imperfect because the legal title is not transferred to the trustees. In such a situation equity will not compel the purported settlor to transfer the property to the trustees: *Donaldson v Donaldson* (1854). The trustees cannot compel transfer (see below) and neither can the beneficiaries (see below).

1.9   As we have seen in Unit 2, the actual transfer of the legal title to the trustees constitutes the trust. It is at this point that a valid trust will have been created. The converse is equally true. If no property is transferred to the trustees then no trust will have been created. There are a number of cases which confirm and support this approach. These include: *Re Bowden* (1936), *Paul v Paul* (1882), and *Re Ralli's Will Trusts* (1964).

Position of volunteer beneficiaries

1.10   In such a situation, the purported beneficiaries will have no rights to sue the purported settlor. This means that such volunteer beneficiaries cannot obtain substantial damages (at common law) for breach of promise on the part of the settlor, and cannot obtain specific performance (in equity) to compel the settlor to carry out his promise.

1.11   Such beneficiaries are 'volunteers', not having given any consideration (value) for the promise by the purported settlor.

1.12   However, there is case law which does establish that volunteer beneficiaries would be able to obtain substantial damages for breach of this promise (breach of contract): *Re Cavendish Browne's Settlement Trusts* (1916).

1.13 This approach was followed in *Williamson* v *Codrington* (1750) (discussed below) where the court awarded volunteer beneficiaries substantial damages for breach of agreement by a purported settlor for failure to create a trust of land in favour of the volunteer beneficiaries.

1.14 Whilst this case is open to a number of interpretations, the view of M. W. Friend in his article 'Trusts of Voluntary Covenants – An Alternative Approach' [1982] Conv 280, is that this case does support the approach that volunteer beneficiaries may be awarded substantial damages.

1.15 However, this conclusion is criticised by Professor David Hayton in *Underhill and Hayton, Law Relating to Trusts and Trustees* 15th edition (ed. David J. Hayton) (1995), Chapter 2.

1.16 His reasoning is as follows. There is no trust because the property has not been transferred to the trustees. As we have seen in Unit 2, in order to create a trust it is necessary for the trust property to be transferred to the trustees. If there is no trust, then the trustees cannot hold any damages they receive on trust for a beneficiary. (The trustees are, of course, entitled to damages for any loss that they, the trustees, have sustained.)

1.17 The consequence is that such damages are held on a resulting trust for the purported settlor. Since it is the purported settlor against whom substantial damages are being awarded, the whole situation is somewhat circular.

1.18 For this reason substantial damages should not be awarded against a settlor.

1.19 Furthermore, Professor Hayton goes on to argue that the settlor will be a sole beneficiary under this resulting trust, and by virtue of the rule in *Saunders* v *Vautier* (1841), discussed previously in Unit 2, the settlor is entitled to call for the legal interest and end the trust.

1.20 There is considerable force in his argument. Such argument supports the conclusion reached in both *Re Pryce* (1917) and *Re Kay* (1939), that since trustees are not able to obtain substantial damages against the purported settlor, they should not bring claims for damages against purported settlors. Such argument, however, was not actually considered in either case. (The position of trustees is discussed immediately below.)

Position of contracting trustees

1.21 It is also established that where the settlor fails to transfer the property to the trustees to hold on trust, the trustees are unable to obtain specific performance against the purported settlor (i.e. are unable to compel the settlor to carry out the promise to transfer).

1.22 This approach has been confirmed by two particular cases, which have been much criticised in academic circles. In the first, *Re Pryce* (1917), in response to a specific request by the trustees, the court directed the trustees that they were not bound to sue the purported settlor so as to obtain specific performance of his or her promise made with them.

1.23 In the second, *Re Kay's Settlement* (1939), the court put the matter more strongly, directing the trustees that they should not sue the settlor so as to obtain specific performance of his or her promise made with them.

Deemed consideration

1.24 Equity does have one established and recognised exception to the rule that volunteers cannot sue. A spouse, children, and grandchildren of the settlor are deemed to have given consideration. The important point is that such children will (it is hoped) give joy, affection and love to their parents and in this way be objects of interest to their parents. Equity does not spell out the way(s) in which they give consideration. It is simply deemed. The authorities which confirm this approach include: *Attorney-General* v *Jacobs-Smith* (1895), *MacDonald* v *Scott* (1893), *Re Cook's Settlement Trusts* (1965).

1.25 For this purpose 'illegitimate' children of the parties are not included within the rule (discussed above) and are not deemed to have given consideration: *Fletcher* v *Fletcher* (1844).

1.26 Section 1 of the Family Law Reform Act 1987, which is designed to improve the position of 'illegitimate' children, does so in terms of construction of a trust. Where, say, the word 'children' is used then, unless there is a contrary intention from the instrument, it will include 'illegitimate' children.

1.27 However, this section does not change the rule in equity that 'illegitimate' children are not within the marriage consideration and so are still deemed not to have given consideration.

1.28 It is possible to argue that the rule as to deemed consideration was simply introduced so as to ensure that parents would be able to leave their property to their 'legitimate' children. These 'legitimate' children, who are deemed to have given consideration, would always be able to enforce the promises made by their parents. Such promises are made in anticipation of their parents' marriage.

1.29 'Legitimate' children are able to sue, even though they would otherwise be volunteers. There are a number of cases which confirm and support this approach. These include: *Attorney-General* v *Jacobs-Smith* (1895), *MacDonald* v *Scott* (1893), *Re Cook's Settlement Trusts* (1965), *Pullan* v *Coe* (1913), *Re Plumptre's Marriage Settlement* (1910), *Re D'Angibau* (1880).

1.30 In the case of a spouse, it is going through a ceremony of marriage and subsequently consummating the marriage that is regarded as the consideration: *Re Ames Settlement* (1946).

1.31 In addition, the law recognises continued love and affection as being consideration: *Re Cook's Settlement Trusts* (1965). It is through undertaking this in advance before the marriage that is the deemed consideration.

1.32 Further, it is not necessary that such persons are parties to the agreement whereby the settlor has agreed to transfer the property to the trustees and thereby set up the trust: *Hill* v *Gomme* (1839). Equity does not adopt the same position as in contract (common law). Being a party is not relevant.

1.33 Simon Gardner in in *An Introduction to the Law of Trusts* (1990), Chapter 4, cites the decision of *Re D'Angibau* (1880) to stress the point that property which subsequently becomes that of a wife, will be held on the trusts of the marriage settlement for the benefit of the 'legitimate' children where they have interests in remainder under those trusts. This shows how significantly 'legitimate' children are favoured.

1.34 Where a valid and binding marriage settlement is made, a wife is able to contract with the trustees and her husband to transfer property into that trust to which she will become entitled in the future: *Williams* v *Commissioners of Inland Revenue* (1965).

1.35 Before the Married Women's Property Act 1882, when women were unable to own their own property, it was essential to have a clause that any property transferred, or left, to a wife after marriage was instead to be held in trust. Historically, it would be husbands, or the parents of the spouses, who would settle property in a marriage settlement on the occasion of their marriage. See generally, Simon Gardner, *op. cit.* above, for the social context in which such trusts operated.

1.36 At various times there have even been tax advantages given to property which is transferred on the basis of the intended marriage: *Rennell* v *I.R.C.*(1962).

Possible solutions – trust of the promise

1.37 One possible solution, to enable volunteer beneficiaries to sue a settlor, derives from the decision in *Fletcher* v *Fletcher* (1844) which involved a promise by a purported settlor to transfer £60,000 to his 'illegitimate' son. This money was never transferred.

1.38 It was decided by the court that there was a completely constituted trust not of the money, but of a promise to transfer the money. This promise was held on trust, and the beneficiaries could enforce this trust.

1.39 There is a fine line between the two concepts. Usually settlors intend that there should be a trust of the property but not of the promise. It is unclear, and remains unclear, what factors pointed to a trust of the promise in *Fletcher* v *Fletcher* (1844).

1.40 One argument is that money is itself a promise by the Bank of England to pay the bearer of the bank-note on demand. It was argued that it is easier to infer a trust of the promise where the property is itself a promise.

1.41 This was the approach taken in *Williamson* v *Codrington* (1750) which concerned an agreement by Sir William Codrington to set up a trust of land in America for two of his 'illegitimate' children. The rents from leasing this land were to be held on trust for Sir William's other 'illegitimate' child, who would receive an annual sum.

1.42 No documents of title to the land were transferred to the trustees. After the death of Sir William, the two children sought to recover substantial damages from the estate for Sir William's failure to transfer the land to the trustees. The third child sought to recover damages for the failure to be paid his annuity.

1.43 The court held that because Sir William had agreed with the trustees to pay an annual sum of money to one of his 'illegitimate' children (derived from the rents from the land) there was a completely constituted trust of this debt from the date of his agreement to set up this trust.

1.44 Similarly, Sir William had made a completely constituted trust (at the time of his promise) in relation to the land. It was therefore not necessary to transfer any documents of title to the trustees. Indeed, Sir William's relationship with his trustees, whereby they were not required to do anything further in connection with the land, pointed to a completely constituted trust of his promise.

1.45 However, the languague used by Sir William in his agreement with his trustees did not indicate a trust of the promise.

1.46 This is a major problem with concluding that a purported settlor has intended a trust of the promise. Usually, settlors only use language indicating a trust of the property. A trust of the promise has been inferred on very weak evidence. This was the position in this case. Sir William had not used language indicating that he had intended to create a trust of the promise.

1.47 In reality, the court felt that since Sir William had sought to provide for his 'illegitimate' children, their interests should be protected.

1.48 Further, the judge made reference to the fact that the mother of the two children who were to have an interest in the land, was brought to England by Sir William, and remained here until he married another woman.

1.49   The completely constituted trust of the promise was used as a mechanism to achieve the just result that the court of equity wanted.

1.50   The importance of looking at the relationship of the parties has been noted by Professor Gareth Jones in a casenote of *Re Cook's Settlement Trusts*, 'The Enforcement of Settlements in Equity by Volunteers' (1965) CLJ 46. He stresses the point that trustees are able to sue and obtain substantial damages for those volunteers for whom the purported settlor is under a moral obligation to provide support.

Possible solutions – actual consideration (love and affection)

1.51   Another possible solution (which follows on from the above approach) is to argue that the various categories of beneficiaries are objects of interest as regards the purported settlor, and so give actual consideration. On this reasoning they are not volunteers and so are able to sue the purported settlor and obtain specific performance or substantial damages.

1.52   It has been suggested by the distinguished academic Roscoe Pound, 'Consideration in Equity' (1919) 13 Illinois Law Review 667, that, historically, equity did consider that natural love and affection counted as consideration. This article was cited in Cases And Materials on Equity: Zechariah Chafee and Edward D. Re (Fifth ed. of Chafee and Simpson's Cases on Equity). 1967.

1.53   The editors put forward a decision – *Sharington v Strotton* (1565) – to support this proposition in the context of two brothers. The love and affection of siblings counted as consideration.

1.54   This is not the position at common law where it is established that natural love and affection do not normally count as consideration. The authorities that support this proposition include: *Jones v Padavaton* (1969), *Balfour v Balfour* (1919).

1.55   By virtue of the Judicature Acts 1875–1879, where there was a conflict between equity and the common law, equity was supposed to prevail, but this did not in fact happen.

1.56   Historically, the rule in equity was overtaken by the rule at common law, so that the common law prevailed. After the Judicature Acts 1875–1879, there was one system in operation, and one system of courts. This new single system of courts followed the common law rule instead of the rule in equity.

1.57   The effect is that at common law it is now not open for volunteer beneficiaries to be able to use the argument that natural love and affection is actual consideration. They are therefore not able to sue the purported settlor for breach of his or her promise to transfer the property to the trustees.

1.58 However, the rule that spouses, children and parents, grandchildren and grandparents, are deemed to give consideration when a trust is set up by their parents (as described above) is firmly established in equity. The equitable rule has not been undermined by the common law position that natural love and affection between any people, whether related or not, does not count as consideration at common law.

Possible solution – the status of a seal

1.59 Another possible solution comes about because of the landmark decision of *Tinsley* v *Milligan* (1994), by which equity may follow the rule at common law where there are different rules in equity and the common law.

1.60 This is important in relation to a document made with a seal. A covenant is a contract made with a seal. Marriage or family settlements were and are usually made by covenant (though the numbers of such transactions have declined for various social reasons).

1.61 Section 1 of the Law of Property (Miscellaneous Provisions) Act 1989 has minimised the importance of a seal generally by providing that no longer will any transaction depend for its validity upon having a seal. However, this act does not change the position in equity, which does not regard a seal as consideration (as we shall see below).

1.62 At common law a seal is regarded as consideration. So, if A is a party to a covenant, then at common law A will be entitled to obtain damages for breach of contract: *Cannon* v *Hartley* (1949). (The remedy of damages is a common law remedy.)

1.63 However, equity took a different view from that of the common law. As we have seen, equity regarded things of substance to count as consideration. Love and affection fell into that category. On the other hand, a seal, being a formal thing, did not count as consideration in equity: *Kekewich* v *Manning* (1851). This meant – and this a crucial point – that equity would not give its remedies. The remedy that a beneficiary would wish to seek would be the equitable remedy of specific performance. This remedy would not be available since equity does not regard a binding contract as having come into existence.

1.64 Since equity did not recognise the creation of a valid contract under its own rules, it could not grant a beneficiary specific performance. Equity accepted the position at common law.

1.65 Simon Gardner in *An Introduction to the Law of Trusts* (1990), Chapter 4, supports this separation of equitable and common law remedies, and the availability of common law remedies.

1.66   After *Tinsley* v *Milligan* (1994), equity could now follow the rule at common law. This would enable beneficiaries, who brought their claim in equity, to enforce the promise of a purported settlor who failed to transfer the property to the trustees.

1.67   It remains unclear whether equity will adopt this approach. Even if it does, beneficiaries will still not be able to compel purported settlors to carry out their promise where the settlor makes an oral promise or ordinary agreement (that is not made by seal).

2 Imperfect gifts

2.1   Equity also uses the other maxim 'equity will not perfect an imperfect gift'. Thus, if the settlor does not transfer the property to the trustee, the trust will not be constituted. For this purpose, an intended trust (one which has failed) is regarded as an imperfect gift. In general terms, the settlor (donor) would be making a gift to the intended beneficiary of the value of the transferred property if the trust was validly created.

2.2   Where the settlor has not transferred the property to the intended trustee there is no valid trust, except where that trustee is appointed executor of the settlor's estate. This would perfect the imperfect trust (gift). Legal title will be obtained by the trustee, and that will constitute the trust. This is known as the 'rule in *Strong* v *Bird*', which derives from a case in 1874.

2.3   Some of the cases, which illustrate the approach in equity that it will not perfect an imperfect gift, will be examined below. See also Unit 2.

2.4   It should be pointed out that with a completely constituted trust the trustee obtains legal title and the volunteer beneficiary the equitable title. Because the trustee has obtained legal title, the beneficiary has rights against the trustee to obtain due performance of the trust.

2.5   In contrast, with an effective gift, the recipient obtains both the legal and the equitable title. These are joined together. It is usual to refer to the recipient as having obtained the property.

2.6   If the person making a transfer of shares does all within his or her power to carry out the transfer, then the gift will be effective. What is required is that the share certificate is transferred to the transferee, and that the share transfer form is signed in favour of the transferee.

2.7   In equity the gift will be effective as soon as the form is signed, even though the change of ownership of the shares still has to be registered: *Re Rose* (1952).

2.8   The reasoning is that the transferor has done all within his power. The transfer is regarded as effective when the share transfer form is signed.

2.9   The registration of the shares by the company is something outside the control of the transferor. The date of registration of the shares is therefore not the relevant date.

2.10   It was important for tax reasons (now inheritance tax) to determine when the ownership of the shares by the transferee had taken place.

2.11   This approach is followed in relation to the transfer of land by way of gift. If the transferor executes a document transferring the land to the transferee, and also gives the transferee the land certificate, then the transfer will be effective and the gift will have taken place at that point: *Mascall* v *Mascall* (1984).

2.12   The transferor will have done all within his or her power, and there will be a valid gift.

2.13   Again, the date of registration of the land (in the appropriate land register) is not the relevant date. The gift is effective even if the transfer has not been registered in the appropriate land register.

2.14   The above two cases are discussed in *Maudsley and Burn's Trusts and Trustees Cases and Materials* (ed. E.H. Burn) (1996), Chapter 3.

2.15   If, because of the county of domicile of the transferor of shares, certain additional consents (such as those of a government department) are required by the transferor in order to transfer shares, the gift will not be effective until such consents are obtained: *Re Fry* (1946).

2.16   The reasoning here is that the transferor has not done all within his or her power. The transferor is able to obtain the necessary consent. This must therefore be done in order for the gift to be effective.

Exceptions to the rule

2.17   There are several exceptions to the rule that equity will not perfect an imperfect gift. These will be discussed briefly below.

- The rule in *Strong* v *Bird* (1874), that if the donee obtains legal title by another route then the gift will be effective. This has been considered above.

- *Donatio mortis causa* (gifts made in contemplation of death in the near future). Such gifts must be conditional on the death of the transferor. In addition, there must be a transfer to the donee of the essential documents of title.

- Proprietary estoppel. Where a donee of land has acted to his or her detriment on an express or implied promise that land will be transferred to him or her: *Grant v Edwards* (1986).

2.18   *Grant v Edwards* will be discussed in Unit 7 in the context of resulting trusts. The carrying out improvements of land by the donee because of such a promise is an example. The donee is able to bring an action to obtain the land even though it has not been (and would otherwise not be) effectively transferred.

2.19   For a detailed discussion of these exceptions see Professor David Hayton in *Underhill and Hayton Law of Trusts and Trustees*, 15th edition (ed. David J. Hayton) (1995), Chapter 2.

Summary

Now you have studied the text and worked through this Unit, you should understand:

☐ **the difference between completely and incompletely constituted trusts**

☐ **what imperfect gifts are.**

Self-assessment questions

1   When is a trust constituted?

2   Is a beneficiary able to sue the settlor if the settlor fails to carry out his promise and does not transfer any property to the trustee?

3   Is a trustee able to sue the settlor if the settlor fails to carry out his promise and does not transfer any property to the trustee?

4   Robin, the chairperson of Minwell Plc, decides, as a philanthropic gesture, to give £2m of his own money to the Minwell pension fund. He promises Adam and Brian, the trustees of the pension fund, that he will transfer the £2m into the fund. However, Robin fails to transfer any money.

   Advise Adam and Brian.

5   David decides to create a discretionary trust for all his children. Sara, aged 28, is his daughter by a former marriage. Tara, aged 20, is his 'illegitimate'

daughter by a relationship that has now ended. He is about to marry Elizabeth who will be his second wife. A week before he marries he agrees with Joe and Mo that they will be the trustees of this discretionary trust. David promises:

'1. To transfer my cottage in the country to my trustees to allow my children, legitimate and illegitimate, to reside in and occupy it.'

'2. To transfer £100,000 to my trustees on discretionary trust to provide income and capital for my children, legitimate and illegitimate, as my trustees shall determine.'

A year later David has not transferred either his cottage or any monies to Joe and Mo.

Advise Sara and Tara as to whether they have any equitable rights which can be enforced.

6   What is the rule in *Strong v Bird* (1874)?

Exam-style questions

1. Joseph recently visited his 10-year-old niece, Mary, and handed over a gold ring which, he told her, had belonged to his mother. As he handed it over, he told her that she was to have the ring. When Joseph left he took the ring with him and it was found amongst his effects when he died shortly afterwards.

    Discuss whether a trust has been validly created.

    [Spring 1995]

2. Explain the maxim 'equity will not perfect an imperfect gift' and, with reference to case law, identify any exceptions.

    [Autumn 1995]

    (The answers are given in the Appendix)

Caselist for Unit 6 Constitution of Trusts

Donaldson v *Donaldson* (1854) Kay 711.

Re Bowden, Hulbert v *Bowden* [1936] Ch 71.

Paul v *Paul* (1882) 20 ChD 742.

Re Ralli's Will Trusts [1964] Ch 288.

Re Cavendish Browne's Settlement Trusts, Horner v *Rawle* [1916] WN 341.

Williamson v *Codrington* (1750) 1 Ves Sen 511.

M. W. Friend, 'Trusts of Voluntary Covenants – An Alternative Approach' [1982] Conv 280.

Professor David Hayton, 'Matters essential to the prima facie validity of an express trust' in *Underhill and Hayton, Law Relating to Trusts and Trustees*, 15th edition (ed. David J. Hayton) Butterworths, London (1995), Chapter 2.

Saunders v *Vautier* (1841) 4 Beav 115.

Re Pryce, Nevill v *Pryce* [1917] 1 Ch 234.

Re Kay's Settlement, Broadbent v *Macnab* [1939] Ch 329.

Attorney-General v *Jacobs-Smith* [1895] 2 QB 341.

MacDonald v *Scott* [1893] AC 642.

Re Cook's Settlement Trusts, Royal Exchange Assurance v *Cook* [1965] Ch 902.

Fletcher v *Fletcher* (1844) 4 Hare 67.

The Family Law Reform Act 1987, section 1.

Pullan v *Coe* [1913] 1 Ch 9.

Re Plumptre's Marriage Settlement, Underhill v *Plumptre* [1910] 1 Ch 609.

Re D'Angibau, Andrews v *Andrews* (1880) 15 ChD 228.

Re Ames Settlement, Dinwiddy v *Ames* [1946] Ch 217.

Hill v *Gomme* (1839) 5 My & Cr 250.

Simon Gardner, *An Introduction to the Law of Trusts*, Clarendon Press, Oxford (1990), Chapter 4.

Williams v *Commissioners of Inland Revenue* [1965] NZLR 395.

The Married Women's Property Act 1882.

Rennell v *I.R.C.* [1962] Ch 329.

Professor Gareth Jones, 'The Enforcement of Settlements in Equity by Volunteers' (1965) CLJ 46.

Professor Roscoe Pound, 'Consideration in Equity' (1919) 13 Illinois Law Review 667.

Cases And Materials on Equity: Zechariah Chafee and Edward D. Re (Fifth ed. of Chafee and Simpson's Cases on Equity) 1967. Brooklyn. The Foundation Press.

Sharington v *Strotton* (1565) 1 Plowd 208.

Jones v *Padavaton* [1969] 1 WLR 328.

Balfour v *Balfour* [1919] 2 KB 571.

The Judicature Acts 1875–1879.

Tinsley v *Milligan* [1994] 1 AC 340.

The Law of Property (Miscellaneous Provisions) Act 1989, section 1.

Cannon v *Hartley* [1949] Ch 213.

Kekewich v *Manning* (1851) 1 De GM & G 176.

Strong v *Bird* (1874) LR 18 Eq 315.

Re Rose, Rose v *I.R.C.* [1952] Ch 499.

Mascall v *Mascall* (1984) 50 P & CR 119.

Maudsley and Burn's Trusts and Trustees Cases and Materials (ed. E.H. Burn), Butterworths, London (1996), Chapter 3.

Re Fry, Chase National Executors and Trustees Corpn Ltd v *Fry* [1946] Ch 312.

Grant v *Edwards* [1986] Ch 638.

7

Trusts of Land

Objectives

After studying the text and working through this Unit, students should be able to:

● **understand strict settlements**

● **understand trusts for sale**

● **appreciate the intentions and interests of co-ownership.**

The Trusts of Land and Appointment of Trustees Act 1996 received its Royal assent on 24 July 1996. This act (referred to below as 'the Act') affects the position with regard to trusts of land.

The Law of Property Act 1925 is referred to in full to distinguish it from the Act above.

1 Strict settlements

1.1   Section 1 of the Act provides that trusts of land can simply be held on ordinary trust. Section 2 provides that, after the commencement of the Act, trusts of land cannot be held as settlements. Instead they can only be held as trusts of land, and this refers also to land held on charitable (public) trusts.

1.2   Land held on charitable (public) trusts will be deemed by the Act never to have been settled land after the Act commences.

2 Trusts for sale

2.1 It is necessary to explain what is meant by a 'trust for sale'. Whenever land is subject to co-ownership, as discussed below, a trust for sale will arise.

2.2 The basic aim behind a trust for sale – which is a statutory creature, created by the Law of Property Act 1925 – is that it will give a purchaser of (registered) land proper and clear title. Any equitable interests in the land are to be 'over-reached'. This means that any beneficiaries will lose their equitable interests in the land. Instead, these will be changed into equitable interests in the purchase monies provided by the purchaser of the land: section 2(i)(ii) of the Law of Property Act 1925.

2.3 The Law of Property Act 1925 lays down a particular requirement concerning the payment of the capital monies for the property by the purchaser. The particular requirement is that such monies must be paid to any two trustees, i.e. any two persons who are the legal owners of the property being sold. A husband and wife could be the two trustees, as could two cohabitees, or a husband and his brother.

2.4 Where this requirement is satisfied, a spouse or cohabitee will lose any rights in the property or the ability to occupy the property. The spouse or cohabitee will be entitled only to a share in the proceeds of sale.

2.5 With a resulting trust, the share is calculated in accordance with the common intention or financial contributions. With a constructive trust, the share is calculated according to the acts of detriment carried out by the spouse or cohabitee.

2.6 An important new power is given to trustees by section 4 of the Act. This provides that trustees will always have the power to postpone the sale of the land in all cases of trusts of land created by 'disposition'; in other words, cases where land is disposed of to another person. Furthermore, the trustees will be able to postpone the sale for an indefinite period. The trustees will not be liable for doing this.

3 Co-ownership

3.1 Whenever land is subject to a presumed resulting trust, see Unit 3, there will be co-ownership, so that both parties acquire an equitable interest. This will be so where there is a common intention between a married couple or cohabitees that each is to acquire an interest in the property in which they live.

Presumed resulting trusts

3.2   The presumed resulting trust is an example of a trust based upon the intention of the parties. The parties will not have properly or totally recorded their agreement. For example, it will come into existence where the parties have both contributed to the purchase price of a property. There will be an implied understanding that both are to have a share in the equitable interest in the property. The presumed resulting trust has been briefly described in Unit 3.

3.3   The use of this trust has important financial implications for parties whose only major asset is the home in which they live. Even for parties with other assets, the home is an important investment.

3.4   Whenever land is subject to a presumed resulting trust, there will be co-ownership so that both parties will acquire an equitable interest. This will be so where there is a common intention between the married couple or cohabitees that each is to acquire an interest in the property in which they live.

3.5   This common intention will be inferred where the spouse or partner has made a substantial financial contribution to the property. Such financial contributions may be direct, in the sense of a direct payment of the mortgage, or indirect, where the spouse's or cohabitee's financial contributions to the household expenses enable the other spouse or partner to pay the mortgage instalments, as in the case of *Burns* v *Burns* (1984).

3.6   In this case the home where the cohabitees lived was bought by mortgage. The cost of the home was £4,900 of which £4,500 was paid by Mr Burns. Ms Burns (who adopted his surname) made no direct contributions to the purchase price. She made no capital contribution and made no financial contributions to the mortgage. Both the legal title to the property and the mortgage were in his (sole) name. Mr Burns was well-off and did not need any financial assistance from Ms Burns. She was not in employment and had no funds with which to make any financial contribution.

3.7   The issue was whether Ms Burns could acquire an equitable interest in the home through looking after the children and carrying out various domestic duties. The Court of Appeal was of the view that neither of these entitled her to an equitable interest in the home. She had not made any financial contribution directly to the capital cost of the home, nor any indirect financial contribution, through paying various domestic bills or other living expenses, which might have assisted Mr Burns in paying the mortgage instalments. In such circumstances, she was not entitled to any share in the home by way of a resulting trust. There was no common intention between the parties that she should have an interest, nor was there any direct or indirect financial contribution by her.

4 Constructive trusts

4.1 Another common type of situation where a constructive trust will arise concerns the purchase of property by spouses or cohabitees. The position of husband and wife is regulated under matrimonial legislation, so that litigated disputes as to the amount of a spouse's equitable interest are rare. Constructive trusts have been previously discussed in Unit 3.

4.2 Imagine a situation where Charles and Dawn are cohabitees living together in a property. Charles informally agrees with Dawn that she is to have a share in the property. If Charles seeks to act contrary to that agreement, then the courts of equity will impose a constructive trust in favour of Dawn. Charles would act contrary to the agreement if he sought to sell the property without telling Dawn, or sought to deny that Dawn had an equitable interest. She will thereby obtain the share in the property which she was promised. This situation has been previously discussed in Unit 3.

4.3 She will obtain an equitable interest, by way of constructive trust, as in the case of *Grant* v *Edwards* (1986). Two requirements are necessary. These have been previously described in Unit 3:

- where there is an informal agreement between Charles and Dawn that Dawn is to acquire an equitable interest in the property

- where Dawn performs acts of detriment in reliance on that agreement.

4.4 In the above case, the property was put into the sole name of the male cohabitee. The reason he gave for doing this was that otherwise this would cause him difficulty in relation to his divorce. This was untrue. His motives were to try to keep the property for himself.

4.5 Because of this, the Court of Appeal was of the view that there was a common intention between both cohabitees that she was to have an equitable interest in the property. He would not have had to resort to this deceit if it had been the parties' intention that he was to have the property for himself.

4.6 Since the female cohabitee had committed acts of detriment in making financial contributions to the payment of the mortgage, she was entitled to an equitable interest in the property. She was awarded a half share to reflect the understanding between the parties, and her financial contributions made on the basis of that understanding.

4.7 The acts of detriment are of a potentially wide scope. In *Ungurian* v *Lesnoff* (1989), Mrs Lesnoff (who was previously divorced) moved into a home in London with Mr Ungurian and various children of both parties. In so doing, she gave up her flat in Poland and her academic career. The High Court held that these were sufficient acts of detriment.

4.8   Helping in the other partner's business may also be sufficient. In *Hammond v Mitchell* (1991), a chance meeting in Epping Forest between Mr Hammond (a businessman separated from his wife) and Ms Mitchell, a 'bunny girl' employed at the Playboy Club, led to further meetings and long-term cohabitation. Their relationship lasted 11 years and gave rise to two children.

4.9   Ms Mitchell argued for a constructive trust in relation to the home in which they all lived. She remembered various conversations with Mr Hammond in which he had said to her, in general terms, that she would have a half share in the home.

4.10   The High Court held these discussions did not precisely identify the share that Ms Mitchell was to have in the home. However, they did amount to an understanding that she was to have some equitable interest in the home in which they lived.

4.11   The High Court expressly took into account her contributions in various ways:

- as the mother of the parties' children and her contributions to their upbringing

- as helper and unpaid assistant to some of Mr Hammond's business ventures.

The result was that she was held to have a half share (equitable interest) in the home. Since she had an equitable interest in a constructive trust no writing was required by virtue of section 53(2) of the Law of Property Act 1925. This section is discussed in Unit 5.

4.12   It would appear that the approach of the courts in cases of constructive trust may be wider than their approach in cases of resulting trust.

4.13   However, in *Lloyds Bank Plc* v *Rosset* (1991) the House of Lords confirmed that there must be some, though not necessarily exact, agreement or arrangement between the parties as to their shares.

4.14   This case concerned a husband and wife who agreed to purchase a property with a view to renovating it. It was paid for by the husband by means of funds from a private family trust and put into the husband's sole name. In consequence, Mrs Rosset did not argue for a resulting trust, because she had not made any financial contributions, but sought to argue a constructive trust.

4.15   The House of Lords confirmed the two-stage approach for a constructive trust to be established:

a) that there is some agreement or arrangement between the parties;

b) that one of the parties has significantly altered his or her position or has acted to his or her detriment because of this agreement or arrangement.

4.16 The House of Lords found as a fact that the parties had not come to any agreement or arrangement as to the equitable ownership before the property was transferred into the husband's name. As a consequence, the House of Lords rejected the wife's arguments and decided that she was unable to establish a constructive trust.

4.17 It is important to note that by section 53(1)(b) of the Law of Property Act 1925, declarations of trust of land must be made in writing. Similarly, by section 2(1) of the Law of Property (Miscellaneous Provisions) Act 1989, a sale or other 'disposition' of an interest in land can only be made in writing.

4.18 However, this is modified by section 53(2) of the Law of Property Act 1925, and section 2(5) of the Law of Property (Miscellaneous Provisions) Act 1989. Resulting or constructive trusts, which come about through operation of the rules described above, do not have to be made in writing. These resulting or constructive trusts will be valid even though the discussions between the parties are exclusively oral and not put into writing at all.

4.19 It will be apparent that there has been considerable case law in this area. There has also been much academic discussion. In particular see Simon Gardner, 'Rethinking Family Property' (1993) 109 LQR 263; David Hayton, 'Constructive Trusts of Homes – a Bold Approach' (1993) 109 LQR 485.

Spouse or cohabitee has an equitable interest

4.20 That the cohabitee has an equitable interest in this situation is confirmed by the case of *Kingsnorth Finance Co* v *Tizard* (1986). The judge accepted that Mrs Tizard had an equitable interest under a resulting trust.

4.21 Furthermore, the land being unregistered, the judge accepted that her equitable interest under a resulting trust was not one which was capable of being registered as a land charge. The buyers of the property in which Mrs Tizard had this equitable interest were held by the court, however, to have notice of her interest.

4.22 The judge's view was that the buyers of the property had, or were taken to have had, information from Mr Tizard – who was trying to conceal his wife's equitable interest – so that they should have made further enquiries. Because they did not do so, they were put on notice of the equitable interest of Mrs Tizard. The concept of notice is discussed in Unit 8.

5 Developments in resulting and constructive trusts

5.1   For an introductory discussion of such developments see generally Professor David Hayton: Unit 9 Resulting and Constructive Trusts of Homes in Fundamental Principles of Law series The Law of Trusts (2nd ed.) 1993.

5.2   For a detailed discussion see Graham Moffat, *Trusts Law Text and Materials*, 2nd edition (1994), Chapter 12.

5.3   As part of this excellent chapter, Graham Moffat looks comparatively at the position taken in a Commonwealth context. He points out that in Canada the approach of the courts in deciding whether there is a resulting or constructive trust is to view them in the context of unjust enrichment.

5.4   The approach is that one partner must have benefited at the expense of the other partner in circumstances where keeping that benefit would be unjust. This concept of unjust enrichment has been briefly considered in Unit 1 when looking at some cases involving cohabitaton and domestic situations.

5.5   There is a further discussion of this theme by Donovan W. M. Waters QC and Simon Gardner in *The Frontiers of Liability*, vol. 2 (ed. P.B.H. Birks) (1994), Chapters 13 and 14 respectively.

5.6   Graham Moffat also points out that in Australia the test of the courts in deciding whether there is a resulting or constructive trust is to use the concept of unconscionability (against conscience).

5.7   One partner will be unable to keep a share in the property where to keep such a benefit would be unconscionable in relation to the other partner. The importance of conscience in equity has been previously discussed in Unit 1.

5.8   There is a further discussion of this theme by The Honourable Sir Anthony Mason, 'The Place of Equity and Equitable Remedies in the Contemporary Common Law World' (1994) 110 LQR 238.

5.9   Sir Anthony Mason, Chief Justice of Australia, makes the point that the key decisions concerning the equitable rights of cohabitees were determined in accordance with the conscience doctrine discussed above.

5.10   In his opinion, there is is not much difference between the unconscionablity doctrine and the unjust enrichment doctrine. In his view these leading cases could have been determined by reference to the alternative doctrine of unjust enrichment that had been used in Canada.

5.11   We have seen the approach in England to the creation of resulting and constructive trusts which has been described earlier on in this Unit. The English courts have not followed either the Australian or Canadian approach. As will be seen from the decision below, there is an important widening of approach in England.

5.12 A recent English decision is *Midland Bank Plc v Cooke* (1995) which is included in *Hayton and Marshall, Commentary and Cases on the Law of Trusts and Equitable Remedies*, 10th edition (ed. D.J. Hayton) (1996), Chapter 6. It is an important case.

5.13 If one partner makes financial contributions to the purchase of a property, he or she thereby establishes the existence of an equitable interest and a presumed resulting trust. The presumed resulting trust has been described in paragraphs 3.2 to 3.7 of this Unit. The court in *Midland Bank Plc v Cooke* decided that these contributions would not be the sole test to determine the extent of the partner's equitable interest. The court is able to look at all the factors to determine the extent of a share, and is not just limited to the financial contributions made.

5.14 This was always the position with regard to constructive trusts. We have seen in paragraphs 4.1 to 4.16 of this Unit that the courts adopted the test of agreement and acts of detriment to determine whether a party had obtained an equitable interest.

5.15 Once an equitable interest had been established then a flexible approach, looking at all the factors, was taken to determine the extent of the share: *Grant v Edwards* (1986).

5.16 This flexible approach was followed and applied in *Hammond v Mitchell* (1991), where the female partner obtained a half-share of the property under a constructive trust. The factors taken into account included:

- financial contributions
- statements made by the parties to each other
- improvements to the property made by one party
- looking after the children of the parties or of the relationship
- assisting in a business activity of the other party
- the general relationship.

5.17 In contrast to the policy approach in *Burns v Burns* (1984), whereby the Court of Appeal wanted to leave matters of reform to Parliament, in *Midland Bank Plc v Cooke* (1995) Waite LJ in the Court of Appeal (delivering the only judgment) was of the opinion that equity is a system of law which would adapt its principles to meet the needs of individuals brought about by social changes.

5.18 The judge realised that he was dealing with an important issue. Large numbers of couples have not formed their intentions sufficiently with regard to the extent of ownership. However, both parties have made direct financial contributions to the purchase price of the property in which they live, usually through mortgage payments, .

5.19   Waite L J's approach has been criticised, in particular by Nicola Glover and Paul Todd, 'The Myth of Common Intention' (1996) LS 325. They argue that this decision is contrary to established precedents.

5.20   Furthermore, they argue that there should be the same rules to determine both the creation of a presumed resulting trust and the extent of an interest under such a presumed resulting trust. In *Midland Bank Plc v Cook* (1995) different approaches were adopted to each of these matters.

5.21   Glover and Todd make the further point in another article – 'Inferring share of interest in home: *Midland Bank v Cook*' (1995) 4 Web JCLI – that the introduction of such an approach would produce an undesirable degree of uncertainty. In their view, a small financial contribution could lead to a large equitable interest being acquired under a presumed equitable trust, if other and wider factors are taken into account.

6 Trust, loan and gift

6.1   There are some domestic arrangements where a loan is intended rather than a trust.

6.2   In one case, H lived with her daughter and son-in-law, P. H provided several hundred pounds to enable an extention to be built. The Court of Appeal confirmed that a loan had been intended by H as she herself had described it as a loan.

6.3   In such a situation, it could not also be a resulting trust, and H had not acquired an equitable interest in the property. H would merely be entitled to repayment of the sum lent: *Hussey v Palmer* (1972).

6.4   In another case, an aunt had provided a substantial amount (£12,000) to her nephew to purchase a property and shop in both his own and his wife's names.

6.5   The High Court (Browne-Wilkinson J, as he then was) decided that the monies provided were either a gift by the aunt to her nephew and his wife, or had been loaned to them. On the particular facts he held that a loan had been made: *Re Sharpe* (1980).

6.6   There was no resulting trust in favour of the aunt as there was not a sufficient common intention between the parties that she should have an equitable interest. In order to acquire such an interest, there would have to be a much more detailed arrangement between the parties.

6.7   In the absence of such plans the aunt did not acquire an equitable interest in the property. The concept of common intention has been discussed previously in this Unit in paragraphs 3.4 and 3.5.

6.8   The need for a common intention in order for an equitable interest to be acquired has been confirmed in subsequent cases: *Spence v Brown* (1988), *Risch v McFee* (1991), and *Bonner v King* (1991). It is a matter for the judge to look at the particular facts and the evidence of the parties.

6.9   An example of such evidence is contained in the decision of *Woodward v Woodward* (1995), where a mother was held to have provided a loan to her adult son, because she had actually said to him that the monies she provided were 'as a loan'.

6.10   A further interesting point in this case is that because the son was an adult, the Court of Appeal decided that there was no presumption of gift between the mother and son. The presumption of resulting trust has been previously discussed in Unit 1.

6.11   A similar approach was adopted in *Sekhorn v Alissa* (1989), where a property was conveyed into the sole name of the daughter (A), who paid a substantial amount (£15,000) by mortgage to the cost of its acquisition, the mother (S) paying the remainder of the purchase price (£21,500).

6.12   The property was then developed into two self-contained flats – the daughter lived in one flat, and the mother in the other.

6.13   In the High Court, Hoffmann J decided that the mother had not intended a gift to her daughter of the monies that she had provided. In particular, on occasion the mother had received rentals, which she had kept, by letting one of the flats. This showed that she was participating in a commercial way.

6.14   There had been no discussions between the parties as to when the monies would be returned to the mother. Hoffmann J. concluded that this pointed against the mother having made a loan to her daughter.

6.15   Importantly, this was an arrangement between two adults. Since the daughter was not a minor there was no presumption of gift. Instead, the presumption was one of trust.

6.16   In particular the presumption was one of resulting trust since the property had been put into the sole name of the daughter. The presumption of resulting trust has been previously discussed in Unit 1.

6.17 The evidence pointed towards a resulting trust, but this presumption of resulting trust was of help to the mother in her claim for an equitable interest. It was held that the mother did acquire an equitable interest. Her share would be an amount equal to the value of the flat in which she lived.

6.18 The theme of these cases should now be apparent. In general, these cases involve domestic situations where monies have been provided by parents or relatives where the exact formal position has not been resolved.

6.19 The courts have three choices. They can find that a gift has been made. They can decide that a loan has been advanced. Or, they can conclude that a resulting trust has been created in favour of the provider of those monies.

6.20 In a different context, a mother lent her son and daughter-in-law a sum of money to pay the deposit for a house purchased by the son and daughter-in-law. The property was put into the son's name alone. The Court of Appeal did infer a common intention between the son and daughter-in-law that they were both to have an equitable interest in that property, because the loan had been lent to them jointly: *Halifax Building Society* v *Brown and Another, Raphael Zorn Helmsley Ltd* v *Same* (1995).

7 Trusts of Land and Appointment of Trustees Act 1996

7.1 For a detailed discussion of this act see Chris Whitehouse and Nicholas Hassall, *The Trusts of Land and Appointment of Trustees Act 1996*, Butterworths (1996).

7.2 See also Nicholas Hopkins, 'The Trusts of Land and Appointment of Trustees Act 1996' [1996] Conv 411.

7.3 See in addition: Richard Wallington 'The Trusts of Land and Appointment of Trustees Act 1996' (1996) NLJ 959.

7.4 The major provisions of this act will now be outlined:

● Trustees of land given the power to postpone a sale of a trust of land. (Section 4(1) – discussed above previously.)

● Trustees of land given the power of an absolute owner in relation to the land held in trust. (Section 6(1).)

● Trustees of land may transfer an interest in land held in trust to a beneficiary who is of full age and mental capacity, even though there is no express provision in the trust document. (Section 6(2).) The trustees are to have regard to the rights of the other beneficiaries in the exercise of this statutory power. (Section 6(5).)

- Trustees of land may delegate their powers under the act to beneficiaries. (Section 9 – discussed previously in Unit 2.)

- Trustees of land to consult with beneficiaries who are of full age and mental capacity so far as is practical. The wishes of such beneficiaries are to be carried out, subject to the general interest of other beneficiaries of the trust. Where there is disagreement amongst the beneficiaries, the majority wish, determined by the value of share in the trust, is to be carried out. (Section 11(1).)

- Trustees of land must not unreasonably exclude or restrict the rights of beneficiaries who have the right under a trust document to occupy (live on) the land. (Sections 12 and 13.)

- Incapacitated trustees of land may be removed and new trustees appointed. (Sections 19 to 21.) These sections have been discussed previously in Unit 2 and will be further considered in Unit 9.

Summary

Now that you have completed this Unit, you should understand:

☐ **strict settlements**

☐ **trusts for sale**

☐ **the intentions and interests of co-ownership.**

Self-assessment questions

1 How may trusts of land may be held?

2 When will a trust for sale arise?

3 What is meant by co-ownership of land?

4 Explain the circumstances in which a person will acquire an interest in land under a presumed resulting trust.

5 Explain the circumstances in which a person will acquire an interest in land under a constructive trust.

6 How do the courts assess the amount (share) of an interest under a presumed resulting trust?

7 How do the courts assess the amount (share) of an interest under a constructive trust?

8 When will a domestic arrangement give rise to a loan rather than a trust?

9 Outline the major provisions of the Trusts of Land and Appointment of Trustees Act 1996.

Exam-style question

John has recently died and your bank has been appointed the executor and trustee of his will. He and his second wife, Martha, lived in his property 'Canada House'. In his will, he bequeathed it to the bank 'upon trust to allow Martha to reside therein as long as she desires...' and, when she ceases to reside there, the bank is to sell it and use the proceeds as part of his residuary estate, which was left to the children of his first marriage (his first wife having died). He also bequeathed another property, 'The Alaska Estate', to Martha for life and, on her death, this property is to pass also into his residuary estate.

a) What does the law require the bank to do as regards the legal title of the two properties?

b) Martha has already indicated that Canada House is too large for her to manage by herself. She is therefore considering moving out, but is reluctant to do so since she cannot afford another home of her own. Discuss who is entitled to sell Canada House and what would happen to the sale proceeds.

(c) Alaska House (part of The Alaska Estate) is run down and needs substantial repairs and improvements. Outline how such costs may be financed and who is responsible for them.

(d) George, one of John's sons by his first marriage, is short of funds despite having recently received his share of his father's residuary estate. He asks the bank to make an advance to him, on account of his future share, from either of the two properties, whenever cash is available. Explain whether the bank can meet such a request.

[Autumn 1995]

(The answers are given in the Appendix)

Caselist for Unit 7 Trusts of Land

The Trusts of Land and Appointment of Trustees Act 1996, sections 4(1), 6(1), 6(2), 6(5), 9, 11(1), 12, 13, 19, 20, 21.

The Law of Property Act 1925, sections 2(i)(ii), 53(1)(b), 53(2)

The Law of Property (Miscellaneous Provisions) Act 1989.

Burns v *Burns* [1984] Ch 317.

Grant v *Edwards* [1986] Ch 638.

Hammond v *Mitchell* [1991] 1 WLR 1127.

Lloyds Bank Plc v *Rosset* [1991] 1 AC 107.

Kingsnorth Finance Co v *Tizard* [1986] 1 WLR 783.

Simon Gardner, 'Rethinking Family Property' (1993) 109 LQR 263.

David Hayton, 'Constructive Trusts of Homes – a Bold Approach' (1993) 109 LQR 485.

Professor David Hayton: Chapter 9 Resulting and Constructive Trusts of Homes in Fundamental Principles of Law series The Law of Trusts (2nd ed.) 1993. Sweet and Maxwell.

Graham Moffat, *Trusts Law Text and Materials*, 2nd edition, Butterworths, London (1994), Chapter 12.

Donovan W. M. Waters QC, 'The Nature of the Remedial Constructive Trust' in *The Frontiers of Liability*, vol. 2 (ed. P.B.H. Birks) Oxford University Press, Oxford (1994), Chapter 13.

Simon Gardner, 'The Element of Discretion' in *The Frontiers of Liability*, vol. 2 (ed. P.B.H. Birks) Oxford University Press, Oxford (1994), Chapter 14.

The Honourable Sir Anthony Mason, 'The Place of Equity and Equitable Remedies in the Contemporary Common Law World' (1994) 110 LQR 238.

Midland Bank Plc v *Cooke* [1995] 4 All ER 562.

Hayton and Marshall Commentary and Cases on the Law of Trusts and Equitable Remedies, 10th edition (ed. D.J. Hayton) Sweet and Maxwell, London (1996), Chapter 6.

Nicola Glover and Paul Todd, 'The Myth of Common Intention' (1996) LS 325.

Midland Bank v *Cook* (1995) 4 Web J.C.L.I.

Hussey v Palmer [1972] 1 WLR 1286.

Re Sharpe (a bankrupt), Trustee of the Bankrupt v *Sharpe* [1980] 1 WLR 765.

Spence v *Brown* [1988] Fam Law 291.

Risch v *McFee* (1991) 61 P & CR 42.

Bonner v *King* [1991] NPC 136.

Woodward v *Woodward* [1995] 3 All ER 980.

Sekhon v *Alissa* [1989] 2 FLR 94.

Halifax Building Society v *Brown and Another, Raphael Zorn Helmsley Ltd* v *Same, The Times,* 8 February 1995.

Chris Whitehouse and Nicholas Hassall, *The Trusts of Land and Appointment of Trustees Act 1996,* Butterworths, London (1996).

Nicholas Hopkins, 'The Trusts of Land and Appointment of Trustees Act 1996' [1996] Conv 411.

Richard Wallington, 'The Trusts of Land and Appointment of Trustees Act 1996' (1996) NLJ 959.

8

The Beneficiary Principle

Objectives

After studying the text and working through this Unit, students should be able to:

- understand the nature of beneficial (equitable) interests

- understand the beneficiary principle

- understand unincorporated associations

- know the class closing rules.

1 The nature of beneficial interest

1.1 A distinction must be made between a personal claim (*in personam*), i.e. a claim made against a person, and a proprietary claim (*in rem*), i.e. a claim made against the asset. This distinction will be dealt with in more detail in Unit 12.

1.2 In *Tinsley* v *Milligan* (1994), Lord Browne-Wilkinson was of the view that the equitable interest in a trust owned by the beneficiary was effectively a proprietary interest. This is because the beneficiary has an interest which may be transferred.

1.3 Furthermore, in a banking context, a bank has the right to combine and set off two separate accounts of the same person, where one is in surplus and the other is overdrawn. However, an individual person's account cannot be combined and set off with a trust account (that is, a bank account with monies held on trust for beneficiaries): *Barclays Bank* v *Quistclose Investments Ltd* (1970).

1.4 The equitable interest is now established as a proprietary right (*in rem*) which will bind third parties who will be subject to it. Where that third party buys an asset in which the beneficiary owns an equitable interest, unless the third party is a *bona fide* purchaser for value without notice (see below), then that third party will take the asset subject to this equitable interest.

1.5   The exception mentioned above is where the third party buyer is a *bona fide* purchaser for value without notice (knowledge). This means that the buyer of an asset in good faith, without knowledge of its defect in title, will acquire both the legal and the equitable interest in that asset. In such a situation, the beneficiary would lose his equitable interest and the buyer would acquire it. (The beneficiary is entitled to recover the proceeds of sale paid to the trustee: *Lake* v *Bayliss*, 1974.)

1.6   Where a third party has notice (knowledge) of another's equitable interest, then the third party will take subject to it: *Kingsnorth Finance Co* v *Tizard* (1986). This case has been dealt with in Unit 7.

1.7   A recent case concerned a father who put funds into a bank account in Antibes in the South of France. The account was in his son's name, which means that legal title was in the name of the son. With these funds, the son purchased property (a flat) in Antibes. Subsequently the son argued that the transfer was a gift to him. Because the relationship was one of father and son, there was a presumption of gift, see the Introduction and in particular the case of *Tribe* v *Tribe* (1995).

1.8   The father brought a claim in the English High Court, and subsequently the Court of Appeal, asserting that this property was held on trust by the son for the father. The son argued (using the Brussels Convention) that the French courts should have exclusive jurisdiction in relation to the father's claim.

1.9   The case ultimately ended up before the European Court of Justice. That court was of the view that the father was really requiring the son to execute the appropriate legal documents which would transfer equitable ownership to the father. Until that was done, the father did not have an action *in rem* (proprietary claim), but merely an action *in personam* (personal claim) against the son.

1.10   The reason for this was that the father was bringing a claim *in personam* against the son. Until his claim succeeded and the son executed the appropriate documents, the father did not have an *in rem* (proprietary) claim. Nor did the father have an equitable interest in the flat which was good against the whole world (except the *bona fide* purchaser for value without notice): *Webb* v *Webb* (1994).

1.11   *Webb* v *Webb* (1994) was discussed by Catherine MacMillan in her casenote: *The European Court of Justice Agrees with Maitland: Trusts and the Brussels Convention*. She makes the point that prior to the ruling by the European

Court of Justice, the Court of Appeal (in an unreported decision), took differing views as to whether the father's claim was *in rem* or *in personam*.

1.12 She also makes the point that the majority of the Court of Appeal (Scott LJ and Taylor LJ) regarded the father's claim as one *in personam* whilst Nourse LJ regarded it as a claim *in rem*. As we have seen the European Court of Justice agreed with the view of the majority.

1.13 For a discussion of trusts in a European Civil Law context, *Hayton and Marshall, Commentary and Cases on the Law of Trusts and Equitable Remedies* 10th edition (ed. D. J. Hayton), (1996) Chapter 12. In this chapter Professor Hayton points out the importance of the maxim (general equitable principle) that equity acts *in personam*.

1.14 In an important early decision, *Penn* v *Lord Baltimore* (1750), it was established that for the courts of equity to be able to rule upon a matter, it was not necessary that the property be located in England. It was sufficient if the defendant was domiciled in England. In such circumstances, equity, by virtue of its own internal rules, would have jurisdiction.

1.15 This approach has been confirmed in *Chellaram* v *Chellaram* (1985) and also in *El Ajou* v *Dollar Land Holdings plc* (1993). In this subsequent case the High Court decided that proceedings could be brought in England to recover misapplied property which had been moved round the world, because the defendant had received that property in England. It was the presence of the defendant in England that was crucial.

2 The Beneficiary Principle

2.1 So far, we have looked at the nature of the beneficiary's interest. There is a further rule in relation to setting up a valid trust which is that there must be ascertained or ascertainable beneficiaries. If this test is not satisfied, the trust is not valid. This important rule is known as 'the beneficiary principle': *Re Denley's Trust Deed* (1969).

2.2 Trusts for purposes are, in general, not allowed unless there are beneficiaries who can enforce the trust. A trust which is set up for a purpose may be directly or indirectly for beneficiaries and so valid: *Re Astor's Settlement Trusts* (1952).

2.3 There have been a number of cases, listed below, where the lack of ascertained or ascertainable beneficiaries has invalidated the trust. In such circumstances the trust could not take effect as a non-charitable express trust.

- a trust to promote the independence of newspapers, to protect newspapers from merging, to control the publication of newspapers, and to provide for the maintenance of good relations between nations: *Re Astor's Settlement Trusts* (1952)

- a trust to conduct research into a 40-letter alphabet: *Re Shaw's Will Trusts* (1952)

- a trust for the inhabitants of the county of West Yorkshire to help economic developement, reduce unemployment, promote organisations concerned with community and youth programmes, assist ethnic minorities, and inform the public of the elimination of county councils: *R v District Auditor, ex parte West Yorkshire Metropolitan County Council* (1986).

2.4 There are certain exceptions where the courts have allowed purpose trusts where there are no ascertained beneficiaries. Such trusts are important concessions to human sentiment. There are several recognised categories:

- trusts for the building, maintenance and repair of graves and tombstones

- trusts for animals and/or pets

- trusts to say masses in private

- trusts for unincorporated associations (see below)

- trusts to advance fox hunting

2.5 Such trusts must comply with the rules relating to perpetuities. These rules have been described in Unit 5. It is established that where the trust instrument provides for the trust to last for as long as is legally allowed, then the trust will be valid.

2.6 These exceptions are considered by Paul Matthews in 'The New Trust: Obligations without Rights?' in *Trends in Contemporary Trust Law* (ed. A.J. Oakley) (1996), Chapter 1.

3 Unincorporated Associations

3.1 In order to be an unincorporated association, four essential requirements must be satisfied: *Conservative Central Office v Burrell* (1982).

- mutual aims and objectives amongst the members of the organisation

- contractual rights and obligations between the members of the organisation

- rules that regulate the control of the organisation and its funds

- the ability to enrol as a member or depart from that organisation.

3.2 There are three main ways in which an unincorporated association may receive a legacy: trust; contract; gift.

Trust

3.3 The leading authority for a trust approach derives from *Re Denley's Trust Deed* (1969) where monies were left on trust to enable a sports ground to be maintained for the use of employees of a particular company.

3.4 Since the purpose would directly or indirectly benefit particular individuals, it was valid.

3.5 Furthermore the trust was to last for only 21 years. This was within the perpetuity period and was not invalidated through lasting too long. The rules relating to perpetuities have been previously discussed in Unit 5.

3.6 In *Re Denley's Trust Deed* (1969), the employees were only seeking to validate the trust. They did not ask for distribution.

3.7 One interesting point is: what is the test for certainty of objects for a purpose trust? This question is not just an academic one, but is relevant to the decision in *Re Denley's Trust Deed* (1969) where the trustees, at their discretion, could allow other persons, who were not employees of the company, to use the sports ground.

3.8 In Unit 4 we have seen that for discretionary express trusts, the trustees must be able to tell of any given individual that he or she is a member of the class.

3.9 It is arguable that purpose trusts are a particular type of trust. They differ from an ordinary express trust in that the settlor provides funds for a particuar purpose, rather than the provision of income or capital for particular beneficiaries.

3.10 However, the test put forward in *Re Denley's Trust Deed* (1969) is that there must be some ascertainable beneficiaries. This test was held to be the test in that case. It was a new test.

3.11 If such analysis is accepted, then it is perhaps appropriate that a different, wider, and easier test to fulfil should be adopted in relation to beneficiaries where a purpose trust is concerned. In *Re Lipinski's Will Trusts* (1976) Oliver J confirmed that this was the test put forward in *Re Denley's Trust Deed* (1969), and that this was the correct test.

3.12 There are problems with the distribution of assets of an unincorporated association amongst its members if a trust analysis is followed. In *Re Denley's Trust Deed* (1969) the employees did not seek to sell the sports ground and distribute any funds received for its sale amongst themselves.

3.13 Hence the case did not, and cannot be an authority which answers whether distribution is possible.

3.14   One authority that might be used to answer the question as to whether distribution amongst the members is possible, is *Saunders* v *Vautier* (1841) discussed in Unit 2. This case decided that in order to distribute funds under an express trust, all the beneficiaries must be ascertained and all must agree to a distribution. If the class is incomplete, or if there are minors or mentally incapacitated beneficiaries, then distribution is impossible.

3.15   There are also authorities which suggest that although the trust is expressed as a purpose, the trust fund can still be divided amongst the beneficiaries who are to benefit through the carrying out of the purpose. Such authorities are contrary to the approach and conclusion in *Saunders* v *Vautier* (1841), since such authorities would allow distribution amongst the beneficiaries. Some of these authorities will now be examined.

3.16   In *Re Bowes* (1896) the testator, John Bowes, left £5,000 on trust to enable his trustees to plant trees for shelter on a particular piece of land known as the Wemmergill estate. The testator provided that if he had chosen, in his lifetime, where the trees were to be planted the trustees were to plant trees as he had decided. The testator also provided that if he had not given instructions about his wishes for planting trees, then the trustees must plant them in accordance with the wishes of the person with the current life interest in the estate.

3.17   There was evidence produced before the court that only 75 acres of the estate could be planted with trees. This would involve an expenditure of no more than £800.

3.18   North J was of the view that the gift was given to benefit the persons entitled to the estate. The gift was not intended to benefit anyone else. In such circumstances they were absolutely entitled to the £5,000.

3.19   A similar approach was taken in *Re Osoba* (*dec'd*) (1979) where income from a property was provided for the deceased's daughter for her maintenance whilst a student.

3.20   The Court of Appeal considered that this purpose was merely an indication of the motives of the testator. There was a presumption that the settlor intended to benefit his daughter to the full value of legacy. On these facts, if the purpose was carried out there would be surplus funds. The fund would therefore be held on trust for the daughter absolutely.

Contract

3.21   An alternative approach is that the members of the unincorporated association are in a contractual relationship with each other. Such an analysis was not possible in *Re Denley's Trust Deed* (1969) for two reasons. First, there was no club in existence which had any rules regulating the position as amongst the employees. Second, the sports ground was clearly left on trust since clear words of trust were used.

3.22 Where a contractual approach is used, this fits in easily with the idea of rules of a club or association which give those members contractual rights between each other: *Re Recher's Will Trusts* (1972).

3.23 This contractual approach was accepted as a matter of general principle in *Re Lipinski's Will Trusts* (1976) where a testator left monies to be used by a club, the Hull Maccabi sports club, to enable it to build or improve its buildings.

3.24 Funds which are left to such a club or association go to increase the general funds of that club or association.

3.25 In order to avoid problems with perpetuities (discussed above and in Unit 5), which would invalidate the bequest, the rules of the club or association must enable or allow the members to: either vest the property in themselves: *Re Lipinski's Will Trusts* (1976); or alternatively, distribute the funds amongst themselves or for some other purpose, *Re Grant's Will Trusts* (1980).

3.26 The rules of the unincorporated association allowed the members of a branch of SOGAT to distribute its funds amongst all the branch members: *News Group Newspapers Ltd and Others* v *Society of Graphical and Allied Trades* (1986).

3.27 Whether distribution is possible depends on the rules of the association. As we have seen, in order to ensure validity and to avoid problems with the rules relating to perpetuity, the unincorporated association must have rules which allow for distribution. Hence, in order for a bequest to be valid, distribution must be possible.

3.28 The contractual approach is therefore much more flexible than the trust approach described above.

3.29 In *Neville Estates* v *Madden* (1962), where the Catford Synagogue had sold some land, the question for the court to determine was the entitlement of the members of the synagogue to the proceeds of sale. It was held that the members were not entitled to such proceeds.

3.30 It was accepted by Cross J that members of an unincorporated association would be able to divide the whole of the property of their association amongst themselves, as a matter of contract, if that was what their rules provided. In such a situation, the unincorporated association could not be charitable.

3.31 *Re Recher's Will Trusts* (1972), part of the testator's estate was left to an organisation called the London and Provincial Anti-Vivisection Society. The point was made by Brightman J that if a donation was made to a particular unincorporated association and words of trust were not imposed, then the donation could take effect as a general addition to the funds of the association.

3.32 Provided the rules of the association allowed, the property of the association, including any donation, could be divided amongst the members. Such division would be on the basis of a contractual relationship amongst the members.

3.33 What is important in the analysis of Brightman J in *Re Recher's Will Trusts* (1972) is that the trust approach is the starting point. Only where no trust has been imposed, because the donor has not used words of trust in his or her bequest, will the court look to a contractual approach.

3.34 However, once a contractual approach has been adopted by the court, it is possible for the donation to be divided amongst the members in accordance with their contractual entitlement.

Gift

3.35 A starting point is *Leahy* v *Attorney General of New South Wales* (1959) where the question was whether a gift to a particular order (group) of nuns was a gift to the individual members of that order. The Privy Councillor, Viscount Simonds, concluded that the gift was not a gift to the individual members.

- First, the gift was to a particular order rather than to individuals within that order.

- Second, there was no evidence to suggest that the donor intended an immediate gift to the individual nuns who currently made up that order.

- Third, the property 'Elmslea' was a property of twenty rooms with outbuildings and grounds of several hundred acres. Such a property was to be used for the general purposes of the order and not to be distributed amongst the nuns who currently made up the order.

3.36 In reaching its decision, the Privy Council considered several precedents. Some of these will be examined below.

3.37 The Privy Council considered an earlier decision, *Cocks* v *Manners* (1871), which concerned the validity of a gift, by the will of Frances Manners, to a Dominican convent at Carisbrook. The testatrix had not imposed any requirement that the gift was to be held for the general purposes of the convent. The court held that the gift was simply given to the superior of the convent to hold as a 'common chest', so that the current members of the convent could divide the fund amongst themselves.

3.38 The Privy Council also considered an earlier decision of *Re Drummond* (1914) which concerned a gift of the residuary estate of James Drummond to a club (originally set up in 1899) for the old boys of Bradford Grammar School. By subsequent codicil (document amending his earlier will and forming part of that will) the donor stated that this gift was to be used by the club for such purpose as the committee of the club might determine, the aims and objectives of the bequest being to benefit old boys of the Bradford Grammar School. In particular, the gift was intended to enable the committee to purchase a club house for use by such old boys.

3.39   Eve J decided that the gift was not a gift to the individual members of the club, but that it was a valid gift for the purposes of the club, as decided by the committee.

3.40   Further, this gift was not invalidated by any perpetuity rule. There was no trust imposed or created which restricted the committee's power to spend the monies given to it.

3.41   The Privy Council also considered an earlier decision: *Re Prevost* (1930) whereby a testator gave the whole of his estate to the trustees of the London Library for the purposes of that institution, including its employees.

3.42   Eve J held that the testator had not created a trust since he had not used words of binding obligation. The gift was valid. Furthermore, the trustees of the London Library could use the sum of money given to them in any way that they wished, and could spend income and capital. They were not obliged simply to keep that money as capital for the purposes of the London Library. For this reason the gift did not offend any rule(s) relating to perpetuity.

3.43   The Privy Council also considered an earlier decision, *Re Ogden* (1933), which concerned a gift of income from part of the residuary estate of Henry Joseph Ogden to political organisations which had as their aim the furtherance of Liberal principles in politics.

3.44   Lord Tomlin held that the executors, who were also trustees, would be able to select organisations falling within this definition. The donor had not imposed a trust since no words imposing a binding obligation had been used. Hence, the donor had intended gifts to the various organisations selected by the executors. Such gifts were absolute gifts for the purposes of the organisations selected. They were valid gifts and not affected by any rule(s) relating to perpetuity.

3.45   The Privy Council also considered an earlier decision, *Re Turkington* (1937), which concerned a gift of Charles Henry Turkington's residuary estate to the Staffordshire Masonic Lodge to enable it to build a temple in Stafford.

3.46   Luxmoore J considered that if the gift had been made to the Masonic Lodge, then there would be no problems as to its validity. The gift would have been a valid gift for the general purposes of the Masonic Lodge and would not be affected by any rule(s) relating to perpetuity.

3.47   However, because no words of trust were used by the testator in relation to his gift, the Masonic Lodge was not under any binding obligation to build a temple. The testator was held to have merely expressed a wish that the Masonic Lodge build a temple. In such circumstances, the residuary estate became the property of the Lodge which could use or deal with the estate in accordance with its constitution.

3.48   If the donor is held to have created a gift, it is apparent from these cases that the gift will go to the general purposes of the organisation and will not be available for distribution amongst the members.

4 Class closing rules

4.1   The class closing rules derive from *Andrews* v *Partington* (1791). The basic idea is that when the first individual beneficiary of a class becomes entitled to his or her interest, for example by attaining a particular age, the class is deemed to close: *Re Chapman's Settlement Trust* (1977). This means that other individuals cannot subsequently become entitled to a share of the trust fund. The rule is designed to promote certainty and enable trustees to distribute.

4.2   The rule may be excluded by specific words to the contrary. An example would be through use of words such as 'whenever born': *Re Edmondson's Will Trusts* (1972) or the imposition of a particular 'closing date': *Re Tom's Settlement* (1987).

4.3   We can take the *Re Denley's Trust Deed* (1969) example where property has been given to employees of a company. If employees who subsequently joined the company were included within the class, this could produce perpetuity problems. (This has been discussed in this Unit and in Unit 5.)

4.4   However, as Paul Matthews points out in his chapter (cited above) section 4(4) of the Perpetuities and Accumulations Act 1964 resolves such difficulty by excluding subsequent members from the class, in our example new employees, where their inclusion would cause invalidity for perpetuity reasons.

Summary

Now you have studied the text and worked through this Unit, you should:

☐ **understand the nature of beneficial (equitable) interest**

☐ **understand the beneficiary principle**

☐ **understand incorporated associations**

☐ **know the class closing rules.**

Self-assessment questions

1 To what extent does a beneficiary of a trust have a right *in rem*?

2 What did the decision in *Webb* v *Webb* (1994) decide?

3 What is the beneficiary principle?

4 How may a bequest to an unincorporated association take effect?

5 Brian wishes that his estate be used in the following ways on his death. To spend £200 on planting trees in the parks where he lives; £5,000 on trust to maintain and improve the buildings of a local sports club of which he is currently a member; £1,000 for the promotion and furtherance of fox-hunting.

   Advise Brian.

6 The Harrow and Healthy Hearts Country Club is in need of additional funds of £10,000 to build a swimming pool. An advertisement is placed in the local press seeking not only new members but also contributions from existing members and the general public. £5,000 is received by cheques and cash as a result of the advertisement. Before any further funds can be obtained, the local and national authorities obtain permission to build a motorway running adjacent to the club. An alternative site cannot be found.

   The club is an unincorporated association, and its members vote to close the club. Under the rules of the club, it is able to dissolve itself. The rules of the club make no provision for the distribution of its assets where it does dissolve itself.

   Advise as to the distribution of the club's assets.

(The answers are given in the Appendix)

Caselist for Unit 8 The Beneficiary Principle

Tinsley v *Milligan* [1994] 1 AC 340

Barclays Bank Ltd v *Quistclose Investments Ltd* [1970] AC 567.

Lake v *Bayliss* [1974] 1 WLR 1073.

Kingsnorth Finance Ltd v *Tizard* [1986] 1 WLR 783.

Webb v *Webb* [1994] 3 All ER 911.

Catherine MacMillan, 'The European Court of Justice Agrees with Maitland: Trusts and the Brussels Convention' (1996) *Conv* 125.

Hayton and Marshall, Commentary and Cases on the Law of Trusts and Equitable Remedies 10th edition (ed. D.J. Hayton) Sweet and Maxwell, London (1996), Chapter 12.

Penn v *Lord Baltimore* [1750] 1 Ves Sen 444.

Chellaram v *Chellaram* [1985] Ch 409.

El Ajou v *Dollar Land Holdings plc* [1993] 3 All ER 717 (High Court).

Re Denley's Trust Deed, Holman v *H.H.Martyn & Co Ltd* [1969] 1 Ch 373.

Re Astor's Settlement Trusts, Astor v *Scholfield* [1952] Ch 534.

Re Shaw's Will Trusts [1952] Ch 163.

R v *District Auditor, ex parte West Yorkshire Metropolitan County Council* [1986] RVR 24.

Paul Matthews, 'The New Trust: Obligations without Rights?' in *Trends in Contemporary Trust Law* (ed. A.J. Oakley) Clarendon Press, Oxford (1996), Chapter 1.

Conservative Central Office v *Burrell* [1982] 1 WLR 522.

Re Lipinski's Will Trusts, Gosschalk v *Levy* [1976] Ch 235.

Saunders v *Vautier* [1841] 4 Beav 115.

Re Bowes, Earl of Strathmore v *Vane* [1896] 1 Ch 507.

Re Osoba (deceased), Osoba v *Osoba* [1979] 1 WLR 247.

Re Recher's Will Trusts, National Westminster Bank Ltd v *National Anti-vivisection Society* [1972] Ch 526.

Re Grant's Will Trusts, Harris v *Anderson* [1980] 1 WLR 360.

News Group Newspapers Ltd and Others v *Society of Graphical and Allied Trades* [1986] ICR 716.

Neville Estates v *Madden* [1962] Ch 832.

Leahy v *Attorney General of New South Wales* [1959] AC 457.

Cocks v *Manners* [1871] LR 12 Eq 574.

Re Drummond, Ashworth v *Drummond* [1914] 2 Ch 90.

Re Prevost, Lloyds Bank Ltd v *Barclays Bank Ltd* [1930] 2 Ch 383.

Re Ogden, Brydon v *Samuel* [1933] Ch 678.

Re Turkington, Owen v *Benson* [1937] 4 All ER 501.

Andrews v *Partington* (1791) 3 Bro CC 401.

Re Chapman's Settlement Trusts, Jones v *Chapman* [1977] 1 WLR 1163.

Re Edmondson's Will Trusts, Baron Sandford of Banbury v *Edmondson* [1972] 1 WLR 183.

Re Tom's Settlement, Rose v *Evans* [1987] 1 WLR 1021.

Section 4(4) of the Perpetuities and Accumulations Act 1964.

9

Trusteeship

Objectives

After studying the text and working through this Unit, students should be able to:

- understand the processes of appointment, retirement and removal of trustees

- know about the different types of trustee

- know about trust corporations

- appreciate the difference between trustees and representatives.

1 Appointment, retirement and removal of trustees

Inherent jurisdiction in equity

1.1   The inherent jurisdiction are rules which equity has developed itself. Equity wished to ensure that its remedies were effective.

1.2   The courts of equity were founded on conscience (see Unit 1 and Unit 8), and the courts will today enforce obligations which bind the conscience of the trustees. The court will make any necessary *in personam* (against the person) orders against trustees where they have acted in an unconscionable way as regards the beneficiaries of a trust.

1.3   A contempt of court order could be granted against the trustee. In addition, equity would grant its remedies against a trustee residing within England even though the trust assets were outside England.

1.4   Such jurisdiction was confirmed in *Chellaram* v *Chellaram* (1985) where the plaintiff beneficiaries wished to remove the defendant trustees.

1.5 If the court felt that in order to protect the rights of the beneficiaries it was necessary to remove trustees and appoint new ones, then it had the necessary powers. Such powers derived from the inherent jurisdiction of the courts.

1.6 The appointment and removal of trustees was governed by English rules of equity even though the system of law (proper law) which governed the interpretation and other obligations of the trust was some other law.

1.7 It was held that the defendant trustees had accepted the jurisdiction of the English courts by accepting the writs served upon them. It followed that the English courts had power to remove the trustees. The court therefore dismissed the application of the defendants to stop the plaintiffs from seeking to remove the defendants as trustees.

1.8 In *Chellaram* v *Chellaram* (1985) Scott J considered an earlier decision, *Letterstedt* v *Broers* (1884) in which Lord Blackburn had stated the general principles upon which the courts of equity will act as follows:

- this was a general jurisdiction, and would depend upon the particular facts

- the interests and welfare of the beneficiaries were the guiding principles

- where the trustees had acted improperly or dishonestly, and endangered the trust assets, they could be removed

- the nature of the duties to be performed by the trustees – whether they were of a particularly personal or delicate nature.

1.9 The court in *Letterstedt* v *Broers* (1884) removed the trustees for two main reasons:

- first, there was continuing friction between the trustees and beneficiaries, as a result of substantial overcharging by the trustees

- second, the trustees would have difficult and delicate duties to perform if they continued to act as trustees.

1.10 In addition, the decision in *Chellaram* v *Chellaram* (1985) confirms that the courts of equity have inherent jurisdiction to appoint new trustees. The courts could not only remove trustees, but could also appoint new ones in place of the removed trustees. The trust assets could be vested in the new trustees. In this way, the rights of the beneficiaries would be protected.

1.11 In *McPhail* v *Doulton* (1971), it was accepted by Lord Wilberforce that, if the trustees were unable to administer a 'discretionary trust' (discussed in Unit 4) the court could appoint new trustees to do so. Such jurisdiction to appoint new trustees was confirmed, by Warner J. in *Mettoy Pension Trustees* v *Evans* (1990), in relation to the inability of existing trustees to exercise a 'fiduciary power' (discussed in Unit 4). On the particular facts, this jurisdiction was not sought.

1.12   The unreported decision of *Richard v The Hon A B Mackay* (14th March 1987), considered in full in 'General Principles Relating to Trustees', in *Maudsley and Burn's Trusts and Trustees Cases and Materials* 5th edition (ed. E.H. Burn) (1996), Chapter 16, lays down some additional principles upon which the equitable jurisdiction is based:

- first, those who are proposing that new trustees be appointed must make out a positive case

- second, if the reason is simply to avoid tax, without any other advantages being shown, the court will not appoint new trustees who are resident abroad

- third, new trustees who are resident abroad may be appointed under the inherent jurisdiction of the court, where the beneficiaries have settled in some other country and it is desired to appoint new trustees in that country.

1.13   Where the existing trustees wish to appoint new trustees, they may simply seek the protection of the court for such an appointment. The court merely needs to be satisfied that the trustees have formed the opinion that this is for the benefit of the beneficiaries or the trust fund, and that this course of action is not so inappropriate that no reasonable trustee could consider it.

1.14   On the facts, the trustees of a trust governed by English law wished to transfer 25% of the trust fund worth over £7m into a new trust in Bermuda, to be run by the leading trust corporation there.

1.15   The court, Millett J, as he then was, did allow these funds to be transferred to the trust corporation in Bermuda, since such a transfer was to the advantage of the beneficiaries.

1.16   The following reasons were advanced by the judge for allowing the transfer of funds:

- first, the beneficiaries of the trust were children of a family that had strong connections with the Far East, and it was likely that such beneficiaries might wish to live in that part of the world as adults. It was appropriate to have a proportion of the trust funds outside the United Kingdom in such circumstances.

- second, Bermuda was a stable area under United States influence

- third, many wealthy families had, in previous years, transferred funds to Bermuda

- fourth, the trust law of Bermuda was analogous to English law, from which it was derived

- fifth, Bermuda allowed free movement of capital

- sixth, the new trustee was the leading trust corporation in Bermuda.

1.17 The law relating to variation of trusts will be considered in detail in Unit 13.

Trustee Act 1925

1.18 Section 36(1) of the Trustee Act 1925 enables the existing trustees, or those persons nominated by the trust instrument, to appoint other trustees in writing:

- where one or more of the trustees have died

- where one or more of the trustees have resided out of the UK for a period greater than a year

- where one or more trustees no longer wish to act as trustees

- where one or more trustees are incapable of acting as trustees by reason of illness or mental disorder

- where one or more trustees are under the age of 18.

1.19 Further, the existing trustees, or those persons nominated by the trust instrument, may appoint other trustees in place of existing trustees.

1.20 By section 25 of the Trustee Act, a trustee who is resident abroad for less than a year is able to delegate his duties to another person by the mechanism of a power of attorney.

1.21 Section 41(1) of the Trustee Act 1925 enables the court to appoint a new trustee whenever it is expedient to do so. In particular, the court may appoint a new trustee as a substitute for a trustee who is incapable of acting as trustee by reason of mental disorder, bankruptcy or insolvency.

1.22 Further, the new trustee can be appointed in addition to, or instead of, the existing trustee(s). Indeed, the new trustee(s) can be appointed even though there are no existing trustee(s).

1.23 By section 37(1)(c) of the Trustee Act 1925, where only one trustee was originally appointed by the trust instrument, a trustee is unable to be discharged from the trust unless there is a trust corporation or at least two persons as trustees to carry out the trust. Trust corporations are considered below.

1.24 Where a trustee wishes to retire from a trust where no new trustee is to be appointed, and there are at least two trustees or a trust corporation (see below) to administer the trust, then that trustee can retire from the trust without the need for a court order, section 39(1) Trustee Act 1925.

1.25 The trustee must, by written document (deed), discharge himself or herself from the trust, and must obtain the consent of the other trustees, section 39(1) Trustee Act 1925.

Trusts of Land and Appointment of Trustees Act 1996

1.26   The Trusts of Land and Appointment of Trustees Act 1996 received the
        Royal Assent on 24th July 1996. This act (referred to in this Unit as 'the
        act') affects the appointment and removal of trustees.

   ● See generally, Chris Whitehouse and Nicholas Hassall, *The Trusts of Land
     and Appointment of Trustees Act 1996, A Practical Guide*, published 1996.

   ● See also, Nicholas Hopkins, 'The Trusts of Land and Appointment of
     Trustees Act 1996', (1996) *Conv* 411.

   ● Briefly discussed, 'Conveyancer's Notebook – Trusts of Land' (1996)
     Conv 77.

   ● Discussed at the bill stage by Wallington, 'The Trusts of Land and
     Appointment of Trustees Bill', (1996) *New Law Journal* 959.

   ● 'General Principles: Capacity; Appointment; Removal; Retirement;
     Control' in *Hanbury and Martin, Modern Equity* 15th edition (ed. Jill E.
     Martin) (1997), Chapter 17.

1.27   The Trusts of Land and Appointment of Trustees Act 1996 provides for
        important additional powers (in addition to those contained in the Trustee
        Act 1925), for the appointment, retirement and removal of trustees. Section
        19 of the act provides that the beneficiaries (where they are of full age and
        capacity, and together they are absolutely entitled to the trust property)
        have the power to remove a trustee.

1.28   Section 19(2) of the act provides that such a direction by the beneficiaries
        may be made in writing.

1.29   Section 20 of the act further provides for the appointment of other trustees
        where three conditions are satisfied:

   ● the beneficiaries must, again, all be of full age and capacity, and together
     be absolutely entitled to the trust property

   ● the trustee must be incapable of carrying out his or her functions due to
     mental disorder

   ● there must be no other person who is both entitled, able and willing to
     appoint a new trustee in place of the incapacitated trustee.

1.30   Section 20(2) of the act further provides that in such situations the
        beneficiaries may give directions in writing to the appropriate person who is
        in legal charge over the affairs of the incapacitated trustee. The directions of
        the beneficiaries will enable the appointment of a new trustee to take place.

1.31   Trustees appointed by section 36 of the Trustee Act 1925, or by section 41
        of the Trustee Act 1925, or by sections 19 or 20 of the act, will have all

the powers, discretions and authority of the original trustee, section 36(7) of the Trustee Act 1925. Section 21(3) of the act makes it clear that section 36(7) of the Trustee Act 1925 applies to trustees appointed by sections 19 or 20 of the act.

1.32 This approach is confirmed by section 43 of the Trustee Act 1925 which provides that any trustee, appointed by a court, shall have the same powers, discretions and authority as if he or she had been validly appointed a trustee by the trust instrument.

1.33 By section 40 of the Trustee Act 1925, the trust property is vested in the new and continuing trustees.

1.34 For a detailed discussion, see generally, 'The death, retirement, or removal of trustees and the appointment of new trustees'. *Underhill and Hayton, Law of Trusts and Trustees*. 15th edition (ed. David J. Hayton) (1995), Chapter 14.

2 Different types of trustees

- See generally, J.G. Riddall, 'Special Forms of Trustee' in *The Law of Trusts* (5th ed.) (1996), Chapter 15.

- 'Appointment of a judicial trustee' and 'The Public Trustee' in *Underhill and Hayton, Law of Trusts and Trustees* 15th edition (ed. D.J. Hayton), (1995), Chapters 15 and 16.

Managing trustees

2.1 The trustees who act in relation to the day-to-day management of the trust are called the 'managing trustees'. Where there is a custodian trustee, the managing trustees will still be responsible for the day-to-day management of the trust.

Custodian trustees

2.2 This concept was created by section 4(2) of the Public Trustee Act 1906. The public trustee acts as a custodian trustee. The trustees of a trust are the 'managing trustees' who are responsible, and continue to remain responsible, for the day-to-day management of the trust even though there is a custodian trustee appointed (section 4(2)(b) of the Public Trustee Act 1906).

2.3 The custodian trustee exercises an additional supervisory function:

- first, all income and capital monies paid out of the trust fund must be paid by, or with the approval of, the custodian trustee (section 4(2)(e) of the Public Trustee Act 1906)

- second, the trust property is vested in the custodian trustee (section 4(2)(a) of the Public Trustee Act 1906)

- third, documents of title relating to the trust are kept by the custodian trustee

- fourth, consent to all proper acts by the managing trustees shall be given by the custodian trustee (section 4(2)(d) of the Public Trustee Act 1906)

- fifth, the managing trustees may appoint additional trustees, and the custodian trustee may apply to the court for the removal and appointment of trustees, described above, (sections 4(2)(f) and 4(2)(g) of the Public Trustee Act 1906)

- sixth, the custodian trustee will continue to act as a trustee until such time as a court order is granted removing the custodian trustee (section 4(2)(i) of the Public Trustee Act 1906).

Judicial trustee

2.4   The office of judicial trustee was created by the Judicial Trustees Act 1896. A judicial trustee may be appointed, by the High Court or County Court, in place of the existing trustees, or as an additional or sole trustee (section 1(1) Judicial Trustees Act 1896).

2.5   Two major situations where the judicial trustee may be appointed are as follows:

- first, where it is necessary to have a person to administer a deceased's estate where the appointed trustees are unable to do this

- second, where there is complex litigation involving a trust fund. An example of this is *Ministry of Health* v *Simpson* (1951) discussed at the end of this Unit.

Settled land

2.6   The position of trustees regarding settled land is completely modified by the Trusts of Land and Appointment of Trustees Act 1996. Section 1 provides that trusts of land made after the commencement of the Act will simply be held as ordinary trusts of land, see Unit 7.

2.7   Sections 6 and 7 of the Act deal with the new general powers that trustees have in relation to trusts of land. In particular, such trustees are to have all the powers that an absolute owner would have. The Act has been outlined in Unit 7.

Bare trustees

2.8   A bare trust is where the trustee holds the trust property for a single beneficiary of full age and mental capacity. In this situation, the sole beneficiary – who is entitled to the whole of the equitable interest – is able to call for the legal interest from the trustee.

2.9   The trustee must agree to the beneficiary's request unless there is some express (or implied) term in the trust instrument to the contrary. When the beneficiary receives the legal interest, he will have both legal and equitable interests, which together equal absolute ownership. The beneficiary will have ended the trust by this action. The leading case is *Saunders* v *Vautier* (1841), discussed in Chapter 2.

Pension funds

2.10   The position as regards the ownership and duties in relation to surplus pension trust funds has been previously discussed in Unit 4. The recent decision of *Jefferies and Others* v *Mayes and Others* (1997) confirms that a power in relation to a surplus in a pension fund can be fiduciary.

2.11   Pension funds are discussed by Professor David Hayton, 'The Administration of a Trust' in *Hayton and Marshall, Commentary and Cases on the Law of Trusts and Equitable Remedies* (D.J. Hayton 10th edition) (1996), Chapter 9, Part 9.

2.12   There is also a discussion of pension funds by Professor Jill E Martin in 'Trusts of Pension Funds', *Hanbury and Martin, Modern Equity* 15th edition (ed. Jill E. Martin) (1997), Chapter 16.

2.13   In addition to the general rules in equity, some of which have been previously described in Unit 4, the Pensions Act 1995 provides an additional statutory framework.

2.14   We will now look at the statutory provisions relating to the removal and suspension of pension fund trustees under occupational pension schemes.

2.15   By section 3(2)(a) of the Pensions Act 1995 where the Occupational Pensions Regulatory Authority is satisfied that a trustee of an occupational pension scheme is in serious or persistent breach of his or her statutory duties under the Pensions Act 1995, then the Occupational Pensions Regulatory Authority may prohibit that person from being a trustee.

2.16   By section 5(1) of the Pensions Act 1995, the trustee must be given not less than one month's notice of the proposed prohibition by the Authority, and must be invited by the Authority to make representations to it.

2.17   By section 4(1)(a) of the Pensions Act 1995, in the above situation, the Authority may suspend the trustee. By section 4(2)(a) of the Pensions Act 1995, the period of suspension must not be for a period greater than 12 months pending an investigation by them.

2.18 By section 5(4) of the Pensions Act 1995, where the Authority suspends the trustee, it must give immediate notice to him or her, and notice to the other trustees as soon as is reasonably practicable.

2.19 By section 6(1) of the Pensions Act 1995, where a trustee continues to act as a trustee whilst prohibited or suspended, then he or she commits a criminal offence.

2.20 By section 7(1) of the Pensions Act 1995, the Authority may appoint another trustee in place of the disqualified trustee.

2.21 By section 8(3) of the Pensions Act 1995, a trustee appointed under section 7 has the same powers and duties as the other trustees.

2.22 By section 9 of the Pensions Act 1995 the Authority has the same jurisdiction and powers of the High Court where it removes or appoints a trustee.

2.23 By section 29(1) of the Pensions Act 1995 a person will be unable to act as a trustee of a pension trust fund where:

- he or she has been convicted of an offence involving dishonesty or deception

- he or she is bankrupt

- he or she has been disqualified from being a director of a company.

2.24 By section 30(1) of the Pensions Act 1995 where a trustee is disqualified for any of the above reasons, then the trustee must cease being a trustee. A trustee who does not cease to be a trustee in such a situation will be guilty of an offence, section 30(3) of the Pensions Act 1995.

2.25 By section 32(1) of the Pensions Act 1995, decisions of pension fund trustees can be made by a majority, unless the trust provides to the contrary.

3 Trust corporations

3.1 There are corporations whose articles expressly enable the undertaking and carrying on of the administration of trusts.

3.2 There is a statutory definition under section 68(18) of the Trustee Act 1925. This includes:

- first, the public trustee (discussed above)

- second, a corporation appointed by the court to be a trustee

- third, a corporation which may be appointed by the court as a result of rules made by statutory instrument under sections 4(1) and 4(3) of the Public Trustee Act 1906.

3.3   In this third situation the trust corporation will be a custodian trustee (discussed above).

3.4   A trust corporation may be appointed a judicial trustee since section 1(3) of the Judicial Trustees Act 1896 enables any fit and proper person to be appointed as a judicial trustee.

4 Trustees and personal representatives distinguished

4.1   A personal representative administers the estate of the deceased. In *Stamp Duties Commissioner (Queensland)* v *Livingston* (1965), the testator Livingston left his estate to his widow. She died whilst the estate was being administered.

4.2   The following principles were established in the Privy Council:

- first, that during administration, the entire ownership of the assets of the estate becomes that of the personal representative

- second, until the estate was administered, the widow had no interest, equitable or otherwise, in any particular asset of the estate

- third, the widow had the right to ensure that the estate was correctly administered.

4.3   An important distinction can now be made. It is established from *McPhail* v *Doulton* (1971), discussed in Unit 4, that the beneficiaries of a discretionary trust are entitled as a collective group to the total equitable interest. This is so, even though such beneficiaries are individually not able to identify a precise share to which they are entitled. The trustee is entitled only to the legal interest. The importance of this distinction has been discussed in Unit 1.

4.4   As we have seen above, in contrast, the personal representatives are entitled to the whole of the estate, both legal and equitable, whilst the estate is being administered.

4.5   We can now turn to another important case in order to make a further distinction. In *Ministry of Health* v *Simpson* (1951) the deceased, Caleb Diplock, made a residuary bequest for charitable or benevolent objects. This gift was not exclusively charitable and so was void since it was not sufficiently certain. As we have seen in Unit 8, there must be some ascertainable beneficiaries in order to have a valid purpose trust. See also, Unit 14 where the law relating to charities will be discussed.

4.5 In the House of Lords, Lord Simonds, the other four Lordships unanimously agreeing, was of the view that where personal representatives had mistakenly transferred funds to various charities, when the estate should have become that of the next of kin, then the next of kin had a personal claim in equity against the charities to whom the estate had been wrongfully distributed.

4.6 Further, the next of kin could claim whether the mistake was one of fact or was one of law: *Ministry of Health* v *Simpson and Others* (1951).

4.7 An alternative, proprietary 'tracing' claim will be dealt with in Unit 12. In order to bring such a claim, a fiduciary relationship must be shown. The nature of a fiduciary relationship will be dealt with in Unit 10.

4.8 For our current purposes, it is sufficient to state that the similarity between trustees administering a trust, and personal representatives administering a deceased's estate is that both are in a fiduciary relationship with those who are entitled to the trust funds or deceased's estate.

4.9 A detailed comparison, showing this distinction between a trustee and a personal representative, is made by Professor Hayton, 'Preliminary definitions – Definitions of trust, trustee, trust property, beneficiary, and breach of trust' in *Underhill and Hayton, Law of Trusts and Trustees* 15th edition (ed. D.J. Hayton) (1995).

Summary

Now you have studied the text and worked through this Unit, you should understand:

☐ **the processes of appointment, retirement and removal of trustees**

☐ **the different types of trustee**

☐ **trust corporations**

☐ **the difference between trustees and representatives.**

Self-assessment questions

1 Describe the position with regard to the appointment, retirement and removal of trustees.

2 Describe the position and powers of the custodian trustee.

3 What is a 'bare trustee'?

4 Describe the position and powers of a trust corporation.

5 Distinguish a trustee from a personal representative.

Exam-style questions

1 Martin and Hazel, who are in their 30s, are the life tenants of a family trust of which various other members of the family are the trustees. They come to your bank and complain that they are not being given any information about the trust, and that they suspect that some of the trustees have arranged to have themselves appointed directors of companies in which the trust has investments. The directors of these companies are known to be receiving high fees, whereas the dividends paid are decreasing. The trust owns land which is leased to one of the companies.

Explain to them how the present trustees could be removed and your bank appointed in their place; and what would be the means of transfer of the trust's assets into the bank's name.

[Spring 1995]

2 Describe the appointment and functions of:

a) a judicial trustee

b) a custodian trustee

c) the public trustee

d) a trustee of a loan stock.

[Autumn 1995]

3 George Fletcher is an important customer of your bank which has assisted him in the setting-up and financing of his various companies.

He wishes to set up a sports and social club for the employees. This would involve buying a plot of land and providing a lump sum endowment. He would like the bank to act as custodian trustee.

Outline to him the advantages and disadvantages of such an appointment and explain what the bank's duties would be.

[Spring 1995]

4   a) By whom, and in what circumstances, may a trustee be removed from office?

    b) Your bank and Elizabeth are the original trustees of a will trust of which the life tenants are all adults and which consists of freehold and leasehold properties, bearer securities and stocks and shares. Elizabeth has been living on a South Sea island for the last six months and has said that she is likely to spend most of her time there in the future. As you are concerned that she fails to answer letters and is out of telephone contact, you have suggested that her son be appointed trustee in her place. The life tenants would prefer her grandson, but you have objected on the grounds of his lack of financial and business experience.

        Explain the following with reasons.

        i)   Assuming that a new trustee is appointed to replace Elizabeth, who has the power to decide on the person to be appointed trustee of this will trust, and who will make the appointment?

        ii) How will the new appointment be made?

        iii) How will the trust property be vested in the new trustees (jointly with the bank)?

                                                            [Spring 1996]

                        (The answers are given in the Appendix)

Caselist for Unit 9 Trusteeship

Chellaram v *Chellaram* [1985] Ch 409.

Letterstedt v *Broers* [1884] 9 App Cas 371.

McPhail v *Doulton* [1971] AC 424.

Mettoy Pension Trustees Ltd v *Evans* [1990] 1 WLR 1587.

The unreported decision of *Richard* v *The Hon A B Mackay* (14th March 1987. Millett J.

'General Principles Relating to Trustees' in *Maudsley and Burn's Trusts and Trustees Cases and Materials* 5th edition (ed. E.H. Burn) Butterworths, (1996), Chapter 16.

Trustee Act 1925 sections 21(3) 25, 36(1), 36(7), 37(1)(c), 39(1), 40, 41(1), 43, 68(18).

Trusts of Land and Appointment of Trustees Act 1996 sections 6, 7, 19, 19(2), 20(2).

Chris Whitehouse and Nicholas Hassall, *The Trusts of Land and Appointment of Trustees Act 1996, A Practical Guide*, Butterworths (1996).

Nicholas Hopkins, *The Trusts of Land and Appointment of Trustees Act 1996*, (1996) *Conv* 411.

Conveyancer's Notebook – Trusts of Land (1996) Conv 77.

Wallington, *The Trusts of Land and Appointment of Trustees Bill*. (1996) *New Law Journal* 959.

'General Principles: Capacity; Appointment; Removal; Retirement; Control' in *Hanbury and Martin, Modern Equity* 15th edition (ed. Jill E. Martin) Sweet and Maxwell (1997), Chapter 17.

'The death, retirement, or removal of trustees and the appointment of new trustees' in *Underhill and Hayton, Law of Trusts and Trustees* 15th edition (ed. D.J. Hayton) Butterworths (1995).

J G Riddall, 'Special Forms of Trustee' in *The Law of Trusts* 5th edition, Butterworths (1996), Chapter 15.

'Appointment of a judicial trustee: The Public Trustee' in *Underhill and Hayton, Law of Trusts and Trustees* 15th edition (ed. D.J. Hayton.) Butterworths (1995), Chapters 15 and 16.

The Public Trustee Act 1906 sections 4(1), 4(2), 4(2)(a), 4(2)(b), 4(2)(d), 4(2)(f), 4(2)(g), 4(2)(i), 4(3).

The Judicial Trustee Act 1896 sections 1(1), 1(3).

Saunders v *Vautier* [1841] 4 Beav 115.

Jefferies and Others v *Mayes and Others, The Times* June 30th 1997.

Professor David Hayton, 'The Administration of a Trust Part 9: The Control of Pension Funds' in *Hayton and Marshall, Commentary and Cases on the Law of Trusts and Equitable Remedies* 10th edition (ed. D.J. Hayton) Sweet and Maxwell (1996), Chapter 9.

Professor Jill E. Martin 'Trusts of Pension Funds' in *Hanbury and Martin, Modern Equity* 15th edition (ed. Jill E. Martin) Sweet and Maxwell (1997), Chapter 16.

The Pensions Act 1995 (c 26) sections 3(2)(a), 4(1)(a), 4(2)(a), 5(1), 5(4), 6(1), 7(1), 8(3), 9, 29(1), 30(1), 30(3), 32(1).

Stamp Duties Commissioner (Queensland) v *Livingston* [1965] AC 694

Ministry of Health v *Simpson* [1951] AC 341.

Professor Hayton, 'Preliminary definitions – Definitions of trust, trustee, trust property, beneficiary, and breach of trust' in *Underhill and Hayton, Law of Trusts and Trustees* 15th edition (ed. D.J. Hayton) Butterworths (1995).

10

Duties of Trustees

Objectives

After studying the text and working through this Unit, students should:

- understand the concept of fiduciaries

- appreciate the strict rule about fiduciaries

- know about remuneration of trustees

- know about general duties of trustees.

1 The concept of fiduciary

1.1 The concept of fiduciary is dealt with at length by L.J Millett in *Bristol and West Building Society* v *Mothew* (1996). The judge makes clear that a fiduciary is someone who acts on behalf of another person with regard to a particular matter. The relationship is one based on trust and confidence. The fiduciary owes particular duties of loyalty to the person for whom he or she is acting.

1.2 In addition, the judge confirms the generally accepted rule that fiduciaries are under an obligation to act in good faith in relation to the person for whom they are acting. In particular, fiduciaries must not place themselves in a position in conflict with duties that are owing to the person for whom they are acting. This will be dealt with below.

1.3 It is also important to emphasise that a trustee is a fiduciary in relation to the beneficiary. This means that the trustee owes all the duties described above to the beneficiary.

1.4 Another important fiduciary relationship in this context is that of director and company.

Director and company

1.5 In *Guinness plc* v *Saunders* (1990) Ward, a director, failed to disclose a commission payment related to the value of a takeover bid for the company of which he was a director. Some of the directors of the company were aware of this commission but it had not been authorised by the full board of directors as required by the articles of the company.

1.6 The House of Lords confirmed that equity forbids trustees or other fiduciaries from making a profit out of their position. This was a strict rule in equity.

1.7 The director was clearly putting himself in a position where he had conflicting interests. The duties to his company conflicted with his own interests. In particular, the profit (in the form of commission) put the director in a conflict with the interests of his company.

1.8 It was held that the director had to return his commission to the company.

1.9 In this case, the High Court, (Browne-Wilkinson VC, as he then was) and the Court of Appeal regarded this case as a 'knowing receipt' case. (The 'knowing receipt' case is dealt with in Unit 16 in the section relating to constructive trusts.)

1.10 Wherever a fiduciary receives trust or company property, then he will hold it on constructive trust (as a constructive trustee) for the beneficiary or company.

Partnerships

1.11 Partners are in a fiduciary relationship with each other. Such duties arise independently of the duties that they owe to each other under their partnership agreement or by statute.

1.12 Where a partner obtained a separate position as a liquidator through being a partner, it was decided that his fees were held on trust for the partnership. Such a result was arrived at irrespective of the contractual position between the partner and the partnership: *Casson Beckman and Partners* v *Papi* (1991).

Agents

1.13 The exact line between an agency relationship and a fiduciary relationship is difficult to draw. Where the agent receives confidential information or is giving specialised advice to his or her principal, then the relationship may become a fiduciary one, as in *Barclays Bank plc* v *Quincecare Ltd* (1992).

1.14 In *Boardman* v *Phipps* (1967) Boardman, although not a trustee, acted as adviser to a trust which owned shares in a company. He became, effectively (though never formally appointed) an agent and negotiated for the purchase of additional shares in that company. Boardman obtained detailed confidential information and knowledge. As a negotiator, he was placed in a central position in relation to the trust.

1.15 It was held by the House of Lords that he was in a fiduciary relationship with regard to the trustees and beneficiaries.

1.16 It was also held by the House of Lords (by a majority of 3 to 2) that Boardman should not have purchased shares in that company for himself, when the trust was unable to purchase these shares. Nevertheless, because he had done so, he had to account to the trust for the profit he made on those shares.

1.17 There is one established exception where the fiduciary is able to make a profit. The House of Lords confirmed that if the fiduciary obtained the full and informed consent of all those to whom he or she owed fiduciary duties, then he or she would be able to make a profit. On the particular facts the testator's widow was one of the beneficiaries. She was in poor health and was therefore not consulted. She did not give her consent and possibly could not have done so.

1.18 This case confirms that there are strict rules with regard to the making of profits by fiduciaries.

2 Rules governing fiduciaries

2.1 The rule that a fiduciary must not place himself in a position where he is in conflict with duties owed to himself and another is a strict rule. This also means that the fiduciary is not able to make a secret (undisclosed) profit from his position.

2.2 In exceptional circumstances the fiduciary may (at the discretion of the court) be allowed to receive remuneration of a fair and just amount for his time and effort. This exception will be further considered in section 3 below.

2.3 The strictness of the rule has been confirmed in one recent decision. The case involved a pension fund for employees of 'Drexel' where the company (employer) had gone into administration. The trustees of the pension fund were employees and hence, also beneficiaries of the trust. The trustees sought to make various distributions of income and capital from the trust.

2.4 Because the trustees feared that they might be in a position of conflict of duty and interest (as both trustees and beneficiaries), they sought directions (advice) from the courts.

2.5 The High Court stated that there were two escape routes.

a) The trustees could ask the court to exercise its discretion in place of them. (This was done in *Marley and Others* v *Mutual Security Merchant Bank and Trust Co Ltd* (1991) and involved the trustees surrendering their complete discretion to the court and placing all the available information before the court so that the court was able to make the decision instead of the trustees.)

b) The trustees who were in a position of conflict of duty and interest could resign and other trustees (new trustees) be appointed instead of these (current) trustees.

2.6 It is apparent that these two escape routes are of a drastic nature and emphasise the strict rule in equity.

2.7 The court declined to give a ruling (answer) to the question of whether the trust instrument itself could allow the trustee to breach any of the trustees' fiduciary duties which would otherwise be owed to the beneficiaries. The court felt that this was a matter for Parliament to resolve by legislation.

2.8 On the particular facts, the appointment of new trustees would lead to delay. The court sanctioned the proposed distributions by the current trustees: *Re Drexel Burnham Lambert UK Pension Plan* (1995).

3 Remuneration of fiduciaries

3.1 As a general rule, trustees are not allowed remuneration for their work unless this is authorised in the trust instrument. The court has discretion to allow remuneration or increased remuneration. This may be done as a matter of the court's own inherent discretion in equity if that was reasonable in the circumstances, as in *Foster* v *Spencer* (1996). In addition, trustees are entitled to their out-of-pocket expenses under section 30(2) of the Trustee Act 1925.

3.2 The House of Lords in *Guinness plc* v *Saunders* (1990) also dealt with the circumstances in which a director is able to receive remuneration. In exceptional circumstances a court of equity may award remuneration to the trustee or fiduciary.

3.3 As regards the remuneration of a director, the House of Lords concluded that this was a matter to be determined by the articles of association of the company and was not a matter for equity. Even if equity did (hypothetically) have jurisdiction to award remuneration to a director, it would not do so on the facts. The reason for this was that receiving of remuneration by the director would encourage him to break his duties.

3.4   In *Boardman* v *Phipps* (1967), discussed above, the House of Lords held that a fiduciary who was not a company director could still be awarded remuneration for his skill and effort even though the fiduciary was in breach of his duties. Boardman was allowed fair remuneration for his time and skill in negotiating and purchasing the shares.

3.5   This approach has been followed in *O'Sullivan* v *Management Agency and Music Ltd* (1985). The Court of Appeal considered that the remuneration which the fiduciary received could include a profit element as well.

4 Jurisdiction to award remuneration to trustees

4.1   After *Boardman* v *Phipps* (1967) it was established that equity could award remuneration to a fiduciary. As we have seen above, the courts had jurisdiction to award remuneration to trustees. This jurisdiction was extended so that fiduciaries as well as trustees could be awarded remuneration.

4.2   This inherent jurisdiction in equity to award remuneration to trustees will now be examined in further detail. We have previously looked at the inherent jurisdiction to remove and appoint trustees in Unit 9.

4.3   The basis upon which remuneration could be awarded was decided in *Re Codd (decd)* (1975). The case involved an only trustee, the National Westminster Bank, which had been appointed under the will of the deceased, and which wanted increased remuneration. This was granted by Graham J, on the basis that it was in the interest of the trust.

4.4   It was decided that the court could increase the general level of remuneration in *Re Duke of Norfolk's Settlement Trusts* (1982). The case concerned a professional trustee who applied to the court for increased remuneration on the basis that he was going to spend a greater amount of time administering the trust than originally anticipated by the settlor. The trustee had bought, next to those properties already owned by the trust, additional properties to develop.

4.5   Evidence was brought before the court that the professional trustee was actually incurring a loss through administering the trust.

4.6   Reasons were advanced by the barrister appointed by the court, in order to protect the interests of the unborn beneficiaries, for not increasing the general level of the trustees remuneration:

   ● first, that there was a contract between the settlor and the trustee as to the remuneration, and that it would be contrary to this contract to raise the general level of remuneration. This argument was rejected by the court. Fox L J considered that in many cases the trustee had not specifically agreed the remuneration.

- second, that if remuneration were awarded it would reduce the equitable interest to which the beneficiaries were entitled. This argument was rejected on the basis that in substance the court was dealing with a claim for increased remuneration and not the variation of equitable interests.

4.7   The position as regards variation of trusts will be dealt with in Unit 13.

4.8   The actions of the professional trustee was clearly in the interests of the trust, and the Court of Appeal increased the general level of remuneration. The court's approach was followed in *Re Berkeley Applegate (Investment Consultants) Harris* v *Conway* (1989).

4.9   The basis of the inherent jurisdiction in equity to award remuneration was affirmed in *Re Keeler's Settlement Trusts, Keeler* v *Gledhill* (1981). The court accepted the general test put forward in those cases involving the interests of the beneficiaries of the trust. However, the court did state that this jurisdiction was to be used only in exceptional circumstances.

4.10   In addition, section 30(2) of the Trustee Act 1925 allows for reimbursement of expenses, by the trust, incurred by the trustee where the trust instrument does not provide for this: *Carver* v *Duncan (Inspector of Taxes)* (1985). Further, the reimbursement of expenses by the trust is only allowed where they have been properly incurred: *Holding and Management Ltd* v *Property Holding and Investment Trust plc* (1989).

4.11   However, this statutory provision does not, of itself, enable trustees to be awarded increased remuneration: *Carver* v *Duncan (Inspector of Taxes)* (1985).

4.12   This approach to section 30(2) of the Trustee Act 1925 was followed in *Foster* v *Spencer* (1996) which has been briefly considered earlier. The facts concerned a cricket club and its sportsground, which included a five-acre field. The membership was on the decline, and the sportsground had fallen into disuse. Unincoporated associations and their winding-up has been previously considered in Unit 8.

4.13   Foster and Sealy, the trustees of club, decided to sell the sportsground. This involved them in spending considerable additional time to arrange this. Foster was a chartered surveyor, and Sealy was the managing director of a construction company.

4.14   The court awarded Foster 5% commission on the sale price of the sportsground. The court recognised that this was greater than the normal rate of commission that an estate agent might be expected to earn. The court awarded such commission for his expertise and for the considerable amount of time spent by Foster, in particular, to obtain planning permission to enable the sportsground to be sold.

4.15 Sealy was awarded £50,000 to represent his work over a ten-year period, which had involved him in dealing with squatters, neighbours, the local authority, and the press.

4.16 In addition Foster and Sealy were awarded interest at 8% per annum, by Paul Baker QC sitting as a judge of the High Court, from 15th December 1992 when the sportsground and five-acre field was sold to a developer.

4.17 The court therefore confirmed that it did have jurisdiction to award not only remuneration, but also a share of the profits made. A similar approach had been adopted in *O'Sullivan* v *Management Agency Music Ltd* (1985) considered above, though the court did not consider this earlier decision.

4.18 The importance of this decision is fundamental to our discussion. If profits or a share of the profits may be awarded, then it undermines the strict rule, discussed previously in this Unit, that a fiduciary cannot receive profits.

4.19 Indeed, in *O'Sullivan* v *Management Agency Music Ltd* (1985), it was decided by the Court of Appeal, as a matter of principle, that remuneration could still be awarded even though its recipient had acted badly. On the facts of the case, the recipient was held to have imposed undue influence upon Gilbert O'Sullivan. O'Sullivan had entered into a contract with Management Agency Music Ltd when a young and unknown composer. Although the contract was rescinded between the parties, the agency were awarded substantial sums, including a profit element, for the work they had carried out for the benefit of O'Sullivan, in particular, in helping to build his successful career.

4.20 A further situation where remuneration can be awarded is where the trust instrument expressly provides. John Mowbray QC, 'Fear not: your charging clause is safe' (1996) Vol 10 No. 2 *Trust Law International* 49, points out that such remuneration will be allowed even though it enables a trustee to gain from his fiduciary position, and even though it produces a conflict of duty and interest. He relies upon various authorities, including express statements in the decision of Lord Templeman in the Privy Council in *Space Investments Ltd* v *Canadian Imperial Bank of Commerce Trust Co (Bahamas) Ltd* (1986), and the decision of the Court of Appeal in *Sargeant* v *National Westminster Bank plc* (1990), which support his approach.

5 Evaluation of the rules relating to fiduciaries

5.1 The rules relating to fiduciary duties are a product of the case law in equity. One notable exception is the Pensions Act 1985 section 39, which reverses the decision in *Re Drexel Burnham Lambert U.K. Pension Plan* (1995) by ensuring that trustees who are also employee beneficiaries of an occupational pension scheme trust are not in a conflict of duty and interest.

5.2 One way of formulating the rule is that put forward in *Chan* v *Zacariah* (1983). This case is considered in detail in 'Constructive Trusts, Section 1, The Fiduciary as Constructive Trustee of Profits' in *Hayton and Marshall, Commentary and Cases on the Law of Trusts and Equitable Remedies* 10th edition (ed. D.J. Hayton) Sweet and Maxwell (1996), Chapter 6.

5.3 In this case the High Court of Australia stated that the principle could be formulated in two main ways:

- first, a person must not put himself in a position where there is a conflict of duty and interest. The rule is strict in that it covers not only actual conflicts but also possible conflicts. A person may be rendered liable to account for profits made simply because there could have been a conflict of duty and interest. The reasons for this rule is that where there is such a conflict a person may be swayed by his own personal interest.

- second, the fiduciary must not misuse his position for his own personal advantage. This includes the use of knowledge or information obtained by the fiduciary. Such an approach is one way of analysing the decision in *Boardman* v *Phipps* (1967). The reason for this rule is simply to stop the fiduciary from misusing his position.

5.4 The rule relating to conflict of duty and interest in intended to be a strict rule. However, this can produce injustice as is shown from the facts of *Hanson* v *Lorenz* (1987). A solicitor agreed with his client to share the profits in relation to some property development. The solicitor was instructed in a professional capacity. Once the profits had been made, the client then sought to keep all the profits on the basis that the solicitor was in a fiduciary position.

5.5 The Court of Appeal declined to award the client all the profits and upheld the agreement. The court was clearly aware that to do otherwise would be unduly harsh. May LJ in the Court of Appeal followed the dissenting judgment of Lord Upjohn in the House of Lords in *Boardman* v *Phipps* (1967) where he made the point that because equity has to be applied in a wide range of situations it would be unwise to have a rigid and inflexible rule. If a fixed rule were adopted it could lead to injustice.

5.6 On the particular facts, the Court of Appeal was able to deal with the case in a narrow way, by finding that the client had consented to the profit being made. We have seen earlier on that this is one of the exceptions to the strict rule that a fiduciary cannot make a profit from his or her position.

5.7 Another possible similar exception to consent is that of acquiescence. If a beneficiary, or person who is owed fiduciary duties, knows about a breach but does not complain about it, then he may be held to have acquiesced: *Re*

Pauling's Settlement Trusts, Younghusband v Coutts & Co (1962). In the particular case, certain beneficiaries who knowingly allowed payments to be incorrectly made by the bank to their mother in breach of trust, were therefore unable to successfully bring a claim for breach of trust for this reason.

5.8 One way to justifiy the strict rule is that it is simply a pragmatic rule which recognises that human nature is fallible: *Regal Cinemas Hastings Ltd v Gulliver* (1967). Further, it was recognised in *British Coal Corporation v British Coal Staff Superannuation Scheme Trustees* (1995) that the rule as to not allowing a conflict of duty and interest is simply a rule based upon common sense.

5.9 Finally, mention needs to be made of the important House of Lords decision: *Target Holdings v Redferns (a firm)* (1995) which lays down an important new principle that in order for a trustee to be liable for a breach of trust, any loss sustained by the beneficiay must be caused by this breach. Such an approach was recognised by Millett L J in *Bristol and West Building Society v Mothew* (1996). These cases will be further considered in Unit 12.

5.10 If we apply this new approach to *Boardman v Phipps* (1967), it produces a startling result. In that case, discussed earlier on in this Unit, Boardman made a profit from the purchase of further shares in a private company, some of which were held in the particular trust for which he acted as agent. Boardman gained the opportunity to buy these shares as a result of his position as agent to the trust.

5.11 The trustees could not have bought such shares since they were unable to do so by the trust instrument. On the basis of the decision in *Target Holdings v Redferns (a firm)* (1995), Boardman would now not be liable since he did not cause any loss to the trust. This would reverse the decision in *Boardman v Phipps* (1967). It is suggested that the House of Lords have done so, although they appear not to have realised this, nor indeed the full implications of their approach in *Target Holdings v Redferns (a firm)* (1995).

5.12 See, generally, the following on fiduciary duties:

- A.J. Oakley, 'Constructive Trusts Imposed as a Result of a Breach of Fiduciary Duty' in *Constructive Trusts* 3rd edition, Sweet and Maxwell (1997), Chapter 3.

- Paul Davies, 'Directors Fiduciary Duties and Individual Shareholders' in *Commercial Aspects of Trusts and Fiduciary Obligations* (ed. Ewan Mckendrick) Clarendon Press, Oxford (1992), Chapter 5.

- The Hon. Mr. Justice B.H. Mcpherson CBE, 'Self-dealing Trustees' and R.P Austin, 'Moulding the Content of Fiduciary Duties' in *Trends in Contemporary Trust Law* (ed. A.J. Oakley) Clarendon Press, Oxford (1996), Chapters 6 and 7.

● For a recent discussion of a number of issues in this area see generally a series of papers: *Pressing Problems In The Law XI. S.P.T.L. Seminars for 1996. Fiduciaries In Context.* Old Library. All Souls.

6 Trustees' general duties in equity

6.1   The beneficiaries are entitled to receive the recorded details of any meetings that take place between the trustees and other relevant information about the trust: *Re Londonderry's Settlement, Peat and Others v Walsh* (1964).

6.2   The beneficiaries have the right to know the investments that comprise the trust fund, as in *Tiger v Barclays Bank* (1952). There is a standard level of beneficiaries' entitlement to information for all trusts, including pension trusts: *Wilson v Law Debenture Trust Corporation plc* (1995).

6.3   The trustees must act in a fair and impartial way and must take into account the needs of all the beneficiaries. The trustees are able to, and should, consider the relationship of the settlor to the particular beneficiary in the exercise of their discretions: *Nestlé v National Westminster Bank plc* (1993). This case is discussed below.

6.4   This duty to act in a fair and impartial way is of importance not only in the way trustees should exercise their discretion with a private express trust but also in relation to a pension trust for employees. Since employers owe a general contractual duty of good faith to their employees, this affects the way that they should administer such a trust: *British Coal Corp v British Coal Staff Superannuation Scheme Trustees Ltd* (1995).

6.5   There may be situations where the trustee is given a fiduciary power which will give considerable discretion to the trustee in terms of distribution of the trust funds.

6.6   In this situation the trustee is not under a duty to distribute the income (or capital). However, the trustee must consider on a regular basis whether to distribute the income or the capital: *Mettoy Pensions Trustees Ltd v Evans* (1991).

6.7   This case concerned a company which was administering a pension scheme trust and which had a fiduciary power in relation to that trust. On the insolvency of the company the surplus in that pension scheme trust was not available for the general creditors of the company, but was only available for distribution amongst the employees.

6.8   Such employees are entitled to the continued exercise of discretion on the part of the trustees. The employees' general interests (as a whole group) are such that they are not to be parted for ever from any surplus by a company which takes a majority shareholding in their company: *Re Courage Group's Pension Scheme* (1987). The position as regards surplus in a pension scheme trust has been previously considered in Unit 4.

7 Delegation of trustees' duties under the Trustee Act 1925

7.1   Trustees are given the right to delegate their decision-making functions. Section 23 of the Trustee Act 1925 allows professional assistance which may be used by the trustees in carrying out their functions. This section also provides that where the trustees act in good faith in doing this, then they will not be liable for any loss incurred to the trust merely by employing an agent.

7.2   Whether the trustee still remains liable for breach of his own duties is not clear. In *Steel v Wellcome Custodian Trustees Ltd* (1988) Hoffmann J, as he then was, concluded that this section gives trustee immunity for the duties that are owed by him to the beneficiary and also for the employment of an agent.

7.3   However, in the Law Reform Committee's *23rd Report on the Powers and Duties of Trustees*, a contrary view was expressed. This was to the effect that a trustee would only gain immunity for the employment of an agent. The trustee would still be liable for the duties that he owed in equity to the beneficiary. It was suggested that the Trustee Act 1925 had not overridden these duties. The trustee would be under a duty to monitor the activities of the agent.

7.4   It is accepted that the Trustee Act 1925 has altered the position that existed prior to the act: *Re Vickery* (1931). Such agents may now be used even if there is no necessity for this.

7.5   Section 22 of the Trustee Act 1925 allows a trustee to employ an accountant to audit the trust accounts.

7.6   Section 25 of the Trustee Act 1925 provides that a trustee may delegate by power of attorney.

7.7   Section 30 provides that a trustee will not be liable for any loss caused to the trust through the deposit of funds of the trust with a bank or deposit-taking institution, or through the deposit of securities with another person, unless such loss is caused by the wilful default of that trustee.

7.8   The meaning of wilful default was discussed in *Re Vickery* (1931). In this case the High Court held that it meant some degree of deliberateness on the part of the trustee. Recklessness or conscious awareness by the trustee that he or she was in breach of his duties would be sufficient.

7.9   It is also established from the High Court decision in *Re Lucking's Will Trusts* (1968) that the employment by the trustee of a person to manage a business owned by the trust falls within section 23, but not section 30, of the Trustee Act 1925.

7.10 Trustee duties of investment will be considered in Unit 11. In so far as trustees delegate their investment functions the rules described above apply to this delegation in the same way that they apply to any other delegation of trustees' duties.

Summary

Now you have studied the text and worked through this Unit, you should understand:

☐ **the concept of fiduciaries**

☐ **the strict rule about fiduciaries**

☐ **remuneration of trustees**

☐ **general duties of trustees.**

Self-assessment questions

1   What is a fiduciary?

2   Is a fiduciary able to place himself in a position where there is a conflict between his duties and his self-interest?

3   Are there any exceptions to the rule that a fiduciary is unable to place himself in a position where there is a conflict between his duties and his self-interest?

4   What duties does a trustee owe to a beneficiary?

5   Under what circumstances, if any, is a trustee entitled to remuneration?

Exam-style questions

1   Martin and Hazel, who are in their 30s, are the life tenants of a family trust of which various other members of the family are the trustees. They come to your bank and complain that they are not being given any information about the trust, and that they suspect that some of the trustees have arranged to have themselves appointed directors of companies in which the trust has investments. The directors of these companies are known to be receiving high fees, whereas the dividends paid are decreasing. The trust owns land which is leased to one of the companies.

Explain to them what rights they have against the present trustees.

[Spring 1995]

2   Your bank is co-trustee with Muriel of the estate of her late father, Frederick. She is life tenant of the residuary estate and has the power to appoint a subsequent life interest to any husband who may survive her. The ultimate beneficiaries are her two children, Tim and Tom, who are both now of age. There is a trust for sale coupled with the usual power to postpone. Among the many assets held are two investment properties, Blackacre and Whiteacre.

a) Muriel has just realised that one of the companies in which the trust is invested is well known for testing its products on animals. She objects strongly, and insists the shares be sold immediately. Would you agree to do so?

b) Muriel, Tim and Tom have suggested that the trust be brought to an end and the assets divided amongst them. How may this be done?

c) Blackacre is now vacant and you wish to sell it. Muriel, on the other hand, wishes to keep it in the family. How would you proceed?

d) Whiteacre is already on the market and the trustees have accepted an offer of £75,000. A third party has now offered £77,000 cash. Muriel refuses to consider this second offer as she feels morally bound by the first acceptance. What would you say to her?

e) Tim has asked for an advance of £6,000 towards the cost of a racing car. Muriel, both as life tenant and as co-trustee, has supported the request. The bank has refused, and Tim has demanded to know why and to see the correspondence on your file. Discuss his right to see it.

[Spring 1996]

3. Describe the powers and responsibilities of trustees to delegate their duties, and to employ agents in the administration of a trust.

[Autumn 1995]

(The answers are given in the Appendix)

Caselist for Unit 10 Duties of Trustees

Bristol and West Building Society v *Mothew (t/a Stapley and Co)* [1996] 4 All ER 698.

Guinness plc v *Saunders* [1990] 2 AC 663. (House of Lords) [1988] BCLC 88 (High Court)

Casson Beckman and Partners v *Papi* [1991] BCC 68.

Barclays Bank plc v *Quincecare Ltd* [1992] 4 All ER 363.

Boardman v *Phipps* [1967] 2 AC 46.

Marley and Others v *Mutual Security Merchant Bank and Trust Co Ltd* [1991] 3 All ER 198.

Re Drexel Burnham Lambert U.K. Pension Plan [1995] 1 WLR 32.

Foster and Others v *Spencer* [1996] 2 All ER 672.

The Trustee Act 1925 section 30(2).

O'Sullivan v *Management Agency and Music Ltd* [1985] QB 428.

Re Codd (decd) [1975] 1 WLR 1139.

Re Duke of Norfolk's Settlement Trusts [1982] Ch 61.

Re Berkeley Applegate (Investment Consultants) Harris v *Conway* [1989] Ch 32.

Re Keeler's Settlement Trusts, Keeler v *Gledhill* [1981] Ch 156.

Carver v *Duncan (Inspector of Taxes)* [1985] AC 1082.

Holding and Management Ltd v *Property Holding and Investment Trust plc* [1989] 1 WLR 1313.

John Mowbray QC 'Fear not: your charging clause is safe' (1996) Vol. 10, No. 2 *Trust Law International* 49.

Space Investments Ltd v *Canadian Imperial Bank of Commerce Trust Co (Bahamas) Ltd* [1986] 1 WLR 1072.

Sargeant v *National Westminster Bank plc* (1990) 61 P & CR 518.

The Pensions Act 1985 section 39.

Chan v *Zacariah* (1983) 154 CLR 178.

'Constructive Trusts', Section 1, 'The Fiduciary as Constructive Trustee of Profits' in *Hayton and Marshall, Commentary and Cases on the Law of Trusts and Equitable Remedies* 10th edition (ed. D J Hayton) Sweet and Maxwell (1996), Chapter 6.

Hanson v *Lorenz* [1987] 1 FTLR 23.

Re Pauling's Settlement Trusts, Younghusband v *Coutts & Co* [1962] 1 WLR 86.

Regal Cinemas Hastings Ltd v *Gulliver* [1967] 2 AC 134.

British Coal Corporation v *British Coal Staff Superannuation Scheme Trustees* [1995] 1 All ER 912. (High Court)

Target Holdings v *Redferns (a firm)* [1995] 3 WLR 352. A.J. Oakley, *Constructive Trusts* 3rd edition, Sweet and Maxwell (1997), Chapter 3.

Paul Davies 'Directors Fiduciary Duties And Individual Shareholders' in *Commercial Aspects of Trusts and Fiduciary Obligations* (ed. Ewan Mckendrick) Clarendon Press, Oxford (1992), Chapter 5.

The Hon. Mr. Justice BH Mcpherson CBE, 'Self-dealing Trustees' and R.P. Austin, 'Moulding the Content of Fiduciary Duties' in *Trends in Contemporary Trust Law*, (ed. A.J. Oakley) Clarendon Press. Oxford (1996), Chapters 6 and 7.

Pressing Problems In The Law XI. SPTL. Seminars for 1996. *Fiduciaries In Context.* Old Library. All Souls.

Re Londonderry's Settlement, Peat and Others v *Walsh* [1964] 3 All ER 855.

Tiger v *Barclays Bank Ltd* [1952] 1 All ER 85.

Wilson v *Law Debenture Trust Corporation plc* [1995] 2 All ER 337.

Nestlé v *National Westminster Bank plc* [1993] 1 WLR 1260.

British Coal Corp v *British Coal Staff Superannuation Scheme Trustees Ltd* [1995] 1 All ER 912.

Mettoy Pension Trustees Ltd v *Evans* [1990] 1 WLR 1587.

Re Courage Group's Pension Scheme [1987] 1 WLR 495.

Steel v *Wellcome Custodian Trustees Ltd* [1988] 1 WLR 167.

Law Reform Committee 23rd Report (The Powers and Duties of Trustees) 1982 Cmnd 8733.

Re Vickery [1931] 1 Ch 572.

Re Lucking's Will Trusts [1968] 1 WLR 866.

Trustee Act 1925 sections 22, 23, 25, 30.

11

Powers of Trustees in Specific Circumstances

Objectives

After studying the text and working through this Unit, students should understand:

- maintenance

- advancement

- the investment of trust funds.

1 Trustees' powers under the Trustee Act 1925 sections 31 and 32 (Introduction)

1.1   Section 31 of the Trustee Act 1925 enables the trustees to provide for the education, maintenance or benefit of a child by providing funds to the child's parents. The statutory power applies unless the trust instrument expressly or impliedly provides to the contrary.

1.2   Section 32 of the Trustee Act 1925 enables the trustees to pay capital sums for the advancement or benefit of a beneficiary who is entitled to the capital, or part of the capital, of the trust. However, the funds advanced cannot exceed one half of the share in the capital of the trust fund to which the beneficiary is entitled.

1.3   The sums previously advanced to the beneficiary must be deducted from the share in the capital to which the beneficiary is entitled.

1.4   Again, the statutory power applies unless the trust instrument expressly or impliedly provides to the contrary. There would be the implied exclusion of Section 32 where a clause gave the trustees the right to advance an amount greater than one half of a beneficiary's share in the trust property.

1.5   It was held by the House of Lords in *Pilkington and Another* v *Inland Revenue Commissioners* (1964) that an advance of a beneficiary's share and placing the capital sums into another trust fund to minimise the effect of taxation, was within the statutory powers given to trustees under section 32.

1.6   Viscount Radcliffe, (in the above case in paragraph 1.5), was of the view that the words 'benefit' and 'advancement' meant the provision of funds that would result in improving the situation of the beneficiary.

1.7   The judge was also of the opinion that even if others might gain indirectly by the advance of a capital share to the beneficiary, it would still be a valid advance.

1.8   However, if the trustee is a bank making the advance and knows that the beneficiary is using the monies to pay off an overdraft with it, then this will be an improper exercise of the power, in the opinion of Wilberforce J in the High Court in *Re Pauling's Settlement Trusts, Younghusband* v *Coutts and Co* (1962). His decision was subsequently upheld by the Court of Appeal on a different point.

2 Maintenance

2.1   The Trustee Act 1925 section 31 is a complex section which has given rise to much litigation. It is a difficult section to interpret, and therefore it is particularly appropriate to look at the views of some leading academics.

2.2   Professor Hayton makes a number of important points in his Unit: Unit 12 *The powers of the trustee: Power to allow maintenance to infants.* Underhill and Hayton *Law of Trusts and Trustees* (15th ed. David J. Hayton) 1995. Some of the points that he makes can be summarised as follows.

● First, the income can be paid for the maintenance, education or benefit of any beneficiary who has not attained the age of majority. For trusts executed before January 1st 1970 this was 21 years of age, which was changed to 18 years of age after this date, Family Law Reform Act 1969 which amended the Trustee Act 1925 section 31.

● Second, the trustees' duty to apply income for the maintenance, education or benefit of the beneficiary is a discretionary power.

● Third, in distributing income for the maintenance, education, or benefit of a beneficiary, the trustees are able to take account of all the circumstances of the case. Obviously, the needs and requirements of the particular beneficiary are of considerable importance.

● Fourth, the trustees may pay over the income to the parent or guardian of the beneficiary, or spend the income to assist the beneficiary directly.

- Fifth, where the trustees do not apply the income for the maintenance of a beneficiary they can accumulate that income. The income and any accumulation of income can be subsequently paid to that beneficiary, section 31(2) of the Trustee Act 1925. The taxation aspects of trusts, in relation to income paid to beneficiaries, will be dealt with in Unit 15.

- Sixth, since the beneficiary is entitled to such income, the beneficiary has an interest in possession. If that beneficiary were to die or transfer his or her interest, then there would be liability to inheritance tax. The taxation aspects of inheritance tax and trusts will be dealt with in Unit 15.

- Seventh, it is a question of construction of the trust document whether the gift is intended to include the right of the beneficiary to accumulated income. Either expressly or impliedly, another beneficiary may be entitled to that income. Alternatively, the trustees may be obliged by the terms of the instrument to accumulate the income for the general purposes of the trust, and not for any particular infant beneficiary.

- Eighth, it is established that the statutory power under section 31 of the Trustee Act 1925 to distribute income for the maintenance of a minor is subject to section 69(2) of the Trustee Act 1925. This section provides that any section in the Trustee Act 1925 can be modified, ousted, or excluded by the trust instrument. In our context this means that the statutory power to distribute income for the maintenance, education or benefit of a beneficiary can be modified, ousted or excluded by the terms of the trust instrument.

2.3   Some of the case law which develops the above points will now be considered. In *Re Delamere's Settlement Trust* (1984), the issue that the court was asked – by originating summons issued by the trustees – was whether section 31 of the Trustee Act 1925 applied to a particular trust fund. An originating summons is a particular process available in cases involving trusts whereby the court can be asked to answer specific questions as to the scope and effect of a trust document.

2.4   Counsel for the defendant beneficiaries, Robert Walker QC, now Robert Walker J, was of the view that section 31 of the Trustee Act 1925 was designed to cover two situations:

- first, where a settlor has created a trust for the distribution of capital, but is not an expert and has not provided any instructions in the trust document for the distribution of income

- second, where a settlor is aware of section 31 and wishes the statutory rules to apply.

2.5   Slade L J in this case gave his analysis of the scope of section 31 of the Trustee Act 1925, and in so doing made a number of points:

- first, that section 69(2) of the Trustee Act 1925 provides that the settlor's wishes are to be supreme

- second, that the provisions of section 31 of the Trustee Act 1925 apply to any type of trust where the beneficiaries have either a vested interest (explained below) or a contingent interest (explained below). Broadly, the vested interest is where the beneficiaries' interest is established and they cannot lose it. A contingent interest is subject to a contingency occuring, and if that contingency does not happen the beneficiaries would lose their interest

- third, that those drafting trust instruments should expressly provide whether section 31 of The Trustee Act is to apply, or is to apply with modifications, or is to be excluded.

2.6 Anthony Oakley, 'Income From The Trust Fund' in *Parker and Mellows, The Modern Law of Trusts* 6th edition (ed. A.J. Oakley) (1994), Chapter 17, also makes a number of important points which can be summarised as follows:

- first, once the beneficiary attains the age of majority, i.e. eighteen, then that is the end of the statutory power under section 31 of the Trustee Act 1925 which enables trustees to apply income for the maintenance, education or benefit of infant beneficiaries

- second, trustees are able to accumulate income by virtue of the terms of the trust instrument and under section 31 of the Trustee Act 1925. However it must be sensible for them to do this

- third, the right to accumulate income (discussed above) is subject to the rules relating to perpetuities and accumulations; the rules relating to perpetuities have been previously discussed in Unit 5.

2.7 Some of the case law dealing with accumulation of income will now be considered.

2.8 In *Re Erskine's Settlement Trusts* (1971), there was an express provision to accumulate income. It was held that such a clause excluded the operation of section 31 of the Trustee Act 1925. Similarly, a provision to accumulate income also excludes the operation of section 32 of the Trustee Act 1925 so that the trustees have no power to advance capital whilst the income is being accumulated: *I.R.C.* v *Bernstein* (1961).

2.9 In *Re Sharp's Settlement* (1973), the High Court was of the view that section 31 of the Trustee Act 1925 should be interpreted in accordance with the intentions of Parliament.

2.10 The issue for the court to determine was what was to happen to the income held in trust for certain beneficiaries after they attained the age of majority (at that time the age of majority was 21). One beneficiary, Joanne, had to attain the age of 21, and so had a contingent interest in the trust. As a consequence of section 31(2) of the Trustee Act 1925 she was entitled to the accumulation of income, even though her interest was contingent.

3 Advancement

3.1 The Trustee Act 1925 section 32 is also a complex section which has given rise to much litigation. It is a difficult section to interpret, and therefore it is particularly appropriate to look at the views of some leading academics.

3.2 Professor Hayton makes a number of points about advancement in his chapter (see above at the beginning of the section on maintenance) which can be summarised as follows:

- first, that capital cannot be advanced to a beneficiary where this would prejudice another beneficiary. In particular, the trustees must weigh up the needs and position of the other beneficiaries when making an advance to one beneficiary; see Unit 10 where the duties of trustees to act fairly as between beneficiaries are considered

- second, capital in the form of cash, shares or land can be advanced to a beneficiary

- third, the trustees must decide whether to exercise their discretion and make an advance for the benefit of the beneficiary.

3.3 Anthony Oakley 'Applications of Trust Capital' in *Parker and Mellows, The Modern Law of Trusts* 6th edition (ed. A.J. Oakley) (1994), Chapter 18, also makes a number of important points which can be summarised as follows:

- first, by disposing of assets in order to make an advance, there may be liability, under general principles, to capital gains tax. The taxation aspects of trusts will be dealt with in Unit 15

- second, the advancement will give rise to liability to inheritance tax. The taxation aspects of trusts will be dealt with in Unit 15

- third, the advancement can be made for moral as well as financial reasons

- fourth, the advancement can be made to beneficiaries of any age

- fifth, the transfer of a beneficiary's interest to a separate fund, which is to be held upon trust for the particular beneficiary, would be a valid advancement and would not be an inappropriate delegation; trustees' duties in relation to delegation have been previously considered in Unit 10

- sixth, where there is an express direction to accumulate in the trust instrument, this will show a contrary intention of the settlor against the distribution of capital; as has been previously stated above, the Trustee Act 1925 section 69(2) provides that there is a statutory power of advancement only to the extent that there is no contrary intention in the trust instrument.

3.4 The case law of importance to understanding the scope of the Trustee Act

1925 section 32 will now be considered.

3.5 The wording of the Trustee Act 1925 section 32 includes transferring monies for 'advancement' or 'benefit' of the beneficiary. There is case law before the Trustee Act 1925 which dealt with the meaning of advancement. Such case gives a good guide as to what would constitute an advancement for the purposes of the Trustee Act 1925 section 32.

3.6 The following would be examples of valid advancements in the light of this case law:

- enabling the beneficiary to furnish his or her home

- enabling the beneficiary to start a career, profession or business

- enabling the beneficiary to emigrate

- to discharge outstanding debts or tax owed by the beneficiary

- purchasing clothes for the beneficiary.

3.7 In examining the scope of the Trustee Act 1925 section 32 attention must be paid to the meaning of the 'benefit' of the beneficiary. This word was considered in the cases below.

3.8 In *Re Moxon's Will Trusts, Downey v Moxon* (1958) the trustees wished to make an advance under section 32 of the Trustee Act 1925 to a beneficiary aged 33. There was no problem with making an advance to someone of that age.

3.9 Dankwerts J was of the view that the advancement of capital for the benefit of a beneficiary gave the trustees the widest possible discretion since 'benefit' was a word with a very wide meaning. However, the trustees must exercise their discretion and must obtain evidence as to why the beneficiary wanted the advancement.

3.10 As a general matter of principle, saving tax (now inheritance tax) would be a legitimate reason for the advancement of capital. As we have seen previously, this approach was confirmed by the House of Lords in *Pilkington and Another v Inland Revenue Commissioners* (1964).

3.11 In *Re Clore's Settlement Trusts* (1966), a trust fund, divided into two separate and equal parts, was set up by Charles Clore for his son Alan, and daughter Vivien. The case involved Alan Clore who wanted the trustees to distribute part of the fund to which he was entitled to charity. Both beneficiaries were entitled to income until the age of 30. After this age each would be absolutely entitled to their half share. Alan Clore was 21 years old at the date of the hearing.

3.12 There was an express clause in the trust which gave the trustees the power to transfer up to two thirds of a beneficiary's interest 'for his or her advancement or benefit in such manner as the trustees in their absolute discretion think fit'. This clause is similar to the power of advancement contained in section 32 of the Trustee Act 1925.

3.13 The trustees sought a determination from the court as to whether it would be correct for them to make a distribution of part of Alan Clore's interest to charity. Alan Clore wished to transfer a capital sum to the Charles Clore Foundation set up by his father.

3.14 The High Court concluded that it was correct for the trustees to make a transfer for the following reasons:

- first, advancement or benefit was wider than mere financial advantage

- second, advancement or benefit extended to assisting the beneficiary to carry out social or moral obligations – an example would be making provision for his or her dependants

- third, as a practical point, a wealthy beneficiary would make large charitable donations, and such assistance would minimise the drain on the beneficiary's personal pocket

- fourth, the beneficiary strongly wished to make this donation.

3.15 In *Re Halsted's Will Trusts* (1937), the express terms of a trust fund enabled the trustees to advance a maximum of half the trust fund to the beneficiary 'for his benefit or advancement in life'. This clause was analogous to the statutory power under the Trustee Act 1925 section 32.

3.16 The trustees wished to transfer half the fund into a new trust for the beneficiary, his wife, and his children. Farwell J was of the view that benefitting the beneficiary's wife and children was also of benefit to the husband beneficiary, who would know that they were provided for. Farwell J. held that the trustees had the discretion to make this advancement.

3.17 A valuation point in *Re Marquess of Abergavenny's Estate Act Trusts* (1981) is of relevance to our discussion of the scope of the Trustee Act section 32. In this case there was an express power in a trust to advance up to half the trust fund, concerning land, to the beneficiary who currently was the 'life tenant'. The position as regards settled land has now been modified by the Trusts of Land and Appointment of Trustees Act 1996. This act has been previously considered in Unit 7.

3.18 Half the trust fund was advanced to Lord Abergavenny, the current life tenant. This was based on values at the time of distribution. Subsequently, the trust fund appreciated considerably. Lord Abergavenny wanted his half share to be altered so that he received a half share of the appreciated fund. The trustees wished to distribute to Lord Abergavenny half of the appreciated current value of the trust fund, thereby making up the shortfall.

The trustees sought the approval of the court to do this. The court declined on the basis that it had no power to authorise such a distribution.

3.19   The principle of the case can of course be extended and applied to section 32 of the Trustee Act 1925. We have seen previously that any capital sums advanced to a beneficiary are subsequently deducted from his share, under this statutory power. The statutory power is drafted in a similar way to the express power given to the trustees in the Abergavenny case. If the same facts came up for judicial decision under the Trustee Act 1925 section 32, one would expect the result to be exactly the same.

4 Trustees' investment duties in equity

4.1   A trustee is expected to conduct the business of investment to the standard of a prudent person in business.

4.2   The trustee must not invest in a risky or hazardous investment, unless this was expressly provided for in the trust instrument.

4.3   Where a trustee makes an investment then he must have full information about it.

4.4   Where the trustee is a trust corporation carrying on business in giving advice and managing trust funds, then the trustee owes a higher standard of care than that described above, *Bartlett and Others v Barclays Bank Trust Co Ltd* (1980).

4.5   In *Nestlé v National Westminster Bank plc* (1993) the Court of Appeal had to consider whether there was a duty on a trustee to maintain the capital value of a trust fund. In the High Court, Hoffmann J (as he then was) in an unreported but important decision in June 29 1988, decided that there was no such duty. This conclusion was upheld by the Court of Appeal. This unreported decision has been fully noted by a case note containing a full transcript in *Trust Law International* Vol 10 No. 4 112 (1996).

4.6   The Court of Appeal laid down some general guidelines:

a) it was not a wise policy for trustees to change their investments frequently

b) a trustee with a power of investment should undertake periodic reviews of the investments held by the trust

c) such reviews should be at least annually.

4.7   In *Cowan v Scargill* (1985) the High Court accepted that where the purpose of a trust is to provide for the financial assistance of the beneficiaries, then their best interests will usually be their best financial interests. Where trustees are proposing to act without treating this factor as of prime importance, then they may be restrained from so doing: *Martin* v *The City of Edinburgh District Council* (1987). Only where moral considerations do not affect the financial interests of the beneficiaries could they be taken into consideration by the trustees: *Harries* v *Church Commissioners for England* (1992).

5 Trustees' investment duties under the Trustee Investments Act 1961

5.1 This act applies where there is no, or no contrary, power of investment in the trust instrument. It applies where trustees wish to invest in 'the wider range category' of investments, (i.e. shares in a company incorporated in the United Kingdom, shares in any building society or in a unit trust scheme). They must then divide the trust fund so that three-quarters is invested in this category. The remaining quarter must be invested in 'the narrower range category' (i.e. gilt-edged and fixed-interest securities). See Part 8 of this Unit in relation to the statutory duties imposed by this act.

5.2 If the trust instrument provides for other or wide powers of investment, then its terms will take precedence. Modern clauses will normally give the trustees greater and wider powers of investment than those provided by the Trustee Investments Act 1961.

5.3 In *Cowan* v *Scargill*, (1985) discussed previously, the High Court considered that the size of the fund was a crucial factor; more diversification would be allowed if the fund was a large one.

5.4 Where the investment clause of a trust instrument is inadequate, then it may be widened by virtue of section 57 of the Trustee Act 1925. In *Mason* v *Farbrother* (1983) the investment clause of a pension fund was amended in a number of ways, after the court heard that other pension funds had wide powers of investment. In particular, the trustees were given the power

● to insure the trust property

● to borrow money

● to lend money

● to invest in freehold or leasehold interests in land.

5.5 Similarly, in *Steel* v *Wellcome Custodian Trustees Ltd* (1988) Hoffmann J as he then was, was prepared to allow investment clauses which allowed for much wider investment than that permitted by the Trustee Investments Act 1961. The judge regarded the Trustee Investments Act 1961 as inadequate and out of touch with modern patterns of investment. Furthermore, the particular charitable trust produced a substantial income, derived from shares in one company. In such circumstances, it was appropriate to allow the inclusion of a clause which would enable the trustees to invest in any assets without restrictions.

5.6 A similar view, that the Trustee Investments Act 1961 was dated and out of touch with current investment practice, had previously been made in *Trustees of the British Museum* v *Attorney-General* (1984). In particular, greater flexibility in making investments should be allowed.

● Trustees should be able to invest in areas which offered considerable opportunities for growth.

● Trustees should be able to invest on short notice and for short durations where appropriate.

● Trustees should be able to invest outside of the United Kingdom.

● Trustees should have flexibility in their powers of investment.

5.7 Megarry VC was prepared to allow a wide investment clause to be inserted into the trust instrument. In addition, he was prepared to allow a clause which would give the trustees wide powers of delegation. The delegation of trustees' duties under the Trustee Act 1925 has been previously considered in Unit 10.

6 Investments allowed by the Trustee Act 1925

6.1 Sections 2 and 3 of the Trustee Act 1925 allow the trustees to purchase redeemable stocks. Section 7 allows the trustees to invest in bearer securities.

6.2 Section 10 of the Trustee Act 1925 allows the trustees to make loans to others. Such a loan may last for a maximum period of seven years.

6.3 Section 19 of the Trustee Act 1925 allows the trustees to insure a building against loss or damage by fire.

7 Investment in land under the Trusts of Land and Appointment of Trustees Act 1996

This act has been previously considered in Units 2, 7 and 9.

7.1 The Trusts of Land and Appointment of Trustees Act 1996 gives trustees of land certain specific powers of investment. In particular, section 6 of this Act provides that trustees of land are to have the same full powers that an absolute owner has.

7.2   By section 6(4) of that act, trustees are able to purchase a legal interest in land. They may do this

    a) as an investment

    b) to provide a property for the beneficiary to reside in

    c) for some other reason.

7.3   Sections 12(1) and 12(2) of the act give a beneficiary the right to occupy land already held on trust, if that land is suitable and available for occupation. By section 13 of the act, the trustees must not unreasonably exclude or restrict this right of the beneficiary.

7.4   This act preserves the general approach in equity, that the wishes of the settlor are of paramount importance. If the trustees are restricted by the trust instrument from investing in a legal interest in land, then they will be unable to do this. The act does not modify the wishes of the settlor. This is expressly provided by section 6(6) of the act.

7.5   Section 8(1) of the act confirms that the act is subject to the wishes of the settlor as regards investing in a legal interest in land. By this section of the act the wishes of the settlor, or the person making the 'disposition', are of paramount importance.

7.6   By section 11 of the act, the trustees are under a duty to consult with the beneficiaries who are of full age and capacity. This duty to consult applies to trustees who are investing trust funds in land.

7.7   By section 9(1) of the act, the trustees of land are able to delegate their duties in connection with that land to any beneficiary who is of full age and capacity and who has an equitable interest in the trust. (For this section, the interest of the beneficiary must, in addition to being an equitable interest, also be an 'interest in possession in land'. This concept is explained in *Pearson* v *I.R.C* (1981) as being the present right to the present enjoyment of the land.

7.8   The act has also affected the position with regard to the variation of trusts of land. Section 6(2) of the act provides that where a beneficiary of a trust of land is of full age and capacity, and has an equitable interest in that trust, then the beneficiary may call for that equitable interest from the trustee.

7.9   Section 6(4) of the act provides that the trustees must transfer the equitable interest to the beneficiary if called upon to do so, unless they are restricted from doing this by the trust instrument.

7.10   If the trustees are restricted in this way, then they will be unable to do so by section 6(6) of the act. By section 8(1) of the act, the wishes of the settlor, or the person making the 'disposition' are paramount.

7.11 There has always been a general inherent jurisdiction to vary trusts in equity. A well-recognised situation in which a trust will be varied is through use of the rule in *Saunders* v *Vautier* (1841). If there are no express or implied terms in the trust to the contrary, then a sole beneficiary has the right to call for the legal title, and is able to end the trust. The rule also extends to the situation where there is more than one beneficiary. However, the beneficiaries must collectively be a complete, closed, total, ascertained, and mentally competent group who are together entitled to the whole of the equitable interest. There must be no unborn or unascertained or unascertainable beneficiaries. This was discussed in Unit 2.

7.12 The statutory jurisdiction to vary trusts under the Variation of Trusts Act 1958 will be considered in Unit 13.

8 Investment duties under the Pensions Act 1995

Investment duties

8.1 The Pensions Act 1995 section 34(1) stated that trustees of an occupational pension scheme will have the power, subject to the express terms of the trust instrument, to make investments as if they were absolutely entitled to the trust assets.

8.2 The Pensions Act 1995 section 35(1) provides that trustees of an occupational pension scheme must provide, on a regular basis, a written statement of the principles upon which investment decisions have been made.

8.3 This statement must contain details of the following:

● the policy adopted by the trustees to ensure that they have delegated their duties properly in relation to the investment of trust funds

● the policy adopted by the trustees as regards the types, and balance between, risk, and anticipated return of investments made, Pensions Act 1995 section 35(2).

8.4 In making investments the trustees and/or fund manager must have regard to two factors under the Pensions Act 1995 section 35:

● first, the necessity for diversification (section 35(2)(a))

● second, their suitability, (section 36(2)(b)).

8.5 A similar principle has been adopted in relation to the Trustee Investments Act 1961 which has been discussed earlier in this Unit. This act is a more general one than the Pensions Act 1995, and covers the investment duties of trustees for all types of trust. It applies to proposed investments falling within the scope of the Trustee Investments Act 1961. This act has been considered previously in this Unit.

8.6 The Trustee Investments Act 1961 section 6(1)(a) provides that the trustees must have regard to the need for diversification of investments, and section 6(1)(b) provides that the trustees must also have regard to the suitability of the proposed investment to the trust.

8.7 The Trustee Investments Act 1961 puts trustees under a statutory obligation to obtain and consider expert advice in relation to making investments, Trustee Investments Act 1961 section 6(2).

Delegation

8.8 The trustees can delegate their powers to a fund manager, the Pensions Act 1995 section 34(2)(a). Such trustees will not be liable for any default or omission by a fund manager where they have taken all reasonable steps to assure themselves that the fund manager:

- has suitable knowledge and expertise

- is currently carrying on his work in a proficient manner, the Pensions Act 1995 section 34(4).

8.9 The general duties of trustees in relation to delegation has been previously considered in Unit 10.

Exclusion of liability

8.10 The Pensions Act 1995 (section 33(1) provides that a failure by the trustees of an occupational pension scheme to exercise proper care and skill in investment matters, cannot be excluded or restricted by the trust instrument.

8.11 The Pensions Act 1995 section 34(6) enables trustees of an occupational pension scheme to exclude or restrict liability for the acts or omissions of a fund manager to whom investment decisions have been delegated. The trustees must be satisfied that the fund manager has the proper experience and is carrying out his work proficiently, the Pensions Act 1995 section 34(6).

8.12 The general position as regards exclusion of liability for breach of trust on the part of trustees will be considered in Unit 12.

Pension surpluses

8.13 The Pensions Act 1995 does not give any new general power to trustees to deal with pension surpluses. The general position in equity is preserved. This has been discussed previously in Unit 4.

8.14 The Pensions Act 1995 section 37(1) does enable trustees to transfer a pension surplus to the employees' company if a number of conditions are fulfilled. The following elements, of particular importance, must all be satisfied:

● first, the occupational pension scheme trust contains the express power to transfer pension surpluses to the employees' company (section 37(1)(a))

● second, the occupational pension scheme is an approved and exempt scheme under the Taxes Act 1988 schedule 22 (section 37(1)(b))

● third, the trustees are satisfied that the transfer of the surplus from the occupational pension fund trust to the employer (company) is in the interests of the employees of the company (section 37(4)(b)).

Summary

Now you have studied the text and worked through this Unit, you should understand:

☐ **maintenance**

☐ **advancement**

☐ **the investment of trust funds.**

Self-assessment questions

Under what circumstances is a trustee able to delegate his duties?

1   Describe the trustees' statutory power of 'maintenance' under section 31 of the Trustee Act 1925.

2   Describe the trustees' statutory power of 'advancement' under section 32 of the Trustee Act 1925.

3   Describe (i) the general law duties, and (ii) the statutory duties of trustees who are to invest trust funds.

4   Describe the statutory powers that trustees of land have under the Trusts of Land and Appointment of Trustees Act 1996 to invest in land.

Exam-style questions

1   a) It has been stated that the duty of a trustee is 'to take such care as an ordinary prudent man would take if he were minded to make an investment for the benefit of other people for whom he felt morally bound to provide'.

        Discuss the continuing force of this statement following court cases in the last 20 years, and whether it applies equally to private trustees and to professional trust corporations.

    b) As a trustee of a will trust, your bank has a co-trustee who runs a jewellery shop. He recently came to see you and recommended that the trustees invest in gold and diamonds which, he is sure, are about to see considerable increases in value. The trust is worth about £200,000, and he suggests an investment of at least £50,000.

        How would you respond?

    c) Discuss the statutory powers available to a trustee for investing in land.

[Autumn 1995]

2   Samuel made a settlement in 1986 which appointed your bank as its sole trustee. It is now worth £400,000 in quoted securities.

    One half of the trust fund was to be held for his grandson James, absolutely, if and when he should attain the age of 25.

    The other half was to be held for another grandson, Richard. Samuel was concerned that Richard's father, who had been made bankrupt some years before, might try to get his hands on Richard's money. As a result the settlement directed the trustee to accumulate the income of Richard's share until he was 45, and only then to release all capital to Richard if he should be living.

    James is now 13 and receiving private education. Richard is a qualified accountant, aged 29.

    How would you respond to the following enquiries?

    a) James's parents ask whether the trustees could pay his school fees from the income arising on his share.

    b) They ask how surplus income is currently dealt with.

    c) They ask how income will be dealt with after James leaves school.

    d) James's main interest is in aircraft and flying; when he leaves school, his parents suggest that he be trained as a pilot and ask for your confirmation that the trustee will make £40,000 available for this purpose.

    e) Richard asks for an advance of £50,000 to allow him to buy into an existing partnership.

[Autumn 1995]

3 Your bank is the trustee of a settlement, the deed of which does not contain any specific investment powers. Describe the powers available to you to invest in:

(a) ordinary shares

(b) land, both as an investment and for the private occupation of a beneficiary. [Spring 1996]

4 Your bank is the trustee of a will trust under which the residuary estate is to be held for such of the testator's grandchildren, Jane, John and Jill, as reach the age of 23. The will does not contain any administrative powers, and the trustees have only the usual statutory powers. The trust fund, invested in quoted stocks and shares, is now worth £250,000.

   a) The parents of Jane, who is now aged 12, wish to send her to a private school and ask the trustees for help in paying the fees. What powers have the trustees to help? What are the taxation consequences of any help they may give?

   b) John, now aged 20, has left school and is considering a career in computers. To this end, he wishes to acquire advanced computer equipment which costs £15,000 and asks the trustees to advance this money to him from the capital of the trust. How should they deal with this request?

   c) Jill will be 18 in two months' time. Explain briefly the effect that this will have on her share and any action that you may wish to consider taking beforehand.

   d) How would your answers to the above questions differ, if at all, if the trust fund consisted of investment properties only?

[Spring 1996]

5. Bernard died some years ago and, in his will, left a life interest in his residuary estate to his daughter, Bertha. She is co-trustee with your bank and, after her death, the estate will pass to a local animal welfare charity.

After the payment of legacies, taxes, etc., the estate consisted of one investment property only. There had been a trust for sale coupled with a power to retain. The property has just been sold for £250,000 to a development company. There are no investment powers in the will.

   a) Explain the procedures and considerations which you feel that the trustees should follow in reinvesting the available money.

   b) Comment briefly on each of the following points made by Bertha, who is a spinster aged 65, when she called to see you about the reinvestment of the proceeds of the property sale.

      i) The trustees should look for another property which might have development value.

      ii) She would like the trust to help her nephew, who is about to get married, to buy a house.

iii) She knows of a local building society which is offering a very good rate of interest on balances of over £100,000 for a fixed term of five years.

iv) Her nephew works as a junior, unqualified member of the staff of a local stockbroking firm; in his spare time he advises Bertha on her own investments and she therefore wishes him to be involved with the trust's investments also.

v) She hates animals, and cannot understand why her father left his money to a charity for them. She does not mind, therefore, if the charity finally receives very little.

vi) She cannot see much future for the UK, and she and her nephew feel therefore that investment should be abroad.

[Spring 1995]

(The answers are given in the Appendix)

Caselist for Unit 11 Powers of Trustees in Specific Circumstances

The Trustee Act 1925 sections 2,3,10,19,31,32,57,69(2).

Pilkington and Another v *I.R.C.* [1964] AC 612.

Re Pauling's Settlement Trusts, Younghusband v *Coutts and Co (High Court)* [1962] 1 WLR 86.

'The powers of trustees: Power to allow maintenance to infants' in *Underhill and Hayton, Law of Trusts and Trustees* 15th edition (ed. D.J. Hayton.) Butterworths (1995), Chapter 12.

The Family Reform Act 1969.

Re Delamere's Settlement Trust, Kenny v *Cunningham-Reid* [1984] 1 WLR 813.

'Income from the Trust Fund' in *Parker and Mellows, The Modern Law of Trusts* 6th edition (ed. A.J. Oakley) Sweet and Maxwell (1994), Chapter 17.

Re Erskine's Settlement Trusts, Hollis v *Pigot* [1971] 1 WLR 162.

I.R.C. v *Bernstein* [1961] Ch 399.

Re Sharp's Settlement, Ibbotson v *Bliss* [1973] Ch 331.

Parker and Mellows, The Modern Law of Trusts 6th edition (ed. A.J. Oakley) Sweet and Maxwell (1994), Chapter 18.

Re Moxon's Will Trusts, Downey v *Moxon* [1958] 1 WLR 165.

Re Clore's Settlement Trusts, Sainer v *Clore* [1966] 1 WLR 955.

Re Halsted's Will Trusts [1937] 2 All ER 570.

Re Marquess of Abergavenny's Estate Act Trusts [1981] 2 All ER 643.

Bartlett and Others v *Barclays Bank Trust Co Ltd* [1980] Ch 515.

Nestlé v *National Westminster Bank* June 29th 1988 Unreported (High Court) [1983] 1 WLR 1260. (Court of Appeal)

Case note of the unreported decision of *Nestlé* v *National Westminster Bank* June 29th 1988. (1996) *Trust Law International* Vol 10 No. 4 112.

Cowan and Others v *Scargill and Others* [1985] Ch 270.

Martin v *The City of Edinburgh District Council* [1987] PLR 9.

Harries v *Church Commissioners for England* [1992] 1 WLR 1241.

The Trustees Investment Act 1961 sections 6(1)(a), 6(1)(b), 6(2).

Mason v *Farbrother* [1983] 2 All ER 1078.

Steel v *Wellcome Custodian Trustees Ltd* [1988] 1 WLR 167.

Trustees of the British Museum v *Attorney-General*

The Trusts of Land and Appointment of Trustees Act 1996 sections 6, 6(2), 6(4), 6(6), 8(1), 9(1), 11, 12(1), 12(2).

Saunders v Vautier [1841] 4 Beav 115.

The Pensions Act 1995 sections 33(1) 34(1), 34(6), 34(2)(a), 34(4), 35(1), 35(2), 35(2)(a), 36(2)(b), 37(1), 37(1)(a), 37(1)(b), 37(4)(b).

12

Breach of Trust

Objectives

After studying this Unit, you should be able to:

- **understand personal remedies**

- **understand proprietary claims.**

1 Personal Remedies

1.1   A beneficiary is able to bring a personal claim against a trustee for breach of trust of the fiduciary or other duties owed to the beneficiary. The type and scope of fiduciary duties have been discussed previously in Unit 10. If the trustee was wrongly to transfer the trust property or other assets to another, then the beneficiary would have a personal claim against the trustee. In addition, or alternatively, the beneficiary would have a proprietary claim against the recipient of the trust property. The proprietary claim will be discussed in Part 7 of this Unit. The beneficiary would not be entitled to double recovery.

1.2   In *Target Holdings Ltd* v *Redferns (a firm)* (1996) there was an admitted negligent breach of trust on the part of the defendants. The question for the House of Lords was the amount which the plaintiffs could recover.

1.3   The House of Lords applied common law principles to determine the amount of breach, even though it was a breach of an equitable right.

1.4   In particular, causative questions were relevant. The defendant's negligent (wrongful) act must cause the damage complained of. The casual connection between the breach of trust by the defendant and the loss to the trust (and hence the beneficiaries) must be established.

1.5 The loss to the trust is to be assessed at the date of trial and not the date of breach. The case was sent for trial, the principles to be applied having been determined.

1.6 This approach has been further developed by the Court of Appeal in *Bristol and West Building Society* v *Mothew* (1996). Millett LJ was of the view that compensation for breach of trust (an equitable claim) was to be the same as a claim in common law where damages would be awarded. In particular, the common law rules of causation, remoteness of damage and the quantum (amount of damages) should be applied to equitable claims for breach of trust.

1.7 In the specific context of breach of an express trust: *Nestlé* v *National Westminster Bank plc* (1993) the Court of Appeal (Leggatt LJ) considered that it must be proved that there was loss. Furthermore, the Court of Appeal (Staughton LJ) considered that even though a trustee may have made errors, such as not being fully aware of his investment powers, it did not necessarily follow that there was a breach of trust. Such powers might not have been exercised by the trustee. Even if they would have been exercised, they might not have resulted in any extra profit being made. Similarly, even if a better balance of investments had ensued, it did not necessarily mean that the trust fund would have reached a higher amount.

1.8 Equity did historically, and still does, give its own remedy for breach of trust. This remedy is liability to account. The defendant trustee, who is in breach of trust, must account to the plaintiff beneficiary for all the profits he makes.

1.9 In contrast, the aim of damages (a common law remedy) is to compensate the beneficiary for loss suffered. However, a beneficiary cannot claim damages and also an account, but must choose between them. The beneficiary is able to elect for the one that is the most advantageous, *Tang Man Sit (dec'd) (personal representative)* v *Capacious Investments Ltd* (1996).

1.10 There is a growing list of cases which cover the amount of damages recoverable for breach of trust. These cases will be examined below. As a consequence, the facts and approach in *Target Holdings* v *Redferns (a firm)* (1996) merits full consideration.

1.11 In particular, some of these cases have involved transactions for the buying of, and lending on, land. In *Target Holdings* v *Redferns (a firm)* (1996), R, the defendant, acted for a client called Crowngate Ltd, C, and also for the plaintiffs, T, in a transaction involving the buying of a property.

1.12 T, who were lenders, loaned £1.7m so that C could buy this property. The property had been negligently overvalued at £2m. This case was not concerned with the issue of overvaluation.

1.13   However, C had in fact purchased the property at £750,000. R knew of this fact, and also of a sub-sale by C to various third parties. Ultimately, R paid over the £1.7m not to C, but to others, to enable them, and not C, to purchase this property.

1.14   In order to facilitate the sub-sale, R had given certain information to T about the transaction which R knew was incorrect.

1.15   It is important to emphasise that the breach by R was paying over the monies lent to the wrong person.

1.16   This was contrary to the agreement between R and T that R would transfer the monies lent by T to C only. For the purposes of the case it was agreed between T and R, that R was a defaulting trustee. R had wrongly paid away the funds lent by T.

1.17   The issue for the House of Lords was the amount of R's liability for this breach of trust.

1.18   In an important decision the House of Lords laid down, unanimously, certain guidelines on the assessment of liability. Lord Brown-Wilkinson gave the only judgement, which was accepted by the other four law lords:

   ● first, that equity and common law had similar rules for the assessment of damages

   ● second, that the defendant's breach must cause the plaintiff's loss

   ● third, that the plaintiff was to be restored to the position he would have been had the breach not occurred

   ● fourth, that the loss suffered by the plaintiff would be assessed at the date of trial and not the date when the breach of trust occurred.

1.19   Having laid down these general principles the House of Lords stated that these rules should be applied at the subsequent trial of the plaintiff's claim.

1.20   Another analogous case is *Mortgage Express Ltd v Bowerman and Partners (a firm)* (1996) where the defendants B were solicitors acting for the plaintiff M, who were lenders. The defendant also acted for H who was the purchaser of a property in Queensway, London. The purchase price was £220,000 and the plaintiff was to advance £180,500. The property had been valued at £199,000 by a professional valuer.

1.21   The seller of the property was in fact purchasing the property himself at £150,000 and was selling on the property to H. The defendant did not disclose this to the plaintiff.

1.22   H obtained and received the loan of £180,500 from the plaintiff. After repaying one installment of this loan H defaulted. The property was repossessed by the building society which subsequently sold it for £96,000, the best price then obtainable.

1.23 The plaintiff building society gave evidence that had it known of the sub-sale it would have obtained another valuation and then discovered that the correct value of the property, at time of the loan, to be only £120,000. The plaintiff would not then have advanced funds to H.

1.24 Sir Thomas Bingham MR was of the view that if a solicitor, in the course of investigating title, discovers facts which would have a material effect on the lending decision, or on the value of the lender's security, then that solicitor must notify the lender of these facts.

1.25 The defendants knew of the sub-sale, and that the seller was only paying £150,000 for the flat. In the opinion of both Sir Thomas Bingham MR and Millett LJ, the defendant was under a duty to report this to the plaintiff since it cast doubt on the valuation of the property. The defendants were negligent in not passing this information on to the plaintiff.

1.26 The plaintiff was awarded £84,500, by the court, representing the difference between the amount of £180,500 it had advanced to the buyer of the property and the amount of £96,000 it received on the subsequent sale of the property after it had been repossessed.

1.27 As M P Thompson points out in his casenote of this decision in (1996) *The Conveyancer* 204, the decision was of importance in that the lender was able to recover the loss it had suffered.

1.28 We know from *Target Holdings v Redferns*, discussed above, that the damages recoverable for breach of trust in equity are the same as the damages recoverable for negligence or breach of contract in common law. Hence, although the claim in *Mortgage Express Ltd v Bowerman and Partners*, discussed above, was a claim for negligence, the decision is of relevance since it gives us the approach of the courts to the assessment of damages both in common law and in equity.

1.29 A similar approach was also taken in *Bristol and West v May and Merrimans* (1996), where Chadwick J accepted that where a solicitor acts for both a buyer and a lender, and becomes aware of a fact which would or could affect the lender's decision to proceed with that loan, then the solicitor will have placed himself in a position of conflict of duty. If the solicitor does not pass on the information, he will be protecting the interests of one client, the borrower, at the expense of the interests of the other client, the lender.

1.30 This factual situation can be distinguished from *Target Holdings v Redferns (a firm)* 1996, discussed above, in that there is not a wrongful transfer of funds to the wrong person, but a failure to inform the lender of facts which might have resulted in a cancellation of the loan.

1.31 The solicitor will be in breach of fiduciary duty, and in breach of the duties he owes to the lender. Fiduciary duties have been previously discussed in Unit 10. The consequence is that the solicitor will be liable for the loss that he caused to the lender by not passing on this information. The solicitor will hold the monies advanced by the lender on constructive trust for the lender. Constructive trusts will be dealt with in Unit 16.

1.32 As a consequence of the conflict of interest giving rise to a constructive trust, the solicitor will be unable to advance them to the borrower. In the absence of full disclosure to the lender, the only action the solicitor can take is to return a sum representing the loan monies to the lender. Once full disclosure is made, the lender is able to give the solicitor new instructions.

1.33 However, this approach was not followed in *Bristol and West Building Society* v *Mothew* (1996) where the defendant solicitor, who acted for a purchaser, obtained a mortgage advance for the purchaser of £59,000 from the Bristol and West Building Society. The defendant solicitor also acted for the building society. The purchase price was £73,000.

1.34 The plaintiff building society required the solicitor to certify that the balance of the purchase price was being provided personally by the buyer, without any additional borrowing, and without a second mortgage. This the defendant solicitor did, even though he knew that the buyer owed monies to Barclays Bank plc, and that a second mortgage and second charge on the property was also arranged with Barclays Bank plc.

1.35 The issue was the measure of damages which should be awarded to the plaintiff. Millett LJ gave the leading judgment in the Court of Appeal, and the other judges agreed with his approach. Millett LJ was of the view that there was a causal link between the defendant solicitor's negligence and the loss suffered by the building society.

1.36 However, where incorrect information is provided, the defendant is liable only for the consequences of the incorrect information.

1.37 Millett L.J. together with the other two judges in the Court of Appeal, declined to follow the approach of Chadwick J in *Bristol and West Building Society* v *May* (1996), discussed above, that the defendant solicitor by acting for both the buyer and the lender was in a conflict of duty situation. In his view the defendant solicitor was not in breach of fiduciary duty and could not be a constructive trustee merely for this reason.

1.38 Further, the misrepresentation made the transaction only voidable not void. The defendant solicitor continued to have the necessary authority to carry out the purchase of the property. The defendant solicitor had not improperly spent trust monies and did not become a constructive trustee.

1.39 In effect the judge made a distinction between careless or negligent conduct where there would be no breach of trust, and hence no liability in equity, and on the other hand culpable or deliberate misconduct where there would be a breach of trust. In *Target Holdings* v *Redferns (a firm)* 1996, discussed above, it was conceded that there was a breach of trust. Such a concession was not made in this case, and can account for the different conclusion.

1.40 The plaintiff was left solely to his claim for damages in common law, since the claim for breach of trust did not succeed in equity.

1.41 In *Hillsdown Holdings plc* v *Pensions Ombudsman and others* (1997) certain pension fund trusts were improperly transferred to the employer company. For a previous discussion about pension fund surpluses, see Unit 4. This raised the extent to which the trustees would be bound by the rule that they were liable to make restoration of the trust fund under the rule in *Target Holdings Ltd* v *Redferns (a firm)* 1996, discussed above.

1.42 Knox J rejected the argument that this rule did not apply because the pension scheme had been ended by this improper act.

1.43 The appropriate remedy was the return of the trust fund, i.e. return of the trust asset.

- For a general discussion of equitable compensation, see generally, C E F Rickett: *Where are We Going with Equitable Compensation?* in *Trends in Contemporary Trust Law* (ed. A J Oakley) 1996, Chapter 8.

- See also, The Honourable Sir Anthony Mason: *The Place of Equity and Equitable Remedies in the Contemporary Common Law World* Vol 110 (1994) LQR 238.

- Anthony Oakley: *The Liberalising Nature of Remedies for Breach of Trust* in *Trends in Contemporary Trust Law* (ed. A J Oakley) 1996, Chapter 10.

- David Capper: *Compensation For Breach of Trust* (1997) *The Conveyancer* 14.

2 Types of breach of trust

2.1 In order to ascertain the breach of trust, it is necessary to examine what duty is owed because, in order for there to be a breach, there must be a breach of some duty.

2.2 One example was shown in *Re Diplock* (1951) discussed in Unit 9 and later in this Unit. The wrongful distribution of income or capital by a trustee would be an important breach of trust. The beneficiaries would be entitled to recover the wrongfully transferred asset. This would entitle them to a proprietary claim which will be discussed subsequently in this Unit. In addition, or in so far as their is a shortfall in the recoverability of the trust assets, the beneficiaries would be entitled to a personal claim against the trustees.

2.3 Another example of breach of trust is where the trustees exercise their discretion incorrectly and do not distribute income or capital as required by the terms of a discretionary trust. This type of situation was considered in Unit 4. As we have seen, the beneficiaries would be entitled to go to the court and ask it to direct the proper administration of the trust in such a situation: *McPhail* v *Doulton* (1971).

2.4 In *Bishopsgate Investment Management Ltd (in liq)* v *Maxwell (No. 2)* (1994), a claim for breach of fiduciary duty was brought against Ian Maxwell for signing blank transfers, below the signature of his brother Kevin, which transferred shares of Bishopsgate Investments Ltd for nil consideration to various companies in the Robert Maxwell empire. Ian Maxwell was a director in Bishopsgate Investments Ltd. which was trustee of various pension fund schemes for the employees of various Robert Maxwell companies.

2.5 This was a breach of Ian Maxwell's fiduciary duties, since his fiduciary powers had been used for an improper purpose. Further, Ian Maxwell had not enquired about the purpose for which the transfers were made. This failure to inquire was also a breach of his fiduciary duties. Breach of directors' fiduciary duties have been previously considered in Unit 10.

2.6 Ian Maxwell was held liable to restore the loss to the pension fund caused by the improper transfers.

2.7 Trustees must also be careful in the employment of agents. If the trustees appoint an agent who cannot carry out his task, or if the trustees never supervise the work of the agent, then the trustees are personally liable for any loss caused to the trust by virtue of their poor supervision. The duties of agents have been dealt with in Unit 10.

2.8 Similarly, trustees must also be careful in their choice of investments. Their general duty is to act as a prudent person of business. If they fail to meet this standard and cause loss to the trust, then the trustees will be liable for the loss caused to the trust through their failure to reach this standard. This type of breach is an example of a negligent breach of trust. The duties of trustees in relation to investments have been dealt with in Unit 11.

2.9 It is also established from the Trustee Act 1925 section 4, that where a trustee merely keeps an unauthorised investment, this will not by itself render the trustee liable. Obviously, if it is an unsound investment, the trustees should sell it for the best price possible as soon as reasonably possible. If it is a sound investment, though unauthorised, then the trustees can keep it.

2.10 In *Foskett* v *McKeown and Others* (1997) a trustee used trust monies to insure his own life. This was an example of a fraudulent breach of trust. However, on the death of the trustee, the beneficiaries were entitled only to a return of the wrongly paid premiums and interest and not any of the benefits under the policies of insurance.

2.11   Where there is a breach of trust then all the trustees will be liable, since liability is joint and several. This also means that any one trustee can be held liable for all the loss caused by the breach of trust. However that trustee is able to recover a proportionate contribution for the loss from the other trustees: Civil Liability Contribution Act 1978.

2.12   In general a starting point is that 'equity is equality', so the trustees are equally liable for the loss caused. However, in particular situations, or where an individual trustee has particular duties or responsibilities, then that trustee can be liable for a greater contribution. The Civil Liability Contribution Act 1978 section 2(1) provides for a contribution between trustees as is 'just and equitable'.

2.13   The guiding test provided by this section is to look at the responsibility of the particular trustee for the loss caused. Say we have a situation where two negligent trustees cause loss to the trust: if one of them is more responsible, then he will be liable for a greater proportion of compensation.

3 Exclusion and limitation of liability

3.1   The decision in *Joseph Hayim v Citibank NA* (1987) is an authority for the view that trustees owe duties of care and skill in carrying out their duties as trustees.

3.2   The Unfair Contract Terms Act 1977 covers standard term clauses in trust instruments which seek to exclude a trustee's failure to exercise these duties of care and skill.

3.3   Such a clause would therefore have to satisfy the requirement of being a 'fair and reasonable clause'. The onus would be on the trustee, who was seeking to rely on the clause to exclude liability, to show that the clause fulfilled this requirement.

3.4   There are obvious difficulties in so doing.

- Beneficiaries place considerable reliance on the actions of trustees.

- Liability for breach of trust on the part of a trustee cannot be excluded under the Trustee Act 1925 (as we shall see below). It would therefore be inconsistent to allow liability for breach of trust to be excluded under the Unfair Contract Terms Act 1977.

3.5   In *Smith v Eric S Bush* (1990), the parties were not in a contractual or trust relationship. The defendant sought to exclude liability for negligence in making a survey of a property which the plaintiff was about to purchase. The House of Lords placed considerable importance upon the fact of reliance by the plaintiff. This case would suggest that a beneficiary's reliance upon the acts and position of a trustee would be regarded by the courts as of importance. (A trustee's position as a fiduciary is described in Unit 10).

3.6   The various reasons that might be put forward, in seeking to show that the Unfair Contract Terms Act 1977 covers exclusion clauses in trust instruments, are discussed by one leading practitioner in his examination of this area: William Goodhart QC Trustee Exemption Clauses and the Unfair Contract Terms Act 1977 (1980) *The Conveyancer.* 333.

3.7   Some doubt has been thrown upon this approach by Charles Harpum (Law Commissioner for England and Wales). Fiduciary Obligations and Fiduciary Powers – Where are We Going? Seminar Paper on Fiduciaries in Context. SPTL *Pressing Problems in the Law* XI 28 September 1996, where he cites *Re Duke of Norfolk's Settlement Trusts* (1982), and argues that the remuneration awarded to the trustee in that case was not on the basis of contract.

3.8   The various reasons, including that of inconsistency as mentioned above, that might be put forward in seeking to show that the Unfair Contract Terms Act 1977 would render an exclusion of liability unreasonable are discussed by Paul Matthews in The Efficacy of Trustee Exemption Clauses in English Law (1989) *The Conveyancer* 42.

3.9   There has been some additional recent academic writing on the scope and effect of trustee exclusion clauses. See generally Richard Nobles: Trustees' Exclusion Clauses in Jersey and England Vol 10, No. 3 (1996) *Trust Law International* 66. In this article, the important unreported decision of Jacob J in the High Court in *Armitage v Nurse and others* 17th July 1995 is considered.

3.10   The author describes the result in this case, namely that the exclusion clause excluded liability for all honest actions of the trustees. Such a clause was valid even though the settlor had enabled his trustees not to follow the terms of the trust, provided the trustees did so honestly.

3.11   Professor David Hayton: The Irreducible Core Content of Trusteeship in *Trends in Contemporary Trust Law* (ed. A J Oakley) 1996, also deals with the unreported decision of the High Court in *Armitage v Nurse and others*. Professor Hayton considers the judgment of Jacob J and emphasises a particular aspect of the judge's decision, where the judge points out that the trustees had expressly undertaken to act on the basis that they would be liable only for fraudulent actions. Obviously, this was an important element in their decision to act as trustees.

3.12   The decision of the High Court found in favour of the defendant trustees (of which one was Richard Nurse). The High Court upheld the validity of the exclusion clause.

3.13   This decision was then appealed by the principal beneficiary, Paula Armitage. This important new decision of the Court of Appeal, *Armitage* v

Nurse and others (1997) will be examined below, where the facts, reasoning, and decision are dealt with in detail.

3.14 Millett LJ gave the leading judgment of the Court of Appeal. The trust had been made in October 1994 as a result of varying a marriage settlement whereby Paula Armitage's mother was a 'life tenant' and Paula Armitage entitled in remainder. This marriage settlement was varied under the Variation of Trusts Act 1958. This act will be considered in Unit 13.

3.15 As a result of this variation, £230,000 was transferred to Paula Armitage's mother and £30,000 plus the land held in trust was transferred to Paula Armitage.

3.16 Paula Armitage alleged a number of breaches of trust. First, that the trustees allowed a family company, G W Nurse & Co Ltd (of which Paula's mother was a shareholder and director) to farm this land. The trustees, in defence, stated that valuable farming services had been provided by this company in return for the payment by the trust.

3.17 Second, that the trustees had not supervised the management of the land owned by Paula Armitage. In support of this allegation, evidence was provided as to the value of the land at the date of partition when the family settlement was varied in 1984, and its value when sold in 1987. In particular, it was alleged that Paula Armitage's interests as beneficiary were not properly taken care of, and that the interests of her mother were always placed first.

3.18 Millett LJ dealt with particular care and detail as to the allegations of breach of trust. In his view, the allegations against the trustees regarding the appointment of G W Nurse & Co Ltd amounted only to an allegation of negligence or gross negligence. As regards the allegation of lack of supervision of this company by the trustees, this allegation was merely one of negligence, and not dishonesty. Further, as regards the alleged wrongful delegation of the trustees' duties to this company, such an allegation did not amount to an allegation of fraud, but only to breach of trust.

3.19 As regards the allegation of preferment of Paula Armitage's mother ahead of Paula Armitage, the allegation did not specifically allege fraud or improper purpose. As drafted, the allegation in relation to the preferment of Paula's mother went no further than to allege negligence.

3.20 When the land apportioned to Paula Armitage had been sold, the sale had been on a commercial basis with professional advice. The alleged claims relating to the value of Paula Armitage's interest in this land could be no more than a claim of negligence.

3.21 In conclusion, the judge was of the view that the allegations of breach of trust did not allege fraud or dishonesty on the part of the trustees.

3.22 Millett LJ dealt with exclusion clauses in trust instruments in a wide-ranging way, and laid down a number of important general principles.

3.23 He looked at the particular clause in the trust instrument, clause 15, which excluded liability except for 'actual fraud' on the part of the trustee. This clause had been deliberately taken from a book of precedents and showed that there was a clear intention to exclude liability in a clear and unambiguous way. It was important that the word 'actual' was used, in the opinion of the judge.

3.24 Millett LJ concluded that the clause excluded liability for breach of trust unless there was dishonesty on the part of the trustee.

3.25 In the judge's opinion, it was the duty of the trustee to act in the interests of the beneficiaries. The judge gave an important definition of dishonesty. If a trustee acted in a way which that trustee did not honestly believe was in the interests of the beneficiaries, then that trustee was acting dishonestly.

3.26 In this regard it does not matter whether the trustee stands to benefit by his actions. Liability for breach of trust does not depend upon a conflict of duty or interest. Such conflicts of duty have previously been considered in Unit 10.

3.27 The simple test is the intention of the trustee. If the trustees intend to promote the interests of the beneficiaries, they are honest. If the trustees do not intend to promote the interests of the beneficiaries, they are dishonest.

3.28 Further, there was no reason of public policy for not giving effect to this exclusion clause. The judge could find no English or Scottish decision which did not allow such a clause. We have previously looked at public policy, in the context of illegality in Unit 1.

3.29 In academic circles it had been argued (in particular see the above article by Professor David Hayton) that there was an irreducible core of trustee obligations which could not be excluded without undermining the whole concept of the trust. It had been argued, and was argued on behalf of Paula Armitage by Peter Weatherill QC, counsel appearing for her, that exclusion clauses should not be allowed for this reason since essential duties of skill and care were being eliminated.

3.30 In the opinion of the judge, the only trustee obligations which could not be excluded were the duties to act honestly and in good faith.

3.31 Finally, in the view of Millett LJ if such exclusion clauses were to be rendered inoperative, then this should be done by parliament.

3.32 Since no allegation of fraud or dishonesty had been alleged against the trustees, and since the valid exclusion clause excluded all claims against the trustees except fraudulent or dishonest ones, it followed that Paula Armitage's claim would be dismissed.

4 Limitation periods

4.1   The Limitation Act 1980 applies to a breach of trust situation. Where there is a breach of trust Section 21(3) of the Limitation Act 1980 provides that action to recover trust property, or the loss arising from this breach, must be brought within six years from the date when legal proceedings could have begun.

4.2   Actions which involve only a claim for breach of fiduciary duty (see Unit 10) are not subject to a limitation period under the Limitation Act 1980: *Nelson* v *Rye* (1996).

4.3   However, where a breach of fiduciary duty does give rise to a constructive trust, then the provisions of the Limitation Act 1980 do apply: *Nelson* v *Rye* (1996).

4.4   There is no statutory period of limitation where the trustee is party or privy to any fraud or dishonesty, or has converted trust property to his own use under Section 21(1) of the Limitation Act 1980.

4.5   In *Kershaw* v *Whelan (No2)* (1997), the plaintiff, Ian Kershaw, was a son whose father had died intestate. However, his father had set up a fund of some £45,000 for distribution amongst the plaintiff, his step-mother and his sister. The trustees had distributed this fund mainly to the step-mother.

4.6   The defendant, Alan Whelan, a solicitor acting on behalf of the step-mother, had written to the trustees administering the fund, supplying what he believed to be correct information about the plaintiff's financial circumstances, and stating that: the plaintiff had lied about his own financial circumstances; the step-mother should benefit exclusively from the fund.

4.7   The plaintiff could not bring a claim in negligence since it was brought too late and barred. However, Mrs Ebsworth J held that this did not stop the plaintiff bringing a claim in equity. In her view, in cases of concealed fraud, where the plaintiff did not know about the fraud, a plaintiff's claim could not become barred. The Limitation Act 1980 did not stop the plaintiff's claim in such circumstances. The plaintiff was allowed to proceed with his claim.

5 Relief from liability

5.1 Section 61 of the Trustee Act 1925 relieves trustees from liability for breach of trust in certain circumstances. The trustee must show three things:

a) that he acted honestly

b) that he acted reasonably

c) that it would be fair to excuse the trustee from liability.

5.2 In *Bartlett v Barclays Bank Trust Co Ltd* (1980), the High Court accepted that the bank had acted honestly. However, the court did not think that the bank had acted reasonably. Furthermore, the court was also of the view that it would not be fair to excuse the bank from liability. The bank was therefore held liable for the net loss suffered by the beneficiaries.

5.3 The general approach of the courts is a strict one, and they do not readily allow trustees relief from liability for their breaches of trust. Where a bank obtained the advice (which was incorrect) from its own solicitors, the Court of Appeal would not relieve the bank from liability, *Re Pauling's Settlement Trusts, Younghusband v Coutts and Co* (1964).

6 Recovery of misapplied funds

Bankers trust orders

6.1 The Chancery Division of the High Court has had to deal with an increasing number of cases involving the misapplication of funds, taken from either a trust or a company.

6.2 To deal with this situation, a bankers trust order has been developed. Bankers trust orders are designed to discover the whereabouts of the plaintiff's monies. Furthermore, such an order is often granted in conjunction with a 'Mareva injunction', that is, an order freezing the bank account(s) of those who possess the plaintiff's monies. Where monies have been wrongfully taken or stolen, then this order may be obtained in addition to a proprietary claim to recover the asset. Such an order is also in addition to a constructive trust which may be imposed against third parties. The proprietary claim is discussed later in this Unit. The constructive trust is described in Unit 16.

6.3 The essential point about such an order is that it is done at the interlocutory stage, that is before any substantive proceedings have taken place. Such an order must be obtained quickly if the plaintiff's monies are not to disappear.

6.4 It is not necessary for the plaintiff to have instituted substantive proceedings to obtain this information: *Bankers Trust Co v Shapira* (1980). The objective behind the order is to obtain information that one or more bank accounts contain the plaintiff's monies: *A v C* (1981).

6.5 However, these two cases establish that for such an order to be granted there must be direct and probative evidence of fraud or wrongdoing.

6.6 The order will be granted only where it will ascertain the whereabouts of the misapplied monies or alternatively will stop such monies from being dissipated: *Arab Monetary Fund* v *Hashim (No. 5)* (1992).

6.7 However, it must be the plaintiff's monies that have been taken. Where funds are stolen from a trust the beneficiaries will be entitled to a bankers trust order. To obtain such an order, either a legal interest or an equitable interest is sufficient. This is established from the case *Arab Monetary Fund* v *Hashim (No. 5)* (1992). For this purpose a fiduciary relationship will not be sufficient.

6.8 Where the plaintiff alleges that his monies have been transferred through a number of bank accounts, then several orders may be granted, as in *Lipkin Gorman (a firm)* v *Cass* (1985).

6.9 Such orders may also be granted in relation the bank account of a third party, as in *Mercantile Group (Europe) AG* v *Aiyela and Others* (1994).

7 Proprietary claims

7.1 In relation to proprietary claims, there have been many new cases. This has generated a considerable amount of academic writing, in particular:

- Sir Peter Millett: Tracing the Proceeds of Fraud. Vol 107 (1991) LQR 71

- Steven Fennell: Misdirected Funds: Problems of Uncertainty and Inconsistency. Vol 57 (1994) MLR 38

- Peter Birks: The English Recognition of Unjust Enrichment (1991). LMCLQ 473

7.2 A beneficiary is able to bring a proprietary claim (*in Rem*) against the third party who has received trust property or some other trust asset. Below is a summary of this new case law. The concept of an *in Rem* (proprietary claim) was considered in Unit 8.

7.3 There are two types of tracing:

a) in common law

b) in equity.

Common law tracing

7.4   Millet LJ in *Jones v Jones* (1996) emphasises that a claim is being made because some property or other asset belonging to another has been taken. However, the judge makes clear that it does not follow that the remedy is proprietary. Indeed, the remedy is not proprietary. The owner does not recover the property or asset but a sum in compensation (damages) for what has been wrongfully taken.

7.5   It is therefore established in common law that the test for bringing a common law tracing claim does not involve the existence of a fiduciary relationship. This concept has been discussed above. It is a concept developed in equity and has traditionally been the basis for bringing a tracing claim in equity. This will be discussed below.

7.6   It is clear that historically the common law tracing claim required an identifiable asset. In consequence, the tracing in common law of monies moved by electronic transfer is difficult. See *Agip (Africa) Ltd v Jackson* (1990) (High Court) and *Agip (Africa) Ltd v Jackson* (1991). (Court of Appeal).

7.7   In *Lipkin Gorman v Karpnale Ltd* (1991) the House of Lords decided that a 'debt' was an item of property and that it would enable a common law tracing claim to be made.

7.8   In *Jones v Jones* (1996) the Court of Appeal (Lord Justice Millett) confirmed that the common law could now follow monies through 'mixed' bank accounts (i.e. where the monies that have been wrongly taken have been mixed with monies belonging to other persons). The common law could follow cheques (physically) as they passed from hand to hand. When the cheques were converted into money, these proceeds were recovered.

7.9   This case (immediately above) decides that, where the asset that is being traced in common law is exchanged for another asset, then:

● the new asset may be recovered

● the profit made in this exchange (if there is a profit) may be recovered as well.

The beneficiary is therefore able to recover both the new asset and any profit made.

Equitable tracing

7.10   A starting point is the judgment of Lord Browne-Wilkinson in *Westdeutsche Landesbank Girozentrale v Islington London Borough Council* (1996). In this important House of Lords decision, Lord Browne-Wilkinson sought to deal with matters of principle. He was of the opinion that:

a) Where there was a trust, the equitable interest of the beneficiary was binding upon third parties

b) In order for a proprietary claim (also called a tracing claim) to be brought by a beneficiary, there must be a separated equitable interest.

This case is discussed at length by Peter Birks: Trusts Raised to Reverse Unjust Enrichment: The Westdeutsche Case (1996) RLR 3.

7.11 The hallmark of a trust is where the equitable interest is separated from the legal interest. In this situation, a beneficiary of a trust is able to bring an equitable proprietary (tracing) claim against third parties who have received, and who still retain, trust property. In such a situation it is also the position that the trustee is in a fiduciary relationship with the beneficiary. (See Unit 10 as to the meaning of fiduciary relationship.)

7.12 The other basis on which a proprietary claim may be brought is the existence of a fiduciary relationship: *Re Diplock* (1948). This has been confirmed in a number of cases including *Chase Manhattan Bank NA v Israel-British Bank (London) Ltd* (1981) and *Agip (Africa) Ltd v Jackson* (1990) (High Court) and *Agip (Africa) Ltd v Jackson* (1991) (Court of Appeal).

7.13 The rule that the person with the equitable interest is entitled to bring a tracing claim has been confirmed in a number of recent decisions. In *El Ajou v Dollar Land Holdings plc* (1993) Millett J wanted to ensure that a tracing claim would be available where a thief stole property or some other asset belonging to an owner who had both the legal interest and the equitable interest joined together. Clearly, the thief is not in a fiduciary relationship with the owner. The judge held that the thief does not obtain the equitable interest in the property or asset belonging to the owner. Because the owner retains, or is able to recover, the equitable interest, he is able to recover the property or asset.

7.14 One example of this proprietary claim occurred in *Barlow Clowes Ltd v Vaughan* (1992). Investors deposited monies with Barlow Clowes Ltd under an agreement to place these monies into one special, separate account. This created a trust relationship between the two parties, *R v Clowes (No. 2)* (1994).

7.15 Upon the insolvency of Barlow Clowes Ltd, the issue was how the remaining assets would be distributed amongst the investors. The Court of Appeal decided that the correct approach was to do what was fair and just. The court did not look at the order in which investors placed monies with Barlow Clowes Ltd. They simply apportioned the total assets available *pro rata* (in proportion) to the amount that each investor had placed with Barlow Clowes Ltd. Furthermore, even where funds have been 'mixed' together, an equitable tracing claim may still be brought. Provided the asset still exists, equity will allow a tracing claim.

7.16   It is also clearly established that where the trust property or other asset has been destroyed, then there cannot be a proprietary claim available to the beneficiary. Thus, where monies are taken from the trust and are placed into a bank account, which subsequently becomes overdrawn, then no proprietary claim will be available to the beneficiary: *Bishopsgate Investment Management Ltd (in liquidation) v Homan (1995)*.

7.17   If the property or other asset being traced in equity increases in value, the increase is recoverable: *A.G Hong Kong v Reid* (1994). The article by Sir Peter Millett (writing in a non-judicial capacity), Bribes and Secret Commissions (1993) RLR 7, was influential in determining the outcome of this case. That the increase in the value of the asset is recoverable is now the position both in equity and in common law. This decision was approved in *Attorney General v Blake (Jonathan Cape Ltd, third party)* (1996), where the High Court held that profits from the sale of a book would be recoverable by a plaintiff.

7.18   Where there is a tracing claim in equity, it will operate through a 'charge' over the property or asset. *El Ajou v Dollar Land Holdings (No. 2)* (1995).

7.19   There are particular equitable tracing defences that a recipient may put forward in relation to an equitable tracing claim. One such defence is that the recipient of the property or other asset is a *bona fide* purchaser for value without notice. This defence is a creation of equity. In general terms, a buyer of trust property or other assets belonging to the trust will obtain the equitable interest in that property. This defence was confirmed in *Boscaven v Bajwa* (1995).

7.20   Another defence emerged from a very important decision of the House of Lords in *Lipkin Gorman v Karpnale* (1991). This case established a new defence of 'change of position in good faith'.

7.21   The defence of 'change of position in good faith' applies irrespective of any representation (statement) on the part of the plaintiff: *Lipkin Gorman v Karpnale* (1991). In order to establish this defence, the following factors must be shown.

a) The defendant must have modified or altered his position in some way.

b) The defendant must have modified his position in good faith, that is to say, without knowledge that he was receiving the property or other asset of another. It follows that if the defendant is acting in bad faith he will not be able to establish the defence. Indeed, the requirement is that the defendant acts in good faith so the onus is on the defendant to show this.

c) The defence is available once the defendant modifies or alters his position in good faith. It is not necessary for the defendant to show that he modified his position in reliance on some statement made to him by the plaintiff. The defence is to be distinguished from a defence based upon estoppel, where an express or implied statement on the part of the plaintiff has to be shown by the defendant.

7.22 This defence of 'change of position in good faith' was discussed in *South Tyneside Metropolitan Borough Council* v *Svenska International plc* (1995). The High Court decided that this new defence would be considered on a case-by-case basis. In particular, this defence is based upon principle and is not based upon discretion (i.e. it is not based upon what is just and fair). In applying the defence the court is bound to follow the rules outlined in the paragraph above. If those rules happen to produce an unfair result, the court is still bound to follow them.

7.23 It is also established that the new defence of 'change of position in good faith' is available to a defendant where a plaintiff seeks to bring a proprietary (tracing) claim in equity against that defendant: *Boscaven* v *Bajwa* (1995).

8 Evaluation of the proprietary claims

8.1 The decision of *Westdeutsche Landesbank Girozentrale* v *Islington London Borough Council* (1996) is an important one and was previously considered in Unit 3. It is important in the context of this Unit since Lord Browne-Wilkinson in the House of Lords not only placed limitations on the role and scope of resulting trusts, but also made clear the application of constructive trusts to the situation of tracing assets in equity.

8.2 Lord Browne-Wilkinson clarified the position that where a thief steals property, this gives rise to a constructive trust, and not a resulting trust. Constructive trusts will be considered in Unit 16. Broadly, the reason for this is that the recipient's, here the thief's, conscience is affected.

8.3 Lord Browne-Wilkinson was able to place a new and different emphasis upon the decision in *Chase Manhattan Bank NA* v *Israel-British Bank (London) Ltd* (1981) previously discussed in Unit 3. In particular the recipient bank that received a double payment, a mistake, knew at the time of this second payment that there was an error.

8.4 Lord Browne-Wilkinson reasoned that the recipient bank's conscience was affected and that it therefore held this second payment on constructive trust for the paying bank. Since there was a constructive trust, a proprietary (tracing) claim was therefore available to the paying bank. This is discussed by Anthony Oakley: The Liberalising Nature of Remedies for Breach of Trust in *Trends in Contemporary Trust Law* (ed. A J Oakley) 1996, Chapter 10.

8.5 This was important because the recipient bank had become insolvent. As we saw in Unit 3, this proprietary claim would rank ahead of other contractual claims, and would take precedence in insolvency.

8.6   There is an Australian authority which supports this approach. In *Black v S. Freedman & Co* (1910), the judge held that a thief holds the stolen property on constructive trust for the owner. The point was made in *Banque Belge pour l'Etranger v Hambrouck* (1921) that equity does not like thieves, and will seek to impose an appropriate remedy against them. This approach was also followed in *A.G. Hong Kong v Reid* (1994), considered in this Unit and also in Unit 5. In particular a constructive trust was imposed against Reid, the recipient of bribes, who had effectively committed deception against the Hong Kong authorities.

8.7   Another point of importance emerges from the decision of the House of Lords in *Westdeutsche Landesbank Girozentiale v Islington London Borough Council* (1996), discussed above. Lord Browne-Wilkinson made it clear that in overruling the decision of *Sinclair v Brougham* (1914), he was not casting any doubt on the decision of the Court of Appeal in *Re Diplock* (1948). It was this Court of Appeal decision which laid down that in order for a tracing claim to be brought, a fiduciary relationship must be shown.

8.8   The need for a fiduciary relationship has been criticised by both judges and academics. In *Agip (Africa) Ltd v Jackson* (1990) Millet J, as he then was, in the High Court, was of the view that a fiduciary relationship should not be the test in order to enable a tracing claim to be brought.

8.9   Professor Peter Birks makes the point, in his article: On Taking Seriously the Difference between Tracing and Claiming *Trust Law International 2*, (1997) Vol 11, No. 1. that one should not confuse the rights of an individual with identifying what has become of his asset. In his view these are distinct questions. For this reason, the use of a fiduciary relationship as a basis for an equitable tracing claim is incorrect.

8.10   The matter became critical in Millett LJ's later decision, *El Ajou v Dollar Land Holdings plc* (1993) where a distinction was made between the agent who steals property or who obtains property by deceiving his principal, where there is a fiduciary relationship, and the situation where a thief deceives the owner, where there is no fiduciary relationship.

8.11   In order to enable the owner to trace in equity in the latter situation, Millett J, as he then was, developed the alternative basis of allowing an equitable tracing claim to be made. This alternative is an equitable interest. Necessarily, an owner has the equitable interest in the property.

8.12   After the House of Lords decision in *Westdeutsche Landesbank Girozentiale v Islington London Borough Council* (1996), discussed above, in the view of Lord Browne-Wilkinson, tracing is allowed simply because the thief's conscience is affected, and the court could impose a constructive trust. It is for this reason that a tracing remedy would be available.

8.13　The *Westdeutsche Landesbank* decision, discussed above, has been followed in *Ghana Commercial Bank v C and Others* (1997), where it was alleged that the defendants had wrongly appropriated the proceeds derived from certain bankers drafts into their own personal accounts. Counsel for the bank argued that there was a fiduciary relationship because the drafts had been stolen, and hence the bank had a proprietary equitable tracing claim. It was argued by counsel for the bank that the bank had a proprietary tracing claim from the moment the receipts from the bankers drafts were placed into the defendants' personal accounts.

8.14　For some of the recent discussions of proprietary remedies, particularly in a commercial context, see the following:

- Gerald McCormack: *The Eye of Equity: Identification Principles and Equitable Tracing* (1996) JBL 225.

- Janet Ulph: *Equitable Proprietary Rights in Insolvency: The Ebbing Tide?* (1996) JBL 482.

- Christa Band: *The Development of Tracing Rules in Commercial Cases* (1997) LMCLQ 65.

- *Laundering and Tracing* (ed. P B H Birks.) 1995.

8.15　*Lipkin Gorman (a firm) v Karpnale Ltd* (1991) is a leading decision on common law tracing. The focus of attention in this case was the legal title or interest. In principle, a tracing claim in common law could be made to follow unmixed monies from the clients' account operated by Cass, a partner in the firm of Lipkin Gorman, solicitors. This account was a chose in action (a debt), and the solicitors had legal title to it. Lord Goff in the House of Lords confirmed that the basis of the common law tracing claim was that of legal title. In this case, no claim for tracing in equity was brought by the plaintiff solicitors.

8.16　In principle the solicitors' claim was for 'money had and received' i.e. broadly, that the another person had received their property. The amount recoverable under this claim is the amount of the plaintiff's property that can be traced in common law.

8.17　In *Jones v Jones* (1996), discussed previously in paragraphs 7.4 and 7.8, Millett LJ confirmed that a plaintiff makes such a claim because the asset originally belonged to him in common law. The plaintiff is seeking to follow his asset. However, the plaintiff's remedy, the common law tracing claim, is only a personal one. In *Jones v Jones* (1996) the claim was brought by a trustee in bankruptcy. Such claims can be brought only in common law.

8.18　Common law tracing does not give a plaintiff any proprietary remedy, in contrast to tracing in equity which is proprietary, and which does allow a claim to be brought in insolvency: Lord Goff in *Lipkin Gorman (a firm) v Karpnale Ltd* (1991).

8.19 One particular difficulty in common law is its inability to trace through mixed bank accounts, i.e. where the owner's monies are mixed with the recipient's monies. This was the view of Scrutton LJ in *Banque Belge pour l'Etranger* v *Hambrouck* (1921).

8.20 However, where there has not been any mixing, then common law tracing is available: *Banque Belge pour l'Etranger* v *Hambrouck* (1921). This approach was confirmed by the Court of Appeal in *Jones* v *Jones* (1996).

8.21 However a contrasting (dissenting) view was put forward by Atkin LJ, as he then was, in *Banque Belge pour l'Etranger* v *Hambrouck* (1921). The judge considered that in the same way that equity could trace into mixed bank accounts, so could the common law. In his view the monies put into the bank account could be identified as the owner's, even after mixing.

8.22 There is support for the approach of Atkin LJ, in *Agip (Africa) Ltd* v *Jackson* (1990), where Millett J, as he then was, considered that monies passing into and out of a bank account could be traced in common law provided that they could be subsequently identified. This approach was followed by Millett LJ in *Jones* v *Jones* (1996) where the judge confirmed that the common law does allow tracing even where assets have been substituted into other assets or their products.

8.23 However, on the facts of *Agip (Africa) Ltd* v *Jackson*, the transfer was made electronically. Both Millett J, as he then was, and the Court of Appeal, accepted that whilst tracing in equity was available, the common law was not able to follow a stream of electrons. It has since been confirmed by Millett J, as he then was, in *El Ajou* v *Dollar Land Holdings plc* (1993) that no claim can be made in common law to trace international transfers of funds made electronically.

8.24 On appeal in *Agip (Africa) Ltd* v *Jackson* (1991) the Court of Appeal considered the decision of Millet J in the High Court, and also the Court of Appeal decision of *Banque Belge pour l'Etranger* v *Hambrouck* (1921). Fox LJ, giving the only judgment in the Court of Appeal, considered that the decision of Atkin LJ gave an incorrectly wide view of the scope of common law tracing.

8.25 In particular, Fox LJ accepted that there was a problem with following the funds from London through the New York clearing system. He was of the opinion that it was up to the House of Lords to enable specifically a common law tracing claim to be made. However, since equity was able to trace, it was not necessary to consider whether the position in common law could be modified by the Court of Appeal to enable a common law tracing claim to be made.

8.26 Millett LJ has argued for the amalgamation of common law and equitable tracing in the course of his judgments and in his article *Tracing the Proceeds of Fraud Vol 107* (1991) LQR 71. In *Bristol and West Building Society* v *Mothew* (1996) Millett LJ makes clear that this would lead to coherent results. In particular the equitable tracing remedy should be used to assist common law tracing claims.

8.27 Millett LJ develops this theme in *Jones* v *Jones* (1996) where he considered that there was no good reason to have dissimilar and diverse tracing rules in common law and in equity.

8.28 Further, in the view of Millett LJ, it was much more irrational not to allow the equitable tracing rules to be used to assist the common law tracing rules. After all, as we have seen in Unit 1, equity developed to mitigate the harshness of the common law rules. Indeed, equity developed remedies where none existed in common law. Therefore, logically equity should allow its own remedies to be used where there is only a partial remedy in common law.

8.29 N.H. Andrews and J.Beatson discuss the possible solutions to this problem in their casenote of *Jones* v *Jones*: Common Law Tracing: Springboard or Swan-Song? Vol 113 (1997) LQR 21. They consider that there are three alternative approaches:

● first, to have different but co-existing rules of tracing in common law and equity, and where possible, eliminate any unnecessary differences;

● second, to merge both systems and have one set of rules;

● third, a more positive role for equity in the elimination of problems with tracing in common law, with equitable rules being used to remedy the defects in common law.

8.30 The Honourable Sir Anthony Mason: *The Place of Equity and Equitable Remedies in the Contemporary Common Law World* Vol 110 (1994) LQR 238 makes an important point, which this author wholeheartedly agrees, that a plaintiff is able to formulate his claim so that he can bring an equitable tracing claim, and/or a common law tracing claim. There may be particular reasons, on particular facts, why one type of claim is pursued and not the other. With differing rules for equitable and common law tracing, this is an important consideration for a plaintiff contemplating bringing a claim for recovery of his misapplied asset.

9 Restitutionary claims

9.1 Although not strictly a common law tracing claim or an equitable tracing claim, it is appropriate to deal with restitutionary claims in this context. The restitutionary claim is available because a recipient will have received the owner's property.

9.2 The decision of *Lipkin Gorman (a firm)* v *Karpnale Ltd* (1991) discussed above in relation to common law tracing, also dealt with this type of restitutionary claim.

9.3 As Professor Peter Birks pointed out in *The English Recognition of Unjust Enrichment* (1991) LMCLQ 473, there are four essential factors of relevance, which he relates to the facts and decision of the House of Lords in *Lipkin Gorman (a firm) v Karpanale Ltd* (1991).

9.4 The first question is: is the defendant enriched? Cass stole funds from the client account of Lipkin Gorman, and gambled them at the Playboy Club. The club gained by this and were clearly enriched.

9.5 The second question is: is the enrichment at the expense of the plaintiff? The answer to this question was yes, since it was at the expense of Lipkin Gorman's client account.

9.6 The third question is: is the enrichment unjust? Lord Goff makes clear that what is unjust is determined as a matter of principle. The enrichment is unjust if the defendant has taken or interfered with some right of the plaintiff. By taking or interfering with the plaintiff's property, namely, the debt owed to the firm of solicitors, the enrichment was unjust. Where property is stolen or misapplied, this factor will nearly always be satisfied.

9.7 The fourth question is: is there some reason why restitution should be partly or wholly denied? In particular, this question raises the issue of the defence of 'change of position'. In Lipkin Gorman, the House of Lords accepted this defence for the first time.

9.8 As a matter of general principle, Lord Goff accepted that the Playboy Club would not have to repay all the sums gambled by Cass, but would only be required to repay the net gains made by it after deduction of the sums won by Cass through his gambling.

9.9 As we have seen in Section 7 of this Unit, this defence has been extended, and is available as a defence to a tracing action.

10 Jurisdictional issues

10.1 Since we are dealing with the recoverability of a plaintiff's assets that have been misapplied, it is appropriate to deal briefly with the jurisdictional problems raised in this situation. This issue is of equal importance and relevance to personal claims brought against defendants for 'dishonest assistance', and 'knowing receipt', which will be dealt with in Unit 16 in the section relating to constructive trusts.

10.2 There have been decisions which have involved questions as to whether English law or another country's system of law applied. The decision of

Webb v *Webb* (1994) involving land in France allegedly held in trust by a son for a father, has been previously considered in Unit 8. One of the issues in this case was whether the courts of France had exclusive jurisdiction in relation to this matter. It was held they did not.

10.3   In addition, the court considered the issue of which of two countries' laws, English or Indian, applied in *Chellaram* v *Chellaram* (1985). Since the defendants had accepted service of an English writ (claim), it was held that English law applied. The beneficiaries were thus able to, and did, invoke the inherent jurisdiction of the English courts to remove and appoint trustees. This has been considered in Unit 9.

10.4   In *Macmillan Inc* v *Bishopsgate Investment Trust plc and others* (1995) certain shares in Berlitz International were pledged to banks as security for various loans made by them to assist the Maxwell empire prior to its collapse. Claims for constructive trust were brought by Macmillan Inc., an American subsidiary company of Maxwell Communications Corporation, against these banks. Macmillan Inc. had previously owned a controlling interest of just over 55% of the shares in Berlitz International. Millett J, as he then was, held that the law of New York applied to determine this dispute, because the transaction had taken place in New York.

10.5   The large number of cases involving misapplied funds has led to a developing case law involving jurisdictional issues.

10.6   In particular, in *El Ajou* v *Dollar Land Holdings plc* (1993), Millett J, as he then was, held that where a plaintiff's assets are transferred around the world, through various jurisdictions, and subsequently arrive back in England, then equitable principles of law would be used to deal with the matter. The plaintiff's assets may be traced in equity since they have been received in England. For this purpose it did not matter that such assets had been moved through a number of jurisdictions.

10.7   Alternatively, if the defendant was resident in England, then equitable principles of English law would be used to deal with the matter. The defendant's conscience would be affected by his wrongful misapplication of the plaintiff's assets. This would enable a plaintiff to bring proceedings for either a tracing claim in equity, or alternatively a personal claim against the defendant for 'dishonest assistance' or 'knowing receipt'. These categories of constructive trust will be dealt with in Unit 16.

10.8   In *The Canada Trust Co and Others* v *Stolzenberg and Others* (1997), the plaintiff, the Canada Trust Co, the trustee of several pension funds, alleged that it had been the victim of a massive fraud. It also asserted that the defendant, S, had committed this fraud.

10.9   The plaintiff sought orders against various banks for documentary evidence of the residence of the defendant. The plaintiff wished to do this in order to establish English jurisdiction as the appropriate jurisdiction in which to bring the claim.

10.10 Lord Justice Millett held that the court did have such jurisdiction. The matter would be referred back to the trial judge to determine whether to grant the plaintiff's request for this documentary evidence. Interlocutory orders (i.e. orders before the main trial) of this type have been considered in Section 6 of this Unit.

Summary

Now that you have completed this Unit, you should understand:

☐ **personal remedies**

☐ **proprietary claims.**

Self-assessment questions

1 Under what circumstances can a beneficiary bring a personal claim against a trustee for breach of trust?

2 What defences are available to a trustee for breach of trust?

3 How is the measure of damages determined for a breach of trust?

4 What is common law tracing?

5 Are funds from several 'mixed' cheques traceable in common law?

6 What is equitable tracing?

7 Harlow Clouds International plc advertises for pension fund trusts and local authorities to invest with it. The company states in its brochure that investments will be made only in 'the best companies' and that 'a return of 10% is guaranteed'. The City Minwell pension fund trust invests £40 million and the Westshire local authority invests £20 million. These are the only two investors. These funds are placed into a mixed trading account. The company misapplies the monies supplied by these two investors, does not invest in safe securities, and goes into liquidation. £10 million remains in this account.

The Harlow Clouds International plc misapplies some of the investors' monies by the following:

a) the director of Harlow Clouds International plc gambles £1 million, in cash, at a Casino

b) a donation of £1 million is made to a local charity to enable it to improve its buildings

c) a yacht costing £1 million is bought for the directors of the company with investors' monies, for the personal use of the directors. The yacht is uninsured and it sinks in a violent thunderstorm.

Advise the City Minwell pension trust and the Westshire local authority as to any tracing rights that each has.

(The answers are given in the Appendix)

Caselist for Unit 12 Breach of Trust

Target Holdings v Redferns (a firm) [1996] 1 AC 421.

Bristol and West Building Society v Mothew [1996] 4 All ER 698.

Nestle v National Westminster Bank plc [1993] 1 WLR 1260.

Tang Man Sit (dec'd) (personal representative) v Capacious Investments Ltd [1996] 1 AC 514.

Mortgage Express Ltd v Bowerman and Partners (a firm) [1996] 2 All ER 836.

M P Thompson (1996): *The Conveyancer* 204.

Bristol and West v May and Merrimans [1996] 2 All ER 801.

Hillsdown Holdings plc v Pensions Ombudsman and others [1997] 1 All ER 862.

C E F Rickett: Where are We Going with Equitable Compensation? *Trends in Contemporary Trust Law* (ed. A J Oakley) 1996. Chapter 8.

The Honourable Sir Anthony Mason: *The Place of Equity and Equitable Remedies in the Contemporary Common Law World Vol 110* (1994) LQR 238.

Anthony Oakley: The Liberalising Nature of Remedies for Breach of Trust. *Trends in Contemporary Trust Law* (ed. A J Oakley) 1996. Chapter 10.

David Capper: Compensation For Breach of Trust (1997) *The Conveyancer* 14.

Re Diplock [1951] AC 251. (House of Lords) [1948] Ch 465. (Court of Appeal).

McPhail v Doulton [1971] AC 424.

Bishopsgate Investment Management Ltd (in liq) v Maxwell (No 2) [1994] 1 All ER 261.

The Trustee Act 1925 sections 4, 61.

Foskett v McKeown and Others [1997] 3 All ER 392.

The Civil Liability Contribution Act 1978 section 2(1).

Joseph Hayim v Citibank NA [1987] AC 730.

The Unfair Contract Terms Act 1977.

Smith v Eric S. Bush [1990] AC 831.

William Goodhart QC Trustee Exemption Clauses and the Unfair Contract Terms Act 1977 (1980) *The Conveyancer* 333.

Charles Harpum: Fiduciary Obligations and Fiduciary Powers – Where are We Going? *Seminar Paper on Fiduciaries in Context. SPTL Pressing Problems in the Law XI* 28th September 1996.

Re Duke of Norfolk's Settlement Trusts [1982] Ch 61.

Paul Matthews: The Efficacy of Trustee Exemption Clauses in English Law (1989) *The Conveyancer* 42.

Richard Nobles: *Trustees' exclusion clauses in Jersey and England* Vol 10. No 3. (1996) *Trust Law International* 66. *Armitage* v *Nurse and others* 17th July 1995. Jacob J. Unreported decision of the High Court.

Professor David Hayton: The Irreducible Core Content of Trusteeship. *Trends in Contemporary Trust Law* (ed. A J Oakley) 1996. Chapter 3. Clarendon Press Oxford.

Armitage v *Nurse and others* [1997] 2 All ER 705.

The Limitation Act 1980 sections 21(1). 21(3).

Nelson v *Rye* [1996] 1 WLR 1378.

Kershaw v *Whelan (No. 2) The Times* February 10th 1997.

Bartlett v *Barclays Bank Trust Co Ltd* [1980] Ch 515.

Re Pauling's Settlement Trusts, Younghusband v *Coutts and Co* [1964] Ch 303.

Bankers Trust v *Shapira* [1980] 1 WLR 1274.

A v *C* [1981] QB 311.

Arab Monetary Fund v *Hashim (No. 5)* [1992] 2 All ER 911.

Lipkin Gorman (a firm) v *Cass. The Times* May 29th 1995.

Mercantile Group (Europe) AG v *Aiyela* [1994] QB 366.

Sir Peter Millett: *Tracing the Proceeds of Fraud* Vol 107 (1991) LQR 71.

Steven Fennell: *Misdirected Funds: Problems of Uncertainty and Inconsistency* Vol 57 (1994) MLR 38.

Peter Birks: *The English Recognition of Unjust Enrichment (1991) LMCLQ 473.*

Jones (F. C.) & Sons (Trustee) v *Jones* [1996] 3 WLR 703.

Agip (Africa) Ltd v *Jackson* [1990] Ch 265 (High Court) [1991] Ch 547 (Court of Appeal)

Lipkin Gorman (a firm) v *Karpnale Ltd* [1991] 2 AC 548.

Westdeutsche Landesbank Girozentrale v *Islington London Borough Council* [1996] AC 669.

Peter Birks: *Trusts Raised to Reverse Unjust Enrichment: The Westdeutsche Case* (1996) RLR 3.

Chase Manhattan Bank NA v *Israel-British Bank (London) Ltd* [1981] Ch 105.

El Ajou v *Dollar Land Holdings plc* [1993] 3 All ER 717 (High Court)

Barlow Clowes International Ltd v *Vaughan* [1992] 4 All ER 22. *R* v *Clowes (No2)* [1994] 2 All ER 316.

Bishopsgate Investment Management Ltd (in liquidation) v *Homan* [1995] 1 WLR 31.

Attorney General of Hong Kong v *Reid* [1994] 1 AC 324.

Attorney General v *Blake (Jonathan Cape Ltd, third party)* [1996] 3 WLR 741.

El Ajou v *Dollar Land Holdings (No 2)* [1995] 2 All ER 213.

Boscaven v *Bajwa* [1996] 1 WLR 328.

South Tyneside Metropolitan Borough Council v *Svenska International plc* [1995] 1 All ER 545.

Anthony Oakley: The Liberalising Nature of Remedies for Breach of Trust. *Trends in Contemporary Trust Law* (ed. A J Oakley) 1996, Chapter 10. Clarendon Press Oxford.

Black v *S. Freedman & Co* [1910] 12 CLR 105.

Banque Belge pour l'Etranger v *Hambrouck* [1921] 1 KB 321.

Professor Peter Birks: On Taking Seriously the Difference between Tracing and Claiming. Vol 11, No. 1. (1997) *Trust Law International* 2.

Ghana Commercial Bank v *C and Others*. *The Times* March 3rd 1997. Gerald McCormack: *The Eye of Equity: Identification Principles and Equitable Tracing* (1996) JBL 225.

Janet Ulph: *Equitable Proprietary Rights in Insolvency: The Ebbing Tide? (1996)* JBL 482.

Christa Band: The Development of Tracing Rules in Commercial Cases (1997) LMCLQ 65.

Laundering and Tracing (ed. P B H Birks) 1995. Clarendon Press Oxford.

N.H. Andrews and J.Beatson (casenote of *Jones* v *Jones*): *Common Law Tracing: Springboard or Swan-Song?* Vol 113 (1997) LQR 21.

Webb v *Webb* [1994] QB 696.

Chellaram v *Chellaram* [1985] Ch 409.

Macmillan Inc v *Bishopsgate Investment Trust plc and others (No 3)* [1995] 3 All ER 747.

The Canada Trust Co and Others v *Stolzenberg and Others*. *The Times* May 1st 1997.

13

Variation of Trusts

Objectives

After studying this Unit, you should be able to:

- **understand the rules relating to variation of trusts.**

1 Inherent jurisdiction

1.1   We have previously considered the inherent jurisdiction in equity to appoint and remove trustees in Unit 9, and to award remuneration in Unit 10. There is also inherent jurisdiction to vary trusts. A leading authority is *Saunders v Vautier* (1841) which enables the court to vary the terms of a trust if all the beneficiaries are ascertainable, of full age and mental capacity, and agree. This important case has been discussed in Units 2, 8, and 9.

2 Trustee Act 1925 section 53

2.1   The court has power by The Trustee Act, section 53, to vest or transfer any equitable interest in trust property owned by an infant, so as to enable income or capital to be applied for the maintenance, education or benefit of that infant. See Unit 11 for a discussion of the circumstances in which trustees can provide income for the maintenance of an infant, or advance capital.

3 Trustee Act 1925 section 57

3.1   The Trustee Act 1925, section 57 is a wide-ranging provision enabling the court to grant additional powers to trustees. Trustees can be granted new powers to buy, invest or spend.

3.2   The Trustee Act, section 57(1) expressly provides that the above powers can be granted by the court only where there is an 'absence' of them in the trust instrument.

3.3   The test laid down by the Trustee Act 1925, section 57(1) is that it must be 'expedient' to do this. This word has been interpreted in the following way: that if the court did not exercise its powers, then real difficulty or inconvenience would result: *Re Municipal and General Securities Co Limited's Trust* (1950). Further, the new powers granted by the court must be for the benefit of the trust fund as a whole: *Re Craven's Estate* (1937).

3.4   An application to the court under the Trustee Act, section 57 can be made by either the trustees or the beneficiaries, Trustee Act 1925, section 57(3).

3.5   This section enables the court to vary a trust to allow for wider powers of investment: *Mason v Fairbrother* (1983). Trustees' powers of investment have been considered in Unit 11.

3.6   In addition the section enables the court to combine two identical charitable trusts into one: *Re Harvey* (1941).

3.7   The powers under this section have been used to vary interests in land. However, since the Trusts of Land and Appointment of Trustees Act 1996, additional powers have been given to beneficiaries to call for their interest in land. These powers will be discussed in section 6 of this Unit.

3.8   The section is still in force despite the Variation of Trusts Act 1958, section 1(6) which expressly states that this act does not affect the jurisdiction under the Trustee Act, section 57. The Variation of Trusts Act 1958 will be considered below.

4 Variation of Trusts Act 1958

4.1   In *Goulding and another v James and another* (1996) it was proposed to vary the interests of certain unborn grandchildren beneficiaries, by increasing their share, and then moving the trust fund offshore to be managed by professional trustees.

4.2   Laddie J dealt with the arguments of counsel and summarised their views as to the principles which guide the court's approach in cases where a variation is sought under this act. First, the court had discretion. Second, it was appropriate to take into account the intentions of the settlor. The judge specifically considered that it was appropriate to take into account the purposes of the trust. However, if the variation was simply a more tax-efficient method of carrying out the intentions of the settlor then, in practice, variation would be approved. Third, applications for variations are in practice almost never refused by a court, if the variation is shown to confer a benefit upon those for whom the variation is sought.

4.3   On these facts, the judge considered that the beneficiaries were seeking to put in place a variation which was the converse of that intended by the settlor. The judge, exercising his powers of discretion, would not allow the variation to take place.

4.4   In *Goulding and another* v *James and another* (1997), the Court of Appeal reversed the decision of Laddie J

4.5   Mummery LJ gave the leading judgment of the Court of Appeal. He looked at a previous decision of the House of Lords: *Re Holmden's Settlement* (1968) which he followed. In the light of this case, the judge laid down a general approach.

4.6   First, the variation of the trust is carried out by the beneficiaries and not the court. Where the beneficiaries are unable to give their consent because they are minors, or they are unascertained or unborn, the court gives its approval, or not, on behalf of such persons.

4.7   Second, the act is an extension of the principle of *Saunders* v *Vautier* (1841), discussed previously in section 1 of this Unit. The act extends the types of beneficiary that are able to give their consent to the variation.

4.8   Brian Green QC, argued that the intentions of the settlor could not outweigh the proposed benefit to the unborn beneficiaries for whom variation was sought. In particular counsel focused on the word 'benefit' which is contained in a proviso to section 1(1) of the act, and which he argued was the guiding principle for the variation of a trust for unborn beneficiaries.

4.9   The judge accepted these submissions, and summarised the general principles upon which the courts will act.

4.10   First, a court has discretion to accept or reject the proposed variation. Second, a variation for beneficiaries who are minors, or who have contingent interests, or who are unascertained or unborn, would only be allowed by the court if it was for the benefit of that class. Third, merely because there is a financial benefit, as shown actuarially, to unborn beneficiaries, does not mean that the court must necessarily approve the variation. The court must weigh up the advantages and disadvantages, must look at the arrangement as a whole, and must consider the potential bargaining position of the unborn beneficiaries. Fourth, the court is under a duty to protect those who cannot protect themselves. Fifth, the intentions of the settlor are not paramount, and the court is able to override them by the statutory jurisdiction given to them under the act.

4.11 The trial judge, Laddie J, had given too much emphasis to the intentions of the settlor, and not sufficient weight to the substantial benefit to the unborn grandchildren beneficiaries.

4.12 The general discretion of the court to vary trusts has been considered in a number of cases. In *Re Weston's Settlements* (1969), changes were sought to an existing trust: first, that under the Trustee Act 1925, section 25, the court appoint two trustees in Jersey in place of the existing trustees who were resident and domiciled in England (discussed in Unit 9); second, that the trust be varied so that property held in trust could be transferred to a similar trust subject to Jersey law.

4.13 Lord Denning MR, in the Court of Appeal, laid down three factors which shape the court's discretion under the act. First, the courts are to protect those who cannot protect themselves, and in so doing must act for their benefit. Second, the courts are able to allow variation of the interests in the trust in order to avoid taxation such as inheritance tax or capital gains tax. Third, the courts should consider the educational and social benefit to the beneficiaries of the variation, and not just the financial benefit.

4.14 In a forthright judgment, Lord Denning recognised that the variation was sought to avoid capital gains tax. He felt that if the variation was truly for the benefit of the beneficiaries, the two sons of the settlor, then it would be sanctioned by the court. He did not consider that it would be in their long-term interest to be uprooted and removed from England.

4.15 Harman LJ considered that the two sons would want other and wider opportunities than those available in Jersey.

4.16 In *Re Remnant's Settlement Trusts* (1970), a trust was created for the various children of two sisters. However, if any of these children married a Roman Catholic, or practiced Roman Catholicism, they would lose their share, and it would accrue to the others.

4.17 Two variations were sought from the court; first, to advance the interests of the children by transferring £10,000 to each of them; second, to delete the forfeiture clause. The legality of such clauses has been considered in Unit 5.

4.18 Harman J allowed both variations. The judge accepted that the continuance of this clause would cause considerable family tension between the two sisters, since the three children of one of the sisters had been brought up as Roman Catholics. The variations would be of benefit to these three children.

4.19 Further, the variations would be allowed, even though they were contrary to the intentions of the settlor who had inserted a forfeiture clause into the trust instrument. This approach, which disregards the settlor's intentions, is entirely consistent with the approach of the Court of Appeal in *Goulding and another v James and another* (1997) discussed above.

4.20   The court has powers of variation, under the Variation of Trusts Act 1958, section 57(1)(b), with regard to beneficiaries 'who may become entitled...to an interest under the trusts'. In *Knocker v Youle* (1986), Warner J held that these words were used in their technical and legal sense. This meant that the prospective next of kin, or a potential future spouse, did not fall within the scope of the act, and the courts had no powers of variation with regard to them.

4.21   On the other hand, a beneficiary with a contingent interest, i.e. contingent on the happening of a future event, would fall within the act, so that the court would have statutory jurisdiction to vary that beneficiary's contingent interest.

4.22   Two further issues regarding variation of trusts were considered in *Re Holt's Settlement* (1969). The first issue was whether writing is necessary to effect a variation under the Variation of Trusts Act 1958. The second issue is whether the Perpetuities and Accumulations Act 1964 is of any importance to a variation made under the Variation of Trusts Act 1958.

4.23   Megarry J, as he then was, was of the opinion that where an interest of a beneficiary was varied under the act, then it was a 'disposition' under the Law of Property Act 1925, section 53(1)(c).

4.24   However, it was argued by Mr Millett, as he then was, one of the counsel in the case, that writing was not required. In his argument, the variation was an arrangement made for valuable consideration, which was specifically enforceable and which gave rise to a constructive trust. It therefore did not need to be in writing by virtue of the Trustee Act 1925, section 53(2).

4.25   Megarry J accepted this argument. The result is that a variation of a trust under the act does not need to be made in writing.

4.26   This approach has been confirmed in *Neville and another v Wilson and others* (1996) which concerned shares in a private company, left by will, which had been settled in trust for various adult and ascertained beneficiaries, with full capacity. The case did not therefore involve the use of the jurisdiction under the act. The Court of Appeal held that the Law of Property Act, section 53(2) eliminated the need for writing.

4.27   However, because there was an oral variation, this case is of direct relevance to variations made under the Variation of Trusts Act 1958, and supports the decision of Megarry J in *Re Holt's Settlement* (1969).

4.28   These sections of the Law of Property Act 1925, and the need for writing, have been previously considered in Unit 5.

4.29   Turning to the second issue raised in *Re Holt's Settlement* (1969), an arrangement, whereby beneficiaries' entitlements are varied by court order under the Variation of Trusts Act 1958, does fall within the Perpetuities and Accumulations Act 1964.

4.30 Megarry J held that it was allowable to put provisions deriving their authority from the 1964 act into an arrangement approved under the 1958 act. The Perpetuities and Accumulations Act 1964 has been previously considered in Unit 5.

5 Variation of trusts of land

5.1 The Trusts of Land and Appointment of Trustees Act 1996, section 6(2) provides that where a beneficiary of a trust of land is of full age and capacity, and has an equitable interest in that trust, then the beneficiary can call for that equitable interest from the trustee.

5.2 Section 6(4) of this act provides that the trustees must transfer the equitable interest to the beneficiary if called upon to do so, unless they are restricted from doing this by the trust instrument, in which case they will be unable to do so by section 6(6) of this act.

5.3 Section 8(1) of this act makes paramount the wishes of the settlor, or of the person making the 'disposition'. The Trusts of Land and Appointment of Trustees Act 1996 has been previously discussed in Units 2,7,9, and 11.

6 Exporting of trusts

6.1 There is no statutory definition of what constitutes the exporting of a trust abroad. It is suggested that there are at least two possible actions that must be carried out in order to export a trust. First, non-resident trustees must be appointed in place of the United Kingdom trustees. Second, the trust property must be transferred to a jurisdiction outside the United Kingdom.

6.2 The statutory and non-statutory jurisdiction to appoint trustees has previously been considered in Unit 9.

6.3 An unreported decision of Millett J, as he then was, in *Richard v The Honourable A B Mackay* 14th March 1987 is of particular importance. Noted as a case report, Vol 11, No. 1, (1997) *Trust Law International* 22, concerned the exporting of part of a trust.

6.4 It has been previously discussed in Unit 9. In addition to wishing to appoint new trustees, the existing trustees wanted to transfer £2 million into Bermudian trusts on broadly the same terms as the English trust. The English trust had assets of £7.5 million held throughout the world. The settlor, Lord Tanlaw, had extensive personal, charitable and business connections with the Far East.

6.5 In particular, the existing trustees wished to provide for the two children, the two defendants, of his current marriage with Lady Tanlaw, who was Malaysian. On the premature death of Lord Tanlaw it appeared probable that Lady Tanlaw would live in the Far East with the two children.

6.6 The trustees were not seeking to avoid any particular tax liability. The trustees wanted greater flexibility, variety, and security for the trust assets.

6.7 While the trustees could currently send trust funds to the Far East, they felt that this could be restricted by the introduction of United Kingdom exchange controls. Bermuda was a stable system, and the money would be available to the children in the Far East if they decided to live there.

6.8 The trustees chose Bermuda, for the transfer of funds, rather than the Far East because of the stability of Bermuda as a jurisdiction. The advantages of this jurisdiction were fully considered when this case was discussed in Unit 9.

6.9 The High Court considered the previous decision of *Re Whitehead's Will Trusts* (1971), and summarised the views of Sir John Pennychuick VC. First, persons who were resident abroad could be appointed as trustees of an English trust. Second, such appointments would be made only in exceptional circumstances, such as a situation where the beneficiaries had settled in some overseas country and the new trustees were to be resident in that country.

6.10 On these facts, Millett J, as he then was, recognised that the beneficiaries, the two children, although resident in England, might possibly choose to live in the Far East in the future, although there were no current plans for them to do so. Further, the new trustees would be resident in Bermuda and not the Far East.

6.11 Millett J considered the approach of Sir John Pennychuick to be too restrictive. In particular, because the trustees were neither seeking the appointment by the court of new trustees under the Trustee Act 1925, nor a variation of the trust by the court under the Variation of Trusts Act 1958. The trustees were simply exercising their discretion, and seeking the approval of the court as a safeguard for themselves.

6.12 In this type of situation, the court merely has to be satisfied that the trustees can properly form the view that the transfer of trust funds is for the benefit of the beneficiaries or the trust. The test was that the proposed transaction was not so inappropriate that no reasonable trustee could entertain it.

6.13 It was also important that the transfer of trust funds should not put such funds at risk, nor deprive the beneficiaries of appropriate protection by a court. Since Bermuda was a jurisdiction analogous to that of the United Kingdom these fears were not realistic on the facts.

6.14 It was also important to consider whether the transfer of funds, and the appointment of new non-resident trustees, was appropriate. Millet J considered that it was for the following reasons: first, the family had strong connections with the Far East; second, the children beneficiaries might wish to live or pursue their careers in the Far East; third, to have some of the trust funds outside of the United Kingdom in a stable jurisdiction was to the benefit of these beneficiaries.

6.15 It was held that the existing trustees were at liberty to transfer a sum, not exceeding £2m, from the English trust to the Bermudian trust.

6.16 In the above case, it was the trustees who made the decision to transfer the trust. Care needs to be taken by a settlor when he creates an offshore trust. In particular, that the settlor does not keep too wide a set of powers in relation to the trust.

6.17 John Mowbray QC Offshore Trusts: Illusion and Reality (1994). *Trust Law International Vol 8 No. 3*, using cases decided in the Jersey Courts, makes the point that if a settlor exercised control over the trustee decisions, including distribution of trust funds and the management of the trust, then the trust might be considered a sham.

6.18 In his view, this was important because the structure of offshore trusts was such that the trust company or organisation based in the offshore jurisdiction was often made subject to the wishes of the settlor by a separate document containing the desires of the settlor.

6.19 Further, the settlor will often be given various powers, such as power to: revoke the trust; appoint financial advisers; remove trustees. In addition, the trust fund will comprise the shares in a company which is controlled by the settlor. John Mowbray's point is that this type of structural arrangement is open to attack on the basis that it is a sham.

6.20 Lastly, mention must be made of the tax implications of transferring trust assets in order to move a trust offshore. An excellent account of this is contained in Exporting Trusts. Parker and Mellows *The Modern Law of Trusts* (6th ed A J Oakley) 1994, Chapter 22. In this chapter, Anthony Oakley makes a number of important points regarding the taxation of this type of transfer. Below is a summary of these points, where trust assets are transferred and the trustees become non-resident in the United Kingdom.

- First, the trust and the trustees are not liable to income tax as regards any or all of the investments made outside the United Kingdom.

- Second, beneficiaries who are resident in the United Kingdom are liable to income tax.

- Third, where income is payable to a company or individual resident overseas, the beneficiary will become liable to income tax: Income and Corporation Taxes Act 1978 section 739.

- Fourth, where income could possibly be paid to an individual resident in the United Kingdom, the beneficiary will become liable to income tax: Income and Corporation Taxes Act 1978 section 740.

- Fifth, there will be deemed to be a disposal in this situation, and the trustees who were previously resident in the United Kingdom will be liable for the capital gains: Taxation of Chargeable Gains Act 1992 section 80(2).

- Sixth, there will be liability for inheritance tax if the settlor was domiciled in the United Kingdom at the time he made the settlement: Inheritance Tax Act 1984 section 6(1). Liability is therefore fixed by this test, and will not be modified because the trust is exported.

7 Miscellaneous statutory jurisdiction

7.1   The Matrimonial Causes Act 1973 section 24 enables trust property to be resettled on the other spouse, or on children of the family, on the occasion of divorce.

7.2   This includes the variation, on the occasion of divorce, of a husband's entitlement under a pension scheme, so that part was transferred to his former wife: *Brooks v Brooks* (1996).

7.3   The Mental Health Act 1983, section 96, enables a court, as it thinks appropriate, to make or vary a trust of which a mental patient is a settlor or a beneficiary.

Summary

Now that you have completed this Unit, you should understand:

☐ **the rules relating to variation of trusts.**

Self-assessment questions

1   Explain and discuss the rule in *Saunders* v *Vautier* (1841).

2   What does Section 57 of the Trustee Act 1925 enable trustees to do?

3   To what extent, and in what ways, can a trust be varied under the Variation of Trusts Act 1958?

4   How can a trust be 'exported'?

5   What are the tax consequences of 'exporting' a trust?

6   When can a trust of land be varied?

Exam-style question

A wealthy customer of your bank, Robert, made a settlement in 1980 with your bank as sole trustee. The settlement, now worth £600,000, is held for such of his children as attain the age of 30.

He has two daughters, Jane aged 20, and Joan aged 14. Jane is at an English university and hopes to remain there as a lecturer after graduation. Joan is at a boarding school in England.

Robert remarried three years ago. His new wife is much younger and is now expecting their first child. After their marriage, they had immediately settled in Jersey. All Robert's assets are now based on that island and he has suggested that the settlement should also be moved there, and that a local professional corporate trustee should be appointed.

Discuss whether or not you can meet Robert's request.

[Spring 1995]

(The answers are given in the Appendix)

Caselist for Unit 13 Variation of Trusts

Saunders v *Vautier* [1841] 4 Beav 115.

Trustee Act 1925 sections 53, 57, 57(1), 57(3).

Re Municipal and General Securities Co Limited's Trust, Re Municipal and General Securities Co Ltd v *Lloyds Bank Ltd* [1950] Ch 212.

Re Craven's Estate [1937] Ch 423.

Mason v *Fairbrother* [1983] 2 All ER 1078.

The Variation of Trusts Act 1958, sections 1(1), 1(1)(b).

Goulding and another v *James and another* [1996] 4 All ER 865.

Goulding and another v *James and another* [1997] 2 All ER 239.

Re Holmden's Settlement Trusts, I.R.C. v *Holmden* [1968] AC 685.

Re Weston's Settlements [1969] 1 Ch 223.

Re Remnant's Settlement Trusts [1970] Ch 560.

Knocker v *Youle* [1986] 1 WLR 934.

Re Holt's Settlement [1969] 1 Ch 100.

The Trustee Act 1925, sections 53(1)(c), 53(2).

Neville and another v *Wilson and others* [1996] 3 All ER 171.

Richard v *The Honourable A B Mackay* 14th March 1987: unreported decision of Millett J, as he then was. Noted as a case report. *Trust Law International* 22 (1997) Vol 11. No. 1.

Re Whitehead's Will Trusts, Burke v *Burke* [1971] 1 WLR 833.

John Mowbray QC: Offshore Trusts: Illusion and Reality (1994). *Trust Law International* Vol 8 No. 3.

Exporting Trusts, Parker and Mellows. *The Modern Law of Trusts* (6th ed A J Oakley) 1996, Chapter 22.

Income and Corporation Taxes Act 1978, sections 739, 740. Taxation of Chargeable Gains Act 1992, section 80(2). Inheritance Tax Act 1984, section 6(1).

The Trusts of Land and Appointment of Trustees Act 1996, sections 6(2), 6(4), 6(6), 8(1).

The Matrimonial Causes Act 1973, section 24.

Brooks v *Brooks* [1996] 1 AC 375.

The Mental Health Act 1983, section 96.

14

An Outline of the Law of Charities

Objectives

After studying this Unit, you should be able to:

● **understand the main features of the law of charities.**

1 Definition of Charity

1.1 The starting point for a definition of charitable trusts is the preamble to the Charitable Uses Act 1601, which gives a definition of what constitutes charity.

1.2 The major objectives of charity given in the preamble can be listed:

● relief of aged, impotent and poor people

● assist the marriages of poor maids

● aid for those unable to pay their taxes

● maintenance of schools of learning, free schools, and scholars in universities

● education and preferment of orphans

● maintenance of maimed soldiers and mariners

● repair of bridges, ports, havens, causeways, churches, sea banks and highways

● relief and maintenance of houses of correction

● relief or redemption of prisoners

● to support and aid young tradesmen

● to aid and assist persons decayed.

1.3   The use made of this preamble will be considered, where appropriate, in various cases below.

1.4   Subsequently, the objectives were grouped into four categories.

1.5   In *Commissioners for Special Purposes of Income Tax* v *Pemsel* (1891) Lord Macnaghten laid down the basic categories of charitable trust: trusts for the relief of poverty; trusts for the advancement of education; trusts for the advancement of religion; trusts for other purposes beneficial to the community.

Poverty

1.6   The phrase 'aged, impotent and poor people' appears in the preamble to the Charitable Uses Act 1601. This phrase has been interpreted in a number of decisions of the courts. The case of *Joseph Rowntree Memorial Trust Housing Association Ltd* v *Attorney General* (1983) involved self-contained accommodation which was provided for retired persons. The High Court confirmed that this phrase was disjunctive, that is to say formed three alternative classes which could be charitable individually.

1.7   Peter Gibson J was of the view that even though rents were paid for this accommodation, its provision could still be charitable. Further, the individuals selected for accommodation did form a class made up of certain elderly persons who had the need for such accommodation. The scheme was ruled to be a charitable one.

1.8   In Re *Niyazi's Will Trusts* (1978) a gift was left to construct, or contribute to the expenditure in building, a 'working men's hostel' in Cyprus. The question was whether 'working men's hostel' had a sufficient connotation of poverty. Megarry VC was of the view that this bequest was a borderline case just falling over the line into the category of charitable.

1.9   The court could take account of the fact that the area where the hostel was to be built was an impoverished area of great housing need. In the light of the fact that it would assist the poor, the bequest was ruled as charitable.

1.10   For all the categories of charity, there must be an element of public benefit. For the category of poverty, there is no formal requirement that the class of potential beneficiaries forms a section of the public.

1.11   In *Re Scarisbrick* (1951) a residuary estate was held on trust for such relations of the testatrix's son and daughter, who in their opinion, shall be 'in needy circumstances'.

1.12   Jenkins LJ considered that poverty was a relative matter. The choice of the children would restrict any uncertainties as to who fell within the class. We saw, in Unit 4, that uncertainty in a trust could be eliminated by the appointment of a third person, other than the trustees, to determine who fell within the class.

1.13 In particular, the fact that the trust was to relieve poverty amongst a class of relatives of the testator did not mean that it was not charitable. The trust was a valid charitable trust.

1.14 This approach was confirmed in *Dingle v Turner* (1972), where income from a residuary estate was to be held in trust in order to provide pensions to poor employees of a particular company, E. Dingle and Co Ltd. It was held by the House of Lords that it was not necessary for the class to form a section of the public, rather than a private class. The crucial factor was the purpose of the trust. If the purpose clearly was to relieve poverty, by assisting the aged or poor, then even though only a small private class benefitted, it was still charitable.

1.15 On the particular facts, the company employed several hundred employees at the death of the testator, and there were a large number of former employees of that company. It was held by the House of Lords that the class did form a section of the public, although this was not the determining factor.

1.16 Since the purpose of the trust was to relieve poverty, the trust was ruled a valid charitable trust.

Education

1.17 In *I.R.C v McMullen* (1981) a trust was created to assist and provide facilities in schools and universities for playing association football and other sports. The aim of the trust was to promote the physical education and development of pupils.

1.18 Lord Hailsham in the House of Lords was of the view that education had the current meaning in English speech. Further, the definition of education was not static, but a developing one in the light of society's values.

1.19 The court followed an earlier decision of *Re Mariette* (1915) in which it was stated that education included physical as well as academic development. For these reasons, the trust was ruled a valid charitable trust.

1.20 In *Re Koeppler Will Trusts* (1986) an institution was set up, called 'Wilton Park' to formulate international public opinion, and promote greater co-operation in Europe and the West. In particular, a number of conferences had been held at Wilton Park. Politicians from a range of political parties had spoken at these conferences which covered matters such as: the environment; Europe; defence and security; the media, public opinion and decision making in government; the future of modern industrial society.

1.21 Slade LJ, accepted the arguments of Christopher McCall QC, on behalf of the charity and considered that the purposes of Wilton Park were educational for the following reasons: there was an exchange of views, knowledge and information; the matters discussed fell within recognised subjects in higher education; the high quality of the speakers. Hence, the Wilton Park project was ruled to be charitable.

1.22 Where there is no exchange of ideas and discussion, the trust will be held not to be charitable. In *Re Shaw's Will Trusts* (1952) the residuary estate of George Bernard Shaw was left on trust to develop a forty-letter alphabet, and replace the current one with it. Since there was to be no element of teaching this alphabet, it was ruled as not being an educational charitable trust.

1.23 If it is simply a non-charitable purpose trust, as this was, it will then fail, since there must be some ascertainable beneficiaries. This has been previously discussed in Unit 8.

1.24 It is also necessary to show some degree of public benefit in order to be an educational charity. On the particular facts, the participants of the various courses had been selected from a large number of countries. They would benefit from the course and be likely to pass on the information to others.

1.25 The need for public benefit was further developed in *Oppenheim v Tobacco Securities Trust Co Ltd* (1951). A trust fund was created to provide, through the distribution of income or capital, education for the employees and former employees of the British American Tobacco Co Ltd.

1.26 In this category of charitable trust, in contrast to the category of poverty, it was necessary that the class of beneficiaries formed a section of the public. Since the class derived from a common employer, they did not form a section of the community. This meant that the trust lacked sufficient public benefit, and was ruled as not being charitable.

1.27 The House of Lords followed the precedents, which established that children of a particular person would also not constitute a sufficient section of the public.

Religion

1.28 In *Re South Place Ethical Society* (1980), an organisation was set up for the study and cultivation of ethical and rational religious principles. Dillon J, as he then was, held that, since ethics involved man's relations with man, and not god, the organisation was not charitable. In his view two essential characteristics of religion were faith and worship.

1.29 Again, it is necessary for public benefit to be shown in order to be a valid charitable trust within this category. The public benefit does not have to be substantial.

1.30   However, a gift for the purposes of the Carmelite Priory in London was held not to be charitable. The nuns spent all their time in prayer and contemplation, and the Priory was not open to members of the public. Lord Simmonds in the House of Lords confirmed that in order to be charitable, it was necessary for public benefit to be shown. On these facts, as a matter of law, no public benefit had been shown: *Gilmour v Coates* (1949).

1.31   The above case was distinguished in *Neville Estates Ltd v Madden* (1962) where there was a sale of certain land by the trustees of Catford Synagogue. If the activities of the synagogue were charitable, the land would be held on charitable trusts, and would require approval of the Charity Commissioners in order to be sold. The issue before the High Court was whether the land was held on a charitable trust.

1.32   Cross J could distinguish *Gilmour v Coates* (1949) on the basis that the synagogue contained members who spent their lives in the outside world. The court would assume that by attending a place of worship, and then mixing with the general public, a public benefit would result. It was held that the trust was a charitable trust.

1.33   In *Re Hetherington (Deceased)* (1990), a gift for saying masses for the testatrix, her husband, and her close relatives was upheld as being charitable. Nicholas Browne-Wilkinson J, as he then was held that the celebration of a religious rite in public was of sufficient public benefit to be charitable.

Other purposes beneficial to the community

1.34   This a wide-ranging category. Some of the important decisions are considered below.

1.35   It is established that a trust for a private, non-profit making hospital is charitable. Such a service was needed by all, and showed a clear and strong public benefit: *Re Resch's Will Trusts* (1969).

1.36   Another trust which was regarded as charitable and of benefit to the community concerned the Incorporated Council of Law Reporting, a manufacturer of law reports, which applied to be registered as a charity.

1.37   Russell LJ recognised that the preamble to the Charitable Uses Act 1601 gave examples which, over the centuries, were regarded as guides in cases coming before the courts. These examples could be used by way of analogy with the particular case arising for decision before the court.

1.38   On other occasions, the courts will look to the general purposes behind the preamble.

1.39   In addition, the judge considered that the courts had power to allow new charitable trusts which had purposes beneficial to the community, even though they did not fall within either the literal wording or the general purposes of the preamble.

1.40   The provision of law reports was not purely an educational purpose, but it did advance the knowledge of law. The Incorporated Council of Law Reporting would therefore be granted charitable status: *Incorporated Council of Law Reporting for England and Wales* v *Attorney-General* (1972).

1.41   In *Scottish Burial Reform and Cremation Society* v *Glasgow Corporation* (1968), the society was an organisation whose objects were to promote, in Scotland, reform in the methods of burial, and introduce inexpensive methods of burial. This organisation was held to be charitable, on the basis that it fell within purposes beneficial to the community, and was within the spirit of the preamble.

1.42   Lord Reid discussed the approach of the courts. Originally, they looked for some analogy between an object in the preamble and the case they were dealing with. Subsequently, they merely sought an analogy between the particular case they were dealing with and some previous decision of the court. Then, if there was a clearly specified object for the benefit of the public at large, the courts would look for any previous case in which there was the slightest resemblance to the situation with which they were dealing.

1.43   A trust to promote a particular industry, trade, or craft, will be held to be charitable. A charitable status can be achieved in a number of ways, by the provision of training or accommodation, or a place of recreation: *Commissioners of Inland Revenue* v *White* (1980).

1.44   Trusts for the provision of sport and recreation are now governed by the Recreational Charities Act 1958.

1.45   Section 1(1) of this act provides that recreational trusts are, and shall be deemed always to have been, charitable. There is an important proviso, namely that the facilities must be provided in the interests of social welfare, and the trust must be of public benefit.

1.46   Section 1(2) of this act states that the interests of social welfare will not be satisfied unless certain conditions are satisfied: first, that the facilities are provided to improve the conditions of life of those for whom those facilities are intended; second, that either of the following are satisfied;

   a) the persons using such facilities have need for them because of their age, disability, income, or social and economic circumstances, or

b) the facilities are also available to females in the general community.

1.47 Section 1(3) of this act provides that where such facilities are provided by village halls, community centres, or women's institutes, they will also be charitable.

1.48 In *Guild* v *I.R.C.* (1992), the scope of this act was considered. The case involved a bequest to a town council to assist it to provide sports in a particular sports centre, or some similar purpose connected with sport.

1.49 Lord Keith rejected the proposition that it was necessary for the facilities to be provided with the object of improving the conditions of life for persons who suffer some form of social disadvantage.

1.50 In his view, it was sufficient if the facilities were provided simply with the objective of improving the conditions of life of members of the general community. On the facts, this was satisfied, and the bequest was ruled charitable.

1.51 Where funds are provided to assist with various disaster situations, the question is whether they are charitable as being for purposes beneficial to the community. In *Re Hobourn Areo Components Ltd's Air Raid Distress Fund, Ryan* v *Forrest* (1946), it was held that such assistance was not a charitable purpose.

1.52 The objective, in this case, was to assist employees of a particular company whose homes had been damaged by air raids. The fund was provided by employees of this company.

1.53 Since the fund was to assist particular employees, it was held by the Court of Appeal, that it was not of sufficient public benefit to be of purposes beneficial to the community. This supports the approach taken in the House of Lords in *Oppenheim* v *Tobacco Securities Trust Co Ltd* (1951) discussed above. Non-charitable purpose trusts of this type have been considered in Unit 8.

1.54 A different approach was taken in *Re North Devon and West Somerset Relief Fund Trusts, Hylton* v *Wright* (1953) because the fund was for the benefit of the general community.

1.55 A fund was created to assist the general community after sudden, violent flooding. The fund was also set up to assist holiday-makers, and anyone else in the community who had suffered. The appeal asked for funds not only from persons who lived in the West Country, but also any person 'who has known and loved Lynmouth and the quiet villages of north Devon and west Somerset'.

1.56 The High Court was of the view that this fund was set up to alleviate hardship and distress caused by this flood not only to the local community, but also to those within the area when the disaster occurred. The fund was held to be a charitable trust.

1.57 It is established that a trust which is designed to achieve certain political objectives will not be held to be charitable. Lord Simmonds gave a reason for this approach in *National Anti-Vivisection Society v Inland Revenue Commissioners* (1948), where he stated that the courts could not tell whether a proposed change in the law would be for the public benefit.

1.58 This approach was followed in *McGovern v Attorney-General* (1982), where Slade J, as he then was, was of the view that Amnesty International could not be a charitable trust since its purposes were political. A further reason was given as to why a trust which sought to change the law would not be held to be charitable. The law as it stands would be regarded as correct, and the purposes of the trust would be considered by the courts as an usurpation of the position of the legislature.

1.59 This reasoning would apply even where the proposed change was to the laws of another country. In addition, this would raise the further question as to whether the trust should be upheld as a matter of public policy, since the trust could jeopardise relations between this country and another country. Issues of this type concerning illegality, and forfeiture clauses, have been previously considered in Units 1 and 5.

1.60 This approach was confirmed in *Webb v O'Doherty and others* (1991) where a student union sought to use funds to support a campaign against the Gulf war.

1.61 Hoffmann J, as he then was, confirmed that it was appropriate following *Attorney-General v Ross* (1986) for a student body to discuss political matters.

1.62 However, there was a distinction between this legitimate activity, and campaigning on a political issue. In his view, the law would allow political persuasion only where it was the minor incidental consequence of carrying out the main educational object. The student union would be restrained by injunction from spending its funds on campaigning in this way.

1.63 Trusts for other purposes which are beneficial to the community must also be of public benefit. Where a residuary estate was left on trust to provide a refuge for animals, the Court of Appeal held that it lacked sufficient public benefit: *Re Grove Grady* (1929). This approach was not followed in the more recent decision of *Re Murawski's Trust* (1971) concerning an animal sanctuary which was held to be charitable.

1.64 These decisions do suggest that what is of public benefit is really a subjective matter. In a trust to assist animals, where one of the purposes was more specific, i.e. to facilitate more humane methods in killing animals, it was upheld as being charitable: *Re Wedgwood* (1915).

Exclusively charitable

1.65 The case law provides that in order to be charitable, the bequest, trust or organisation, must be exclusively charitable. This follows as a result of the important decision in *Chichester Diocesan Fund and Board of Finance (Incorporated) v Simpson* (1944) where a residuary estate was left for charitable or benevolent objects. It was held by the House of Lords that 'benevolent' was not only not charitable, but uncertain. These words were alternatives, and the bequest was not exclusively charitable. The bequest was held void, and went to the next of kin.

1.66 This decision has been reversed by the Charitable Trusts (Validation) Act 1954. Where property could be used for some purposes which are exclusively charitable, and also for other purposes which are not exclusively charitable, then it will still be charitable: section 1(1) of the act. Section 1(2) of this act deems the whole of the declared objects to be charitable. This act applies after December 16th 1952.

2 Cy-près

2.1 We have seen the inherent jurisdiction of the courts to appoint and remove trustees in Unit 9, to award remuneration in Unit 10, and to allow the variation and exporting of a trust in Unit 12. There is also the inherent jurisdiction of the courts to enable property left on charitable trusts to be applied for an analogous purpose in certain situations. This is called *cy-près*. This has been further developed by various acts of parliament, in particular, sections 13 and 14 of the Charities Act 1993.

Initial failure

2.2 There can be a situation where a person leaves property by will to a charity which is in existence when the will is made but not at the date of death. It may have ceased to exist altogether, it may have moved, or it may have merged with some other institution. There can also be a situation where a person leaves property by will to a charity which has not yet been set up, but which will be, if sufficient funds are raised. For one reason or another, sufficient funds are not raised.

2.3 If a charitable intention on the part of the donor (testator) is shown, then the monies or property left by the testator can be applied *cy-près*.

2.4 Say, we have a fund to provide a 'soup kitchen' for the sick and needy in a particular area, and the soup kitchen is not set up because there are insufficient funds to purchase, or lease, the land on which this soup kitchen could be set up.

2.5   If it can be seen that in effect the donation is given for charitable purposes in a particular area, a scheme of *cy-près* will be ordered by the court. The monies could go to other charities in that area which are concerned with provision for the sick and needy, or alternatively charities with similar object outside the area: *Biscoe v Jackson* (1887).

2.6   If the testator leaves monies or property to a number of charitable institutions, this will show a general charitable intention.

2.7   In contrast, if the testator leaves property to a particular charitable organisation, identifying with care that particular charity, which has ceased to exist at death of the testator, it will be difficult for the court to find a general charitable intention: *Re Harwood* (1936).

2.8   If the residuary estate is left for charitable purposes which cannot be applied *cy-près* because there is no charitable intention, then the estate will go on resulting trust for the next of kin.

2.9   There is also a further rule that if the bequest is to an unincorporated charity, that it must take effect as a gift for a charitable purpose. Thus, where a particular charitable body has ceased to exist, if that body was unincorporated, a general charitable intention, although difficult, can more readily be inferred: *Re Finger's Will Trusts* (1972).

Subsequent failure

2.10   A different situation from the above is where the money or property is validly left to a charity, which exists at the date of death of the testator. If that charity subsequently ceases to exist, and the donation still exists as a separate entity and can be identified, then the monies or property can always be applied *cy-près*: *Re Slevin* (1891).

2.11   In *Re Slevin* (1891), the cessation of the charity took place a short period after the donation took effect, and could still be identified.

2.12   Similarly, where monies were left to provide a stained glass window in a place of worship, then if only part of those monies are used to carry out that purpose, and there is a surplus, then the surplus could be applied *cy-près*. In this situation, it was not necessary for charitable intention to be shown: *Re King* (1923).

Charities Act 1993 section 13

2.13   This section adds to and widens section 13 of the Charities Act 1960, which also provided for *cy-près* to take place in certain circumstances.

2.14   This new section enables *cy-près* to take place, on direction of the court, where any of the alternative following circumstances apply, so that the original purposes of the charitable gift:

- first, cannot be carried out;

- second, provide only a partial use for the property given;

- third, can be more effectively carried out in conjunction with other similar purposes;

- fourth, cannot any longer be carried out in the particular area laid down by the terms of the gift;

- fifth, are now adequately provided by other means, or are no longer charitable, or can no longer be effectively and suitably carried out: Charities Act 1993, section 13(1).

2.15 By the Charities Act 1993, section 13(5), a trustee is placed under a duty to ensure that property held on trust for charitable purposes is applied *cy-près*. The general duties of trustees have been considered in Unit 10, and breach of trustees' duties considered in Unit 12.

2.16 For the possible use of section 13 of the Charities Act 1993, as regards independent schools, see Joseph Jaconelli: Independent Schools, Purpose Trusts And Human Rights (1996) *The Conveyancer* 24.

Charities Act 1993 section 14

2.17 This section provides for the operation of *cy-près* for property given, by unknown or disclaiming donors, for specific charitable purposes which fail.

Charities Act 1993 section 16

2.18 Where a court directs a scheme to be applied, it can refer the matter to the Charity Commissioners for them to set up a scheme on such terms as they deem appropriate: Charities Act 1993, section 16(2).

Charities Act 1993 section 74 and 75

2.19 These sections apply to unincorporated charities. Section 74 enables a charity whose annual gross income is below £5,000 to transfer all of its property or modify its objects. Section 75 enables a charity whose annual gross income is below £1000 to spend its capital.

Charities Act 1993 section 33

2.20 Where there is a closure of a charity, then proceedings can be brought by any person 'interested' in that charity, or by two or more inhabitants in the area of that charity if it is a local charity: Charities Act 1993, section 33(1).

2.21 A school, run by Buckfast Abbey for those aged between 8 and 13, was closed, against the strong objections of a large number of parents. They claimed that the correct procedures for closing the school had not been followed.

2.22 These facts are summarised from a short case-note of the unreported decision of Arden J in *Gunning* v *Buckfast Abbey* 9th June 1994, by Richard Nolan. He makes the point, in this case-note, that this section enables a large number of individuals to bring proceedings, with permission of the Charity Commissioners, to secure the correct administration of that charity. Case summary: Who is interested in charity? *Gunning & Others* v *Buckfast Abbey Trustees Registered & Another*, Vol 9, No. 4 (1995) *Trust Law International* 130.

3 Charities Act 1993

3.1 See, generally, the discussion of the provisions of this act by Jean Warburton 1993 Vol 1. *Current Law* 1994.

3.2 The actual wording of many of the important sections in this act are contained in Hayton and Marshall: *Commentary and Cases on the Law of Trusts and Equitable Remedies* (10th ed. D J Hayton) 1996, and in Maudsley & Burn's: *Trusts & Trustees Cases & Materials* (Fifth ed. E H Burn) 1996.

General

3.3 The Charities Act 1993, section 3 provides for a system of registration of charities. The Charities Act 1993, section 4(1) provides that an institution will be conclusively presumed to be a charity whilst on, and for the period it was on, that register.

3.4 Section 4(3) of this act gives a right of appeal to the Chancery Division of the High Court against any decision of the Charity Commissioners:

- to register

- refusal to register

- to remove from the register

- not to remove from the register.

3.5 Where an institution has been held by the courts not to be a charitable institution, that decision can be subsequently considered anew by the Charity Commissioners. This applies where the circumstances of the charity have changed, or where a later judicial decision in a different case affects the previous ruling by the courts: Charities Act 1993, section 4(5).

Appointment and removal of trustees

3.6 This has been previously discussed in Unit 9. The particular provisions of the Charities Act 1993 which relate to the appointment or removal of trustees will now be considered.

3.7 By the Charities Act 1993, section 2(1) there is an officer known as the 'official custodian' whose function is to act as trustee for charities. The Charity Commissioners, who regulate charities, can appoint an official custodian: Charities Act 1993, section 2(2).

3.8 Property held in charitable trust can be vested in the official custodian: Charities Act 1993, sections 21 and 22.

3.9 Section 18 of this act enables the Charity Commissioners, where there has been misconduct or mismanagement in the administration of a charity, to suspend any trustee for a maximum period of no longer than 12 months. In this situation the Charity Commissioners can appoint additional trustees as they consider necessary for the proper administration of that charity: section 18(1) Charities Act 1993.

3.10 A person shall be disqualified from being a trustee of a charity where any of the following are satisfied. Where he has:

- been convicted of any offence involving dishonesty or deception

- been made bankrupt

- been removed from the office of trustee under section 18 (discussed immediately above)

- been disqualified as a company director: Charities Act 1993, section 72(1).

3.11 A person who acts as a trustee of a charity whilst disqualified commits a criminal offence: Charities Act 1993, section 73(1).

3.12 The trustees of a charity can apply to the Charity Commissioners to be incorporated: Charities Act 1993 section 50(1). The Charity Commissioners can grant approval for this, if they consider such incorporation to be in the interests of the charity: Charities Act 1993 section 50(1)(b). Various provisions connected with such incorporation are contained in sections 51 to 62 of the act.

Investment

3.13 The position as regards trustees' duties in relation to making investments has been previously considered in Unit 11. This part of this Unit is concerned with charitable trustees' duties of investment.

3.14 There is a general power to enable the trustees of a charity to obtain advice from the Charity Commissioners: Charities Act 1993, section 29(1). A trustee who acts on such advice will be deemed to have acted in accordance with the terms of the trust: Charities Act 1993, section 29(2). The general position as regards breach of trust has been previously considered in Unit 12.

3.15 This section would enable trustees of a charity to obtain advice from the Charity Commissioners in relation to the making of investments.

3.16 Section 29 is a re-enactment of section 24 of the Charities Act 1960. The Charity Commissioners have stated in their annual report in 1986, in relation to section 24, that they will give advice where it is necessary for the proper administration of the charity, or to prevent a misapplication of its funds.

3.17 Section 24(1) of the Charities Act 1993 enables common investment schemes, for any two or more charities, to be introduced. These schemes will be under the control of trustees appointed to manage such funds.

3.18 Section 25(1) of the Charities Act 1993 enables common deposit funds, for any two or more charities, to be introduced. These schemes will be under the control of trustees appointed to manage these deposits.

3.19 Section 28(1) of the Charities Act 1993 enables the Charity Commissioners to give directions in relation to dormant bank accounts of charities, where the trustees of that charity, or the charity itself, cannot be found. An account is deemed to be dormant if no transaction has been carried out within 5 years immediately before the date that the Charity Commissioners have been informed that the account is dormant by a deposit-taking institution (including a bank) or building society.

3.20 The Secretary of State can make orders enabling trustees to invest funds equally between narrower and wider range investments, as provided by the Trustee Investments Act 1961: Charities Act 1993, section 70(1)(a). This act has been previously discussed in Unit 11. The Secretary of State is given the power to further relax the rules relating to investments in shares and gilts: Charities Act 1993, section 70(1)(b).

3.21 The Secretary of State can make orders enabling trustees to invest in other types of property: Charities Act 1993, section 71.

Land

3.22 Before dealing with particular sections of the Charities Act 1993 relating to charitable trusts of land, it is appropriate to deal briefly with two other statutes which relate to land held on charitable trusts.

3.23 Trusts of land held on charitable trusts are now simply held on trust, and not as settled land: Trusts of Land and Appointment of Trustees Act 1996. This act has been previously considered in Unit 7.

3.24 There are no restrictions on numbers of trustees of land: Trustee Act 1925, section 34. Trusteeship is considered in Unit 9.

3.25 Sections 36(1) and 36(2) of the Charities Act 1993 provide that land held on charitable trust cannot be sold, leased or disposed of without court order, or approval of the Charity Commissioners, where the sale is to a connected person such as the donor of the land, an officer, employee or trustee of the charity.

3.26 Jean Warburton makes the point, in her annotations to the act in *Current Law*, that where the sale would amount to a breach of the trustees' fiduciary duties, then court order or approval would be required.

3.27 It is established that a trustee cannot sell property to himself. If this is done, the sale can be avoided by the beneficiary, who can seek to set it aside by court order, however fair the transaction: *Tito v Waddell (No. 2) (1977)*.

3.28 This rule is known as the self-dealing rule: *Re Thompson's Settlement, Thompson v Thompson* (1986). Vinelott J was of the view in this case that the self-dealing rule is an application of a wider principle that a person cannot put himself in a position where there is a conflict of duties. Fiduciary duties, including conflict of duty and interest, have been previously considered in Unit 10.

3.29 Where the trustees propose to sell land held on charitable trust, they must, before the agreement to sell:

● obtain a written report from a qualified surveyor acting exclusively for the charity on the proposed sale

● advertise the property to be sold unless advised not to do this

● after consideration of this report, satisfy themselves that they have the best terms which can reasonably be obtained: sections 36(3)(a), 36(3)(b), 36(3)(c) of the Charities Act 1993.

3.30 Trustees are able to mortgage land held on charitable trust, provided that they have obtained proper advice in writing on the following matters: Charities Act 1993, sections 38(1) and 38(2).

3.31 The following matters must be advised in writing:

● whether the loan is necessary

● whether the terms of the loan are reasonable

● whether the charity is able to repay the loan: sections 38(3)(a), 38(3)(b), 38(3)(c).

3.32 The person giving the advice must be a person who is believed by the trustees to be properly qualified and experienced, and who has no conflict of duty and interest, sections 38(4)(a), 38(4)(b) of the Charities Act 1993.

3.33 Where the trustees change, property can be vested in the new trustees: Charities Act 1993, section 83(1).

Summary

Now that you have completed this Unit, you should understand:

☐ **the main features of the law of charities.**

Self-assessment questions

1 What is a charitable (public) trust?

2 What is a trust for the relief of poverty?

3 What is a trust for the advancement of education?

4 What is a trust for the advancement of religion?

5 What is a trust for other purposes beneficial to the community?

6 What is the *Cy-près* doctrine?

7 Describe the major provisions of the Charities Act 1993

Exam-style question

A retired member of the staff of your bank has recently died and it has been found that she left a home-drawn will appointing the bank as executor and trustee. The residuary estate is to be divided into three parts and the will states that the trustee is to hold both the capital and income of one such part for each of the following purposes:

a) 'to encourage the preservation of the world's rainforests',

b) 'to assist the Vicar and Churchwardens of St John's Church, Birmingham (her local church) in parish work'.

c) 'to provide sports equipment and prizes (in memory of her late husband) for snooker tournaments for staff of your bank under the age of 25'.

Discuss each of these trusts and explain whether any of them are charitable.

[Autumn 1995]

(The answers are given in the Appendix)

Caselist for Unit 14 An Outline of the Law of Charities

The Charitable Uses Act 1601.

Commissioners for Special Purposes of Income Tax v Pemsel [1891] AC 531.

Joseph Rowntree Memorial Trust Housing Association Ltd v Attorney General [1983] Ch 159.

Re Niyazi's Will Trusts [1978] 1 WLR 910.

Re Scarisbrick, Cockshott v Public Trustee [1951] Ch 622.

Dingle v Turner [1972] AC 601.

I.R.C v McMullen [1981] AC 1.

Re Mariette, Mariette v Aldenham School Governing Body [1915] Ch 284.

Re Koeppler Will Trusts, Barclays Bank Trust Co Ltd v Slack [1986] Ch 423.

Re Shaw's Will Trusts, National Provincial Bank Ltd v National City Bank [1952] Ch 163.

Oppenheim v Tobacco Securities Trust Co Ltd [1951] AC 297.

Re South Place Ethical Society [1980] 1 WLR 1565.

Gilmour v Coates [1949] AC 426.

Neville Estates Ltd v Madden [1962] Ch 832.

Re Hetherington (Deceased), Gibbs v McDonnell [1990] Ch 1.

Re Resch's Will Trusts, Le Cras v Perpetual Trustee Co Ltd [1969] 1 AC 514.

Incorporated Council of Law Reporting for England and Wales v Attorney-General [1972] Ch 73.

Scottish Burial Reform and Cremation Society Ltd v Glasgow Corporation [1968] AC 138.

Commissioners of Inland Revenue v White, Re Clerkenwell Green Association [1980] TR 155.

The Recreational Charities Act 1958, sections 1(1), 1(2), 1(3).

Guild v I.R.C. [1992] 2 AC 310.

Re Hobourn Areo Components Ltd's Air Raid Distress Fund, Ryan v Forrest [1946] Ch 86.

Oppenheim v Tobacco Securities Trust Co Ltd [1951] AC 297.

Re North Devon and West Somerset Relief Fund Trusts, Baron Hylton v Wright [1953] 1 WLR 1260.

National Anti-Vivisection Society v Inland Revenue Commissioners [1948] AC 31.

McGovern v Attorney-General [1982] Ch 321.

Webb v *O'Doherty and others. The Times* February 11th 1991.

Attorney-General v *Ross* [1986] 1 WLR 252.

Re Grove Grady, Plowden v *Lawrence* [1929] 1 Ch 557.

Re Murawski's Trust, Lloyds Bank Ltd v *Royal Society for the Prevention of Cruelty to Animals* [1971] 1 WLR 707.

Re Wedgwood, Allen v *Wedgwood* [1915] 1 Ch 113.

Chichester Diocesan Fund and Board of Finance (Incorporated) v *Simpson* [1944] AC 341.

The Charitable Trusts (Validation) Act 1954, sections 1(1), 1(2).

Biscoe v *Jackson* (1887) 35 Ch D 460.

Re Harwood, Coleman v *Innes* [1936] Ch 285.

Re Finger's Will Trusts, Turner v *Ministry of Health* [1972] 2 Ch 286.

Re Slevin, Slevin v *Hepburn* [1891] 2 Ch 236.

Re King, Kerr v *Bradley* [1923] 1 Ch 243.

The Charities Act 1993, sections 2(1), 2(2), 3, 4(1), 4(3), 4(5), 13, 13(1), 13(5), 14, 16, 16(2), 18, 18(1), 21, 22, 24(1), 25(1), 28(1), 29, 29(1), 29(2), 33(1), 36(1), 36(2), 36(3)(a)(b)(c), 38(1), 38(2), 38(3)(a)(b)(c), 38(4)(a)(b), 50(1), 50(1)(b), 70(1)(a), 70(1)(b), 71, 72(1), 73(1), 74, 75, 83(1).

Joseph Jaconelli: Independent Schools, Purpose Trusts And Human Rights (1996) *The Conveyancer* 24.

Who is interested in charity? *Gunning & Others* v *Buckfast Abbey Trustees Registered & Another* Vol 9, No. 4. (1995) *Trust Law International* 130.

Jean Warburton 1993 Vol 1. *Current Law* 1994 Sweet and Maxwell.

Hayton and Marshall *Commentary and Cases on The Law of Trusts and Equitable Remedies* (10th ed. D J Hayton) 1996 Sweet and Maxwell.

Maudsley & Burn's *Trusts & Trustees Cases & Materials* (Fifth ed. E H Burn) 1996 Butterworths.

The Trustee Act 1925, section 34.

Tito v *Waddell (No 2)* [1977] Ch 106.

Re Thompson's Settlement, Thompson v *Thompson* [1986] Ch 99.

15

An Outline of the Taxation Aspects of Trusts

Objectives

After studying this Unit, you should be able to:

● **understand how tax affects trusts.**

1 Introduction

1.1　Funds can be put into a trust for a range of reasons. An obvious reason, would be where it was felt that a beneficiary was not mature enought to manage his affairs, and the trust enables others to take the decisions as to how to invest the capital of the trust fund, and how much income or capital to distribute to that beneficiary. More may be advanced to the beneficiary as he gets older, or has greater need of funds.

1.2　This policy has been adopted in relation to the Trusts of Land and Appointment of Trusts Act 1996, where the trustees are able to delegate their functions to a beneficiary who is absolutely entitled to an interest: Trusts of Land and Appointment of Trustees Act 1996, section 9(1). This act also enables consultation to take place between trustee and beneficiary, where the beneficiary is absolutely entitled and is over the age of 18: Trusts of Land and Appointment of Trustees Act 1996, section 11(1). This act has been previously discussed in a number of Units.

1.3　Other reasons for setting up a trust include those of privacy and confidentiality. With a secret trust, which will be discussed in Chapter 16, this can be a prime reason. The will of the testator, or testatrix, is a public document, but the terms of any fully or half (partly) secret trust will remain confidential.

1.4　A large estate can be put into trust to enable other professionals to manage it, particularly for choosing investments. The duties of trustees have been considered in Units 10 and 12, and the duties with regard to making investments have been considered in Unit 11.

1.5   An obvious reason for setting up a trust is not simply for convenience, but to avoid or minimise taxation. We have already seen, in Unit 14, that trust funds can be partially or totally exported. In some cases, taxation plays a partial or central reason for this.

1.6   The approach of the courts to tax avoidance is a crucial matter, and will be discussed immediately below, before a detailed account is given of the various taxes that effect trusts.

2 Tax Avoidance

2.1   There are a large number of important decisions on this. One recent and relevant one of the House of Lords is *Inland Revenue Commissioners* v *McGukian* (1997). The case concerned Mr McGukian and his wife who were both resident and domiciled in the United Kingdom. They each owned half of the capital of a particular company Ballinamore, (B) which had accumulated a substantial surplus.

2.2   In order to avoid tax, the shares in B were transferred into a trust, and the trustee was a company called Shurltrust (S) based in Guernsey. This company then asssigned (transferred) the rights to receive the income from the shares in B to another company Mallardchoice, (M) incorporated in the United Kingdom. M was associated with a Mr Taylor, the tax consultant who devised the scheme.

2.3   Subsequently, B declared a substantial dividend of just over Ir. £400,000 which was paid by cheque to M. M paid 99% of this sum (deducting a small amount for commission) to S by a cheque.

2.4   The Inland Revenue sought to attack the scheme on the basis that it was caught by section 478 of the Income and Corporation Taxes Act 1978, briefly considered previously in Unit 13.

2.5   Lord Brown-Wilkinson recognised that a number of conditions had to be satisfied in order for this anti-avoidance of tax section to apply:

- first, that a transfer of assets has been made by the taxpayer by virtue of which income has become payable to a person outside the United Kingdom

- second, a non-resident person receives income

- third, the tax payer or his assistant has power to enjoy the income of the non-resident

- fourth, because of these arrangements, the taxpayer has power to enjoy this income.

2.6   The first, third and fourth factors were agreed. The issue before the House of Lords was whether the second factor was satisfied. The taxpayer's argument was that when Shurltrust received 99% of B's dividends, it had received capital.

2.7   Their Lordships unanimously held that the scheme was a pre-ordained, circular series of steps designed to avoid taxation. Such steps were then to be disregarded. It followed that the 'real' transaction was paying a dividend to S. The second factor was satisfied, and the taxpayer was liable to tax.

2.8   This case shows the use of a trust to seek to avoid taxation, although the particular scheme did not succeed.

3 Income Tax

3.1   The author wishes to acknowledge the particular assistance derived from Income Tax: Maudsley and Burn's *Trusts & Trustees Cases and Materials* (Fifth ed. E H Burn) 1996, Chapter 13.

3.2   In general terms, it is the trustees who are liable for income tax, and further, are liable to pay income tax on the whole of the income produced by the trust fund.

3.3   In general terms, the beneficiaries become liable for income tax when they receive income from the trust.

3.4   Professor Edward Burn makes the point that trusts can be distinguished from individuals in that individuals are liable to higher rate income tax whereas trusts are usually taxed at basic rate only. However, he makes the further point that the trustees can be liable to pay an additional rate of 10% where no beneficiary is currently entitled to receive trust income. A discretionary trust, considered in Unit 4 would be a classic example of the type of situation where the additional rate is payable.

3.5   Professor Burn makes an additional point that, in contrast to the above, where a beneficiary does have an interest in possession in the trust, then it is the beneficiary who is liable to pay income tax, and not the trustees. This concept, and the important decision: *Pearson* v *I.R.C.* are dealt with in Unit 11.

3.6   Say the trust fund makes £1,000 gross income and the trustees pay all of it to a particular beneficiary. The trustees deduct 24% basic rate tax, i.e. £240 and transfer £760 net to the beneficiary. If the beneficiary is liable to a higher rate of 40% tax, then further income tax of 16% of £1,000 will be payable by the beneficiary.

3.7 Professor Burn deals with a number of anti-avoidance of tax provisions. In particular he deals with the Finance Act 1995, section 660A whereby a settlor will be deemed to have an interest in a trust if income could become payable to the settlor.

3.8 A previous anti-avoidance of tax provision gave rise to litigation. In *Re Vandervell's Trusts (No. 2)* (1974) Vandervell (V) wished to make a gift of income to the Royal College of Surgeons to enable a Chair in Pharmacology to be set up for a short initial time, until another benefactor came along and gave further funds.

3.9 He transferred shares to them and put the shares into their name so that they could take the income as a result of being the legal and equitable owners of these shares. Once the Chair had been set up for a period of time, he wished the shares to be returned, because he would no longer be funding that Chair.

3.10 In order to do this he created an option, which would enable the shares to be returned into his ownership. V did not particularly want the shares back, so he created an option which could be exercised by a company, called Vandervell Trustees Ltd, VT, a trust, which had been specifically created for the benefit of V's children.

3.11 However, when the option was created, V did not spell out the terms upon which VT would exercise this option. In particular, he did not specify in whose favour the option would be exercised.

3.12 This was quite important, for if V failed to divest himself of his interest in the shares he would then be liable to additional income tax under the provisions of the Income Tax Act 1952

3.13 There was considerable litigation in the matter, and the Inland Revenue sought to assess V to higher (additional) rates of income tax.

3.14 In *Vandervell v I.R.C.*(1967) Lord Wilberforce in the House of Lords, and Lord Denning MR in subsequent proceedings in the Court of Appeal, in *Re Vandervell's Trusts (No. 2)* (1974) were of the view, that:

● first, this option was vested in VT

● second, it was vested on trusts which were not defined at the time the option was created but which would possibly be defined later.

3.15 Since V had not sufficiently declared who were to be the beneficiaries of this trust, there was an automatic resulting trust in his favour to fill the gap in this equitable ownership. Automatic resulting trusts have previously been considered in Unit 3. V therefore kept an equitable interest in these shares and was liable to income tax.

3.16   In *Re Vandervell's Trusts (No. 2)* (1974) Lord Denning MR confirmed that when V expressly and clearly declared, together with VT that the shares were held on trust for his children and that all dividends were those of his children, then he had divested himself of any equitable interest in those shares. At this point V was no longer liable for income tax.

3.17   If a similar situation to Vandervell were to come before the courts today, it is suggested that for the period when V was a beneficiary under a resulting trust of the shares in Vandervell Products Ltd, he could have received a dividend in relation to those shares, and would, potentially, be liable for income tax under the Finance Act 1995, section 660A as a beneficiary with an interest in a trust.

4 Capital Gains Tax

4.1   The author wishes to acknowledge the particular assistance derived from Capital Gains Tax: Maudsley and Burn's *Trusts & Trustees Cases and Materials* (Fifth ed. E H Burn) 1996, Chapter 14.

4.2   Professor Burn makes the point that setting up a trust will be a disposal, by the settlor, of all the property transferred into the settlement: the Taxation of Chargeable Gains Act 1992, section 70. The settlor will be liable for any chargeable gains at that point. Once the trust is set up, then, as a general principle, the normal rules relating to chargeable gains apply to that trust.

4.3   We know as a matter of general trust law that once the trust is constituted, the settlor will lose his entire ownership. The legal interest will move to the trustee, and the equitable interest will move to the beneficiary: *Paul v Paul* (1882). This has been previously considered in Unit 2.

4.4   Professor Burn deals with two exceptions to these general rules relating to capital gains in his chapter. They are of importance, and require elaboration.

4.5   First, where a settlor retains an interest in a trust, then he is liable for capital gains instead of the trustees: the Taxation of Chargeable Gains Act 1992, sections 77(1) and 77(2). The trustees are normally liable for any chargeable gains if the settlor does not retain any interest in the trust.

4.6   Second, where a beneficiary becomes 'absolutely entitled' to the trust property, then there is a disposal: the Taxation of Chargeable Gains Act 1992, section 71(1).

4.7   An illustration of this can be seen in the decision in *Harthan v Mason (Inspector of Taxes)* (1980) involving the meaning of 'absolutely entitled' under previous legislation. The Taxation of Chargeable Gains Act 1992 was a codification of previous legislation.

4.8   A trust of property was set up for Edward Harthan, Victor Harthan and Dora Harthan (two brothers and a sister) in joint equal shares. As a result of the subsequent death of Victor Harthan, Edward and Dora became jointly entitled in equal shares. The property was sold.

4.9   Fox J, as he then was, held that Edward Harthan was 'absolutely entitled' to an interest (half share) in the trust and was liable to pay capital gains with regard to this half share. Fox J held that he was still 'absolutely entitled' to a half share in the trust property even though he was a beneficiary.

5 Inheritance Tax

5.1   The author wishes to acknowledge the particular assistance derived from Inheritance Tax: Maudsley and Burn's *Trusts & Trustees Cases and Materials* (Fifth ed. E H Burn) 1996, Chapter 15.

5.2   The Inheritance Tax Act 1984 and the Finance Act 1986 taxes transfers or deemed transfers of capital by the owner.

5.3   Professor Burn makes the point that where a beneficiary is entitled to an interest in possession in a trust (this concept, and the important decision *Pearson* v *I.R.C.* are dealt with in Unit 11), and if anything happens to, or affects the interests of, the beneficiary so that he:

● first, ceases to be entitled to that interest, other than on the occasion of the death of the beneficiary

● second, assigns, transfers or disposes of that interest

● third, enters into a surrender of that interest

then a transfer of value will occur: Inheritance Tax Act 1984, sections 49 to 57.

5.4   Professor Burn makes the additional point that where a beneficiary is not entitled to an interest in possession (such as a discretionary trust dealt with in Unit 4), then it will be subject to a tax charge every 10 years from the date of its creation: Inheritance Tax Act 1984, section 64.

5.5   Professor Burn makes the further point that certain types of trust, with no interest in possession, are given favoured treatment, and are not liable for this 10 year charge. These include:

● first, charitable trusts

● second, compensation funds held for employees or those in a particular profession

● third, discretionary trusts for employees of a particular company, or their relatives, or their dependants (the trust in *McPhail* v *Doulton*, dealt with in Unit 4 would fall into this category)

- fourth, accumulation and maintenance trusts (the Trustee Act 1925, section 31 dealing with duties of maintenance of minors has been previously dealt with in Unit 11)

5.6 Professor Burn deals in some detail with the definition and advantages of accumulation and maintenance trusts. Below is a summary of his main points.

5.7 In order to qualify as an accumulation and maintenance trust, certain conditions must all be fulfilled:

- first, no beneficiary has an interest in possession (see above in this Unit)

- second, at least one beneficiary will gain an interest in possession in, or become absolutely entitled to, the trust property

- third, income not distributed is accumulated (see Unit 11 where the statutory duties of trustees as regards maintenance and accumulation have been previously considered)

- fourth, the beneficiaries have a common grandparent.

5.8 Where these conditions are satisfied, then this trust will have a number of advantages:

- first, no liability for the 10 year charge

- second, no liability for the trustees or beneficiary, when the beneficiary becomes absolutely entitled to the trust fund or acquires an interest in possession

- third, no liability for the trustees or other beneficiaries on the death of any beneficiary.

5.9 Further, a transfer by a settlor into an accumulation and maintenance trust will constitute a 'potentially exempt transfer' (PET), so that if the settlor survives for seven years after this transfer, it will be totally exempt from Inheritance Tax.

5.10 Recently, a scheme to avoid Inheritance Tax failed in the Court of Appeal by a majority of two to one. Lady Ingram, (I) made a gift of a property known as 'Hurst Lodge' together with 60 acres of agricultural land to Mr Macfadyen, M. M agreed with I to create, and did create, a trust of this land for I's three daughters, and the children of her deceased son.

5.11 Since she wanted to continue to live at Hurst Lodge, and continue to receive rents from the property, she was leased the property for a nil rent for twenty years.

5.12 The arguments of her heirs was that the value of Hurst Lodge was not its freehold, but merely its leashold, value.

5.13 Nourse LJ, giving judgment for the majority, thought that the scheme failed because I could not grant a lease to herself. Millett LJ, dissenting was of the opinion that the tax avoidance scheme worked, even though it was highly artificial. In his opinion, it was not for the courts to close any loophole, but rather, a matter for parliament.

5.14 Robert Venables QC, counsel for the children, is reported in *The Times* July 29th 1997, from where a summary of the facts of this case is derived, as saying that the Court of Appeal decision would cost the beneficiaries 'hundreds of thousands'. The case is expected to go on appeal to the House of Lords, and will be a test case for many taxpayers.

Summary

Now that you have completed this Unit, you should understand:

☐ **how tax affects trusts.**

Self-assessment questions

1 What is tax avoidance, and what is the general attitude of the courts to it?

2 Describe the effect of income tax upon a trust.

3 Why did an automatic resulting trust arise in the Vandervell litigation, and what effect did it have?

4 Describe the effect of capital gains tax upon a trust.

5 Describe the effect of inheritance tax upon a trust.

Exam-style questions

1 Describe the taxation implications involved in the making, the administration and the termination of:

a) a discretionary settlement,

b) an accumulation and maintenance settlement,

c) an interest in possession trust.

In each case your answer should refer to inheritance tax, capital gains tax and income tax.

[Spring 1995]

2   In 1980, Dai Evans and his wife, Megan, were divorced. As part of the divorce arrangement, Dai made a settlement of some of his assets, including one of his farms, which was then worth £400,000. Megan was given custody of the only child of the marriage, their daughter Blodwyn, then aged 15.

Your bank was appointed trustee of this settlement, under which the income was to be paid to Megan for life, then Blodwyn for life and, after her death, the capital was to pass to such of Blodwyn's children as attain the age of 30. If these trusts failed, the deed provided that the trust funds were to revert to Dai, or to his estate if he were then dead.

When the settlement was made, Megan moved to the farm which had been settled and she farmed the land for the rest of her life.

The following events have subsequently occurred.

i)   In 1989, when Blodwyn married, the trustees advanced £200,000 to her under certain express powers contained in the deed.

ii) In 1990, Dai died.

iii) In 1991, Megan died. The trustees afterwards let the farm and land to a tenant who not only farmed the land but also ran a haulage business from the premises.

iv) In 1994 Blodwyn died, leaving an only child, Gwyneth, aged 1 year.

Required:

Outline the inheritance tax and capital gains tax consequences of each of the above events (i) to (iv). No calculations or figures are required but indicate any reliefs which may be available.

[Autumn 1995]

(The answers are given in the Appendix)

Caselist for Chapter 15 An Outline of the Taxation Aspects of Trusts

Inland Revenue Commissioners v *McGukian* [1997] 1 WLR 991.

The Income and Corporation Taxes Act 1978, section 478.

Income Tax: Maudsley and Burn's *Trusts & Trustees Cases and Materials* (Fifth ed. E H Burn) 1996, Chapter 13.

The Finance Act 1995, section 660A.

Re Vandervell's Trusts (No. 2) [1974] Ch 269.

In *Vandervell* v *I.R.C.* [1967] 2 AC 291.

Capital Gains Tax: Maudsley and Burn's *Trusts & Trustees Cases and Materials* (Fifth edition E.H. Burn) 1996, Chapter 14.

The Taxation of Chargeable Gains Act 1992, sections 70, 71(1), 77(1), 77(2).

Paul v *Paul* (1882) 20 ChD 742.

Harthan v *Mason (Inspector of Taxes)* [1980] STC 94.

Inheritance Tax: Maudsley and Burn's *Trusts & Trustees Cases and Materials* (Fifth edition E H Burn) 1996, Chapter 15.

Inheritance Tax Act 1984, sections 49 to 57., 64.

General report of the case involving Lady Ingram: *The Times* July 29th 1997.

16

Miscellaneous

Objectives

After studying this Unit, you should understand:

- **trusts to evade creditors**

- **secret trusts**

- **constructive trusts.**

1 Trusts to evade creditors

1.1 In the Introduction to Unit 1, we looked at the circumstances in which a trust will be rendered invalid due to illegality. In general terms, if a trust is set up and then put into effect in order to defraud creditors deliberately, it is then invalid: *Tribe* v *Tribe* (1996). This Unit should be consulted.

1.2 The Insolvency Act 1986 is also of relevance in this context. In Unit 3, we looked at *Re Kayford* (1975) where a special earmarked account was set up in order to protect customers who had sent in monies to purchase goods. We saw that this arrangement could be rendered voidable by the Insolvency Act 1986 if the transaction was at undervalue, or was a preference. Again, paragraphs 4.23 to 4.26 of Unit 3 should be consulted.

1.3 As a general principle, a trust cannot oust the rights of creditors by providing that a beneficiary's interest will not be available to meet the beneficiary's debts. The Trustee in Bankruptcy will obtain the beneficiary's interest and will use the funds or assets to pay the creditors. Such a clause would either be held to be illegal (see above and Unit 1) or contrary to public policy. The circumstances in which a trust or clause of a trust would offend public policy have been previously considered in Unit 5.

1.4   A particular form of statutory protection, known as the protective trust, is valid. The beneficiary's interest comes to an end should he become bankrupt, so that there is no interest which can be taken by the Trustee in Bankruptcy.

1.5   This protective trust is given effect by the Trustee Act 1925, section 33. This protective trust is created where the 'principal beneficiary' has an interest for his life or such other specified period set out in the trust instrument, and the income is held on trust for that 'principal beneficiary': section 33(1)(i).

1.6   If something happens, including bankruptcy of that principal beneficiary, which would cause the principal beneficiary to be deprived of the right to receive that income, a particular type of discretionary trust will automatically come into existence.

1.7   This means that the principal beneficiary's life interest will end, and cannot be taken by his creditors.

1.8   For the remaining period, the income is held upon trust for the maintenance, support, or benefit of the following persons (described immediately below) as the trustees in their absolute discretion think fit: section 33(1)(iii).

1.9   This trust that comes into existence is a discretionary trust for particular beneficiaries. Discretionary trusts have been previously considered in Unit 4.

1.10   There are various categories of persons who are the potential objects of the trustees discretion, depending upon whether the principal beneficiary is married and/or has children.

1.11   Where the principal beneficiary is married, the potential objects are the principal beneficiary, his spouse, and his legitimate or illegitimate children: section 33(iii)(a).

1.12   The word children in the Trustee Act 1925, section 33 was the only word included in this section. As Professor Jill Martin points out in Protective Trusts: Hanbury and Martin *Modern Equity* (Fifteenth ed. Jill E Martin) 1997, Chapter 7, this would include legitimate or illegitimate children of the principal beneficiary: the Family Law Reform Act 1987, section 1. This section has been previously considered in Unit 6, paragraph 1.26.

1.13   If the principal beneficiary is not married and has no children, then the income is held on trust for the principal beneficiary and the next of kin: section 33(1)(iii)(b).

1.14   Professor Jill Martin also makes the point in her chapter, that where an event happens, whereby the principal beneficiary loses his interest in the income, there is no liability to inheritance tax: the Inheritance Tax Act

1984, section 88. Liability to inheritance tax has been previously considered in Unit 15.

1.15 It should be noted that the life interest does not come to an end, if the statutory power to advance capital under the Trustee Act 1925, section 32 is exercised. This section has been previously considered in Unit 11. Similarly, the life interest of the principal beneficiary does not end if an express power, contained in the trust instrument, to advance capital is exercised.

2 Secret Trusts

2.1 These are trusts which take effect through the operation of a will. In general terms, the rules which relate to trusts also relate to secret trusts. There are a number of examples of this, some of which are listed below:

- first, 'the three certainties' apply to such a trust

- second, a secret trust can be a discretionary trust like any other express trust

- third, a secret trust can be for only such length of time as allowed by the rules relating to perpetuities and accumulations.

2.2 Such trusts have to be set up in accordance with very specific rules, which will result in invalidity if not followed. Since such trusts operate through a will, the courts have taken a strict approach, so as not to undermine unnecessarily the rules relating to wills.

2.3 An obvious reason for the use of such trusts is to obtain confidentiality. The terms, and the beneficiaries, of such trusts can remain secret.

2.4 Historically, there is evidence, as a result of research by N G Jones: *Trusts for Secrecy: the Case of John Dudley, Duke of Northumberland* (1995) CLJ 545, that such trusts were originally used because of worries about political, not religious, oppression.

2.5 The modern theory relating to such trusts is that they are 'constituted', once the executor of the will receives the property to be held in secret or half-secret trust. Constitution of trusts has been previously considered in Unit 6. The interests of the beneficiaries take effect at the point in time when the trust is constituted.

Fully secret trusts

2.6 Such trusts were allowed so as to stop possible fraud on the part of the secret trustee, who could otherwise take the property left by the testator or testatrix, since the will is absolute. Such a trust is an example of a constructive trust (see section 3 below): *Thynn* v *Thynn* (1684)

2.7 It is for this reason that fully secret trusts, and also half (part) secret trusts operate outside (*dehors*) the will, and are not subject to the Wills Act. It is for this reason that a beneficiary of both a secret or a half-secret trust is allowed to witness the will: *Re Young* (1951).

2.8 If such trusts are constructive, then if land is left by a secret trust, the trust will be valid. The Law of Property Act, section 53(1)(b) requires the manifestation and proof by writing. If there is a lack of writing, the gift of land will be saved by the Law of Property Act, section 53(2). This formality has been previously considered in Unit 5.

2.9 In *Ottoway* v *Norman* (1972) which concerned a mutual will (analogous to a secret trust – see below in section 3), the court did not hear any argument on this question and upheld the disposition. This case is of limited value in determining this difficult issue of whether wrting is required.

2.10 Such a trust is created where the will is absolute because of the express language of the will (on its face). An example would be 'to Bob absolutely'. In addition there must also have been an oral or written communication and acceptance between the testator or testatrix and the secret trustee at any time prior to the death of the testator, which contains the following:

● first, a definite trust obligation

● second, certainty of subject matter

● third, certainty of objects.

2.11 Acceptance by the secret trustee can occur through acquiescence, i.e. by not objecting to being a trustee: *Moss* v *Cooper* (1861).

2.12 If there is no oral or written communication at all between the testator and the secret trustee, the secret trust will fail: *Re Boyes* (1884).

2.13 It is established that communication by a sealed letter, not to be opened by the secret trustee until after the testator's death, will be effective: *Re Keen's Estate, Evershed* v *Griffiths* (1937).

Half-secret trusts

2.14 These were allowed at a later stage by the courts: the House of Lords decision in *Blackwell* v *Blackwell* (1929). The reason is to compel the half-secret trustee to carry out the promise he has agreed to with the testator, and not to stop fraud.

2.15 A half-secret trust is partially expressed on the will. The word 'trust' can appear, though not the terms of the trust nor the names of the beneficiaries. The will is not absolute on its face; there are words indicating that a half-secret trust is to take effect. An example would be 'to Benita on the terms that I have previously communicated to her'.

2.16 In addition there must also have been an oral or written communication and acceptance between the testator or testatrix and the secret trustee at any time prior to, or contemporaneously with, the testator making the will, which contains the following:

- first, a definite trust obligation

- second, certainty of subject matter

- third, certainty of objects.

2.17 There is clear authority, although criticised, which establishes that communication must be prior to, or contemporaneously with the testator making the will: *Re Keen's Estate, Evershed v Griffiths* (1937).

2.18 In addition, the terms of the will must not require a communication to be made after the will is executed: *Re Bateman* (1970). A correct form of words would be as follows: 'as I have previously communicated prior to the making of this will'.

2.19 Further if property is left by half-secret trust to a number of trustees, there must be oral or written communication (and acceptance) by all the trustees: *Re Spence (deceased)* (1949). The trustees will hold the property jointly: *Re Stead* (1900).

2.20 If T, the testator, agrees to leave £1,000 to S, the secret trustee, then T cannot leave £2,000 to S. The additional amount must be agreed by S. If this is not done, only the £1,000 is held on trust: *Re Cooper* (1939).

2.21 It is established that communication by a sealed letter will be effective: *Re Keen's Estate, Evershed v Griffiths* (1937).

2.22 Acceptance by the secret trustee can occur through acquiescence, i.e. by not objecting to being a trustee: *Blackwell v Blackwell* (1929)

2.23 Since there is a trust on the face of the will, the trustee is unable to obtain any property or monies for himself or herself: *Re Rees* (1950). Any surplus, must go on resulting trust for the next of kin: *Re Cooper* (1939)

2.24 See generally, *Secret Trusts and Mutual Wills Constructive Trusts* (Third Edition A J Oakley) 1997, Chapter 5.

3 Constructive Trusts

3.1 We have previously seen, in Unit 3, that a constructive trust is imposed as a remedy against inequitable, unconscionable or improper conduct. Lord Browne-Wilkinson in *Westdeutsche Landesbank Girozentrale* v *Islington London Borough Council* (1996) has indicated that there is the need to develop a general 'remedial' constructive trust in English law.

3.2 We have also seen a number of situations where a constructive trust will be imposed:

- first, where there is a specifically enforceable contract, and possession is not taken by the buyer, such as with land or shares, the seller will hold the item sold on constructive trust for the buyer (previously considered in Unit 5): *Lloyds Bank plc* v *Carrick and another* (1996)

- second, as between cohabitees or spouses, where one party has acted to his own detriment in reliance of a common intention that he is to have an equitable interest in the home (previously considered in Unit 7)

- third, where a thief steals, or obtains property by deception, so that his conscience is deemed to be affected, he will hold the property on constructive trust for the owner (previously considered in Unit 12)

- fourth, where a bank receives monies which it knows it is not entitled to receive, so that its conscience is affected, it will hold those funds on constructive trust for the owner (previously considered in Units 3 and 12).

- fifth, secret trusts (previously considered in section 2 of this Unit)

3.3 Some additional categories, not mentioned in previous Units, where a constructive trust will be imposed are:

- first, where monies are borrowed in order to enable a borrower to purchase a property, the borrower may fail to make repayments; in this case the lender is able to sell the property at a time of his choice for the best price obtainable; the lender will hold the sale proceeds on constructive trusts after paying off the amount outstanding on the loan, and any other loan, and necessary expenses and costs: the Law of Property Act 1925, section 105

- second, where the recipient of a gift of property kills the donor, a constructive trust will be imposed to ensure that the donee will not obtain the gift, but holds it on constructive trust for another, such as the next of kin: *Re Jones (deceased) Jones* v *Midland Bank Trust Co Ltd and Others* (1997)

- third, where two persons agree to make irrevocable and unaltered mutually binding wills, a constructive trust can be imposed by the courts to carry out this agreement: *Re Goodchild (decd)* (1997)

- fourth, where a person acts as a trustee *de son tort*, i.e. acts as though he is a trustee, and receives trust property or makes a profit at the expense of the trust; an example is *Phipps v Boardman* (1965), where Lord Denning in the Court of Appeal considered Tom Boardman to be a trustee *de son tort*, the decision of the House of Lords being previously considered in Unit 10

- fifth, the categories of 'dishonest assistance' and 'knowing receipt' (considered in detail immediately below).

3.4   The categories of 'dishonest assistance' and 'knowing receipt' have been developed by the courts as a response by them to tackle the growing commercial fraud that has taken place. Not all the cases litigated on these two categories have involved commercial fraud.

3.5   We saw in Units 8 and 12 that a tracing action, (an *in rem* proprietary claim) can be used to recover misapplied funds or property. The categories of 'dishonest assistance' and 'knowing receipt' are also used to recover misapplied funds. The difference is that liability in constructive trust, and for both these categories, is a personal remedy. An owner of funds is seeking to render personally liable the person who has helped misapply those funds either by assisting in their disposal or by receiving them. This claim is *in personam* – see Unit 8 where this concept is discussed.

Dishonest Assistance

3.6   There will be a general overview of this category before it is analysed in detail.

3.7   The category has four elements:

- first, the assets or other properties that have been misapplied must belong to a trust or company

- second, there must be a breach of trust by the trustee or, in the case of a company, a breach of fiduciary duty on the part of the director or senior employee of that company

- third, there must be assistance by the stranger (the person sought to be rendered liable as a constructive trustee) in the misapplication of funds or property

- fourth, there must be dishonesty on the part of the assister.

3.8   This category seeks to render liable a person who helps in the misapplication. Liability is being imposed on a secondary party who will be rendered personally liable, in particular, for all the loss sustained as a consequence of helping in the misapplication.

3.9   It can be seen that this category has an *actus reus*, i.e. requirement for certain actions to be carried out – elements 1 to 3. In addition, there is a *mens rea*, i.e. requirement for a particular state of mind – element 4.

3.10 The first element is a starting point. Assets are, in general terms, held in trust or by commercial organistions. This formulation makes liablility possible.

3.11 We saw in Unit 12 that a fiduciary relationship – of any type – is necessary for a tracing claim to be brought. The various types of fiduciary relationship have been previously considered in Unit 10. A similar principle operates here.

3.12 However, not all categories of fiduciary relationships count for liability under this category. There are four of importance that are established categories of fiduciary relationship for the purposes of this category:

● first, a trustee relationship

● second, the relationship of director and company

● third, the relationship of senior employee and company

● fourth, an agent who acts for the trust or company.

3.13 The extension to senior employees was confirmed, in the High Court, in *AGIP (Africa) Ltd* v *Jackson* (1990). It is not always directors of companies who misapply their company's funds. The extension to senior employees, such as the company's accountant in that case, enabled various third parties to be ultimately rendered liable for assisting in that misapplication.

3.14 This leads naturally onto the second element, that of a breach of trust or fiduciary duties. The decision of the Privy Council in *Royal Brunei Airlines Sdn Bhd* v *Tan* (1995) – now a landmark decision in this area – considerably reformulated liability. The trustee, director, senior employee or agent merely needs to misapply funds. A breach of trust or fiduciary duty (see Units 10 and 12) is all that is required. A minor or technical breach will be sufficient.

3.15 The third element is that of assistance by the stranger, the person sought to be rendered liable as a constructive trustee. The focus of attention, it is suggested quite correctly, is directed to that of the assister.

3.16 Assistance has not been comprehensively defined. It broadly means helping in the misapplication of trust or corporate assets. It is established that transferring funds would constitute assistance, *Baden Delvaux and Lecuit* v *Société Générale* (1983). It is not necessary for funds to have been received in order to constitute assistance. It is now established after *Royal Brunei Airlines Sdn Bhd* v *Tan* (1995) that encouraging or inducing a misapplication of funds would be sufficient.

3.17 The fourth element concerns the mental intention on the part of the assister, i.e. the third party sought to be rendered liable as a constructive trustee. *Royal Brunei Airlines Sdn Bhd* v *Tan* (1995) established, for the first time, that the assister must be dishonest.

3.18 For this purpose, this means dishonesty in a civil context, since we are dealing with personal liablility as a constructive trustee.

3.19 In *Royal Brunei Airlines Sdn Bhd* v *Tan* (1995), Brunei Airlines appointed Borneo Leisure Travel Sdn Bhd (BLT) as its agent to sell passenger and cargo transportation. It was agreed between Royal Brunei Airlines and BLT that the monies (less commission) that BLT received were to be held on express trust by BLT for Royal Brunei Airlines. However, there was no arrangement – as there should have been, in order to fully protect Royal Brunei Airlines – that these monies should be put into a separate account. The effect of earmarking funds into special, separate accounts has been considered in Unit 3.

3.20 Royal Brunei Airlines sought to make Tan, the managing director and main shareholder in BLT, personally liable as a constructive trustee for 'dishonestly assisting' in the misapplication of funds by BLT. The monies received from the sales of passenger and cargo transport were placed into a general current bank account of BLT, and used by it to pay salaries, overheads and other expenses, and to minimize its overdraft with the bank. Royal Brunei Airlines had not received payment for the sums owing by BLT to it. BLT became insolvent with no monies in its general trading account.

3.21 Lord Nicholls gave judgment in the Privy Council. He explained at length what was meant by dishonesty. In particular, if a person deliberately or willfully took another's property or was reckless as to the rights of others, that would be a very strong indication of dishonesty.

3.22 The test was an objective one, and dishonesty was to be determined by the courts. The court, in determining whether the defendant was dishonest, would have regard to the personal attributes, experience and intelligence of the defendant.

3.23 On the facts, Tan had instructed BLT to use the monies of Royal Brunei Airlines, which he knew to be theirs and which he knew were held on trust for them, thereby committing a breach of trust. In the view of the Privy Council he was dishonest and liable as a constructive trustee. This meant he was personally liable for the monies that BLT owed Royal Brunei Airlines.

3.24 This crucial test of dishonesty, and the decision in Royal Brunei Airlines Sdn Bhd, has been the subject of much academic discussion.

3.25 Charles Harpum in his case note of the decision: *Accessory Liability for Procuring or Assisting a Breach of Trust* (1995) LQR 545, believes that the decision could pave the way for a general form of secondary liability for assisting or encouraging a breach of any duty, analogous with some of the economic torts such as inducing breach of contract.

3.26 Simon Gardner in *Knowing Assistance and Knowing Receipt: Taking Stock* (1996) LQR 56, is critical of the reason put forward by Lord Nicholls for the introduction of dishonesty as the test, namely that mere knowledge is not a sufficient reason for liability to be imposed. In his view neither dishonesty nor knowledge (this concept will be discussed below) is a sufficient or adequate test for the imposition of liability.

3.27 Professor Peter Birks in his case note of the decision: *Accessory Liability* (1996) LMCLQ1 is of the view that the test of knowledge on the part of the assister is a more preferable test to that of dishonesty now adopted by the courts.

3.28 As Anthony Oakley points out in: Constructive Trusts Imposed as a Result of a Disposition of Trust Property in Breach of Trust. *Constructive Trusts* (Third ed. A J Oakley) 1997, Chapter 4, Lord Nicholls makes clear that knowledge of the assister is no longer to be the essential ingredient of liability.

3.29 However, Lord Nicholls did not make clear what importance knowledge was now to have. It was this point that emerged as being unclear in a subsequent decision: *Brinks Ltd (formerly Brink's-Mat Ltd) v Abu-Saleh & Others* (1996).

3.30 Brinks Ltd, formerly known as Brink's-Mat Ltd, were the victims of an armed robbery at its warehouse near Heathrow Airport.

3.31 Mr Black, a security guard at Brinks Ltd was prosecuted for, and found guilty of, robbery with violence. He gave valuable assistance and inside information about relevant security matters to enable the robbers to commit the raid successfully.

3.32 In order to recover the proceeds of the stolen goods, Brinks Ltd brought claims to make 57 defendants liable in constructive trust for laundering the proceeds.

3.33 Two of the defendants, Mr and Mrs Elcombe, had previously been acquitted on criminal charges of laundering the proceeds of the robbery. The civil claim against Mr Elcombe was settled out of court, but agreement could not be reached regarding Mrs Elcombe.

3.34 The Elcombes carried on an antiques business which sold much of their stock to a Mr Parry. Mr Elcombe and Mr Parry later formed a new company which also dealt in antiques. They were on good business terms.

3.35 Mr Parry was prosecuted and found guilty of handling stolen goods.

3.36 In the civil case against Mrs Elcombe, after much evidence, Rimer J made certain crucial findings of fact:

- first, Mr Parry knew as a fact that he was laundering the proceeds of this robbery. Further, there was a 'real possibility' that Mr Elcombe knew this too

- second, Mrs Elcombe believed that the monies were legitimately derived from Mr Parry's business activities but were being taken abroad to Zurich for tax evasion reasons

- third, Mrs Elcombe escorted her husband in four of his six trips abroad to Zurich, during which he laundered over £3m.

3.37 Rimer J was of the view that Mr Black, although not an officer or director of Brinks Ltd, was an employee in a fiduciary position in relation to his employer because of the valuable information he possessed. Further, he was in breach of his fiduciary duties when he used that knowledge to aid others to rob his employer.

3.38 In order to render Mrs Elcombe liable as a constructive trustee under the 'dishonest assistance' category, it was necessary to show that there was a breach of fiduciary relationship on the part of an employee who had important information.

3.39 Rimer J was also of the view that Mrs Elcombe, by going on trips to Zurich with her husband, was not providing assistance so as to render her liable as a constructive trustee. She was 'welcome company' who was happy to enjoy the expenses paid by Mr Parry. Further, Mr Elcombe went on two trips by himself, which showed that her presence was not necessary.

3.40 Finally, Rimer J dealt (*obiter*) with the issue of knowledge on Mrs Elcombe's part, which it was not strictly necessary for him to decide.

3.41 In so doing, Rimer J gave his interpretation of *Royal Brunei Airlines Sdn Bhd v Tan* (1995). He considered that the Privy Council had not intended to eliminate the need to show that the defendant knew what was going on.

3.42 In *Royal Brunei Airlines Sdn Bhd* v *Tan* (1995) Tan had actual knowledge of what was happening, so that in that particular case, knowledge was not an issue. In the view of Rimer J it was necessary to show that Mrs Elcombe had knowledge of the facts giving rise to liability.

3.43 In the view of Rimer J, Mrs Elcombe believed that monies were being laundered for dishonest tax evasion reasons concerning Mr Parry's business. However, in his view, she did not know that Mr Elcombe was laundering, on her trips with him, monies derived from the Brink's-Mat robbery.

3.44 Since Mrs Elcombe had not assisted in the laundering process, she was not liable as a constructive trustee for 'dishonestly assisting'.

3.45 Anthony Oakley in The Liberalising of Remedies for Breach of Trust. *Trends in Contemporary Trust Law.* (ed. A J Oakley) 1996 Chapter 10, makes the point that Millett J, as he then was, in *Agip (Africa) v Jackson* (1990), took a contrary position, namely that it was not necessary for the assister to be aware of the precise nature of the fraud or of the identity of the victim. Further, Oakley points out that Millett J was of the clear opinion that the potential assister cannot simply say that he thought that it was merely a case of breach of exchange control or tax evasion.

3.46 John Stevens in his case note of Brinks Ltd: *Deliminating the Scope of Accessory Liability* (1996) Conv 447, is of the opinion that the case was correctly decided. Merely because she knew of some illegality was not sufficient for liability to be imposed against her, since she believed the monies were being transferred to the rightful owner.

3.47 Perhaps it is possible to reconcile Millett J's approach by arguing that Mrs Elcombe, who was a non-professional, unlike the defendants in *Agip (Africa) v Jackson* (1990), did not know that there was a fraud being perpetrated on an individual, although she did know that the state authorities would suffer by what was going on.

3.48 *Royal Brunei Airlines Sdn Bhd v Tan* (1995) has also been considered by the New Zealand High Court, in *Cigna Life Insurance New Zealand Ltd v Westpac Securities Ltd* (1996).

3.49 The plaintiff, Cigna Life Insurance Ltd, C, wished to invest surplus monies in short term investments in the money market. It authorised its 'trusted servant', an employee who was the trainee accountant in the firm, to make investments with the defendants, Westpac Securities Ltd, W at negotiable interest. This employee had access to all documents in a small office, the company C, being a relatively small orgainisation.

3.50 The cheques transferring C's monies should have gone from C's numbered account directly to Westpac's bank. Instead, this trusted employee opened his own numbered account, and deposited four cheques from C into this account between February and November 1987. The first and third amounts were repaid to C with interest but the second and third, totalling $680,000 were not repaid. The fraud was discovered in August 1988.

3.51 The plaintiff, C, sued the defendant W, as a constructive trustee. C brought an action against W on the basis that W had 'dishonestly assisted' the employee to steal from his employer C.

3.52 W's defence was the following:

● first, the employee was known to W's dealers as C's accountant

● second, the employee used C's deposit forms

- third, the cheques were signed by C's company secretary as well as the employee.

3.53 Hence, W had no grounds for suspicion and did not make any checks.

3.54 Greig J in the High Court of New Zealand was of the view that as a consequence of the decision in *Royal Brunei Airlines Sdn Bhd* v *Tan* (1995), dishonesty was now an essential ingredient of liability.

3.55 On these facts, Greig J was of the clear opinion that there was no evidence at all of any dishonesty on the part of W or its staff.

3.56 They were neither aware of, nor did they know, nor shut their eyes to any circumstances which might have indicated, any fraud on the part of C's employee. It followed that the claim in constructive trust by C against W could not succeed.

3.57 A recent unreported decision of *H.R.* v *J.A.P.T.* decision of Lindsay J of March 19th 1997, gives further guidance on the question of dishonesty. This decision is discussed in a case note by David Pollard: *Liability of Directors of a Corporate Trustee* (1997) TruLI 48, from where the following information and facts are derived.

3.58 A trustee company, which managed the employer's pension fund trust, agreed to lend the employer £3m. No provision was made for the employer to pay interest or for security to be given to the trustee company.

3.59 Subsequently, three months later, the trustee company, on behalf of the pension fund trust, agreed to purchase the employer's principal place of business for £3.5m. The purchase price was greater than the market price obtainable.

3.60 A further sum of £0.5m was paid by the trustee company to bring forward the date of completion of this sale. The trustee company did not obtain independent advice regarding these two transactions concerning the purchase of the employer's business premises. Completion was in fact not brought forward, and the purchase occurred at the original date. The trustee company subsequently sold the property for £2.2m.

3.61 The person who determined the price for all transactions was a director of both the trustee company and the employer's company. Subsequently, the employer went into receivership.

3.62 Various claims, including breach of fiduciary duties, were brought against this director. A further claim, with which we are concerned, was a claim against the director for 'dishonestly assisting' in a breach of trust on the part of the trustee company. The director sought to strike out this claim on the basis that it disclosed no cause of action against him. Lindsay J refused to do this.

243

3.63 Lindsay J was of the following opinion:

- first, the involvement in a transaction by a person who knows it is a misapplication of pension fund trust assets to the disadvantage of the beneficiaries would be dishonest

- second, such action involved the director in taking a commercially unacceptable risk which would harm the rights of others, namely the beneficiaries of the pension fund trust, and showed a reckless disregard for their rights.

3.64 The position as regards pension fund trusts and pension fund surpluses have been previously considered in Units 4, 9, 10 and 11.

3.65 Where there is liability for 'dishonest assistance', it is suggested that there will be liability for all the loss that results. We know from Unit 12 that causation issues are now relevant in equity. It is suggested that they should now be of relevance in determining the amount of liability under the 'dishonest assistance' category.

3.66 It is also suggested that an analogy can be drawn between 'dishonest assistance' and 'fraudulent misrepresentation' at common law. In *Smith New Court Securities Ltd v Scrimgeour Vickers (Asset Management) Ltd* (1996), Lord Browne-Wilkinson laid down the approach of the House of Lords as to the amount of liability in cases of fraudulent misrepresentation. His approach can be applied to situations of 'dishonest assistance' as follows:

- first, the defendant is liable to make reparation for all the damage directly flowing from his 'dishonest assistance'

- second, although the damage need not have been forseeable, it must have been directly caused by the 'dishonest assistance'

- third, the plaintiff is entitled to recover consequential losses.

3.67 Where these three elements are satisfied, the assister will be liable to account to the trust or company for the loss or damage caused to it. There is not a true constructive trust, since the assister does not necessarily have to have received any trust, or company, property.

Knowing Receipt

3.68 There will be a general overview of this category before it is analysed in detail.

3.69 This category has four elements:

- first, the existence of a trust or fiduciary relationship

- second, misapplication of funds or assets by the trustee or fiduciary

- third, receipt of those misapplied funds by the stranger, that is the person who is sought to be rendered liable as a constructive trustee

- fourth, requisite knowledge on the part of the stranger.

3.70 This category seeks to render liable a person who receives misapplied funds. Liability is being imposed on a secondary party who will be rendered personally liable, in particular, for all the trust or company funds or assets that he has received.

3.71 It can be seen that, as with 'dishonest assistance' this category has an *actus reus*, i.e. requirement for certain actions to be carried out – elements 1 to 3. In addition, there is a *mens rea*, i.e. requirement for a particular state of mind – element 4.

3.72 Again, as for 'dishonest assistance', the first element is a starting point. Assets are, in general terms, held in trust or by commercial organistions. This formulation makes liablility possible.

3.73 We saw in Unit 12, that a fiduciary relationship – of any type – is necessary for a tracing claim to be brought. The various types of fiduciary relationship have been previously considered in Unit 10.

3.74 However, not all categories of fiduciary count as a basis for liability under this category. A similar principle operates here for the category of 'knowing receipt', as it does for 'dishonest assistance'. There are four of importance that are established categories of fiduciary relationship for the purposes of this category:

- first, a trustee relationship

- second, the relationship of director and company

- third, the relationship of senior employee and company

- fourth, an agent who acts for the trust or company.

3.75 The extension from a trust situation to directors and senior employees of a company was confirmed, in a Court of Appeal decision involving a 'knowing receipt' claim: *Rolled Steel Products (Holdings)* v *British Steel Corp and Others* (1986).

3.76 This leads naturally onto the second element, that of a breach of trust or fiduciary duties. The trustee, director, senior employee or agent merely needs to misapply funds. A breach of trust or fiduciary duty (see Units 10 and 12) is all that is required. A minor or technical breach will be sufficient. This need for a misapplication has always been the approach for the 'knowing receipt' category.

3.77 An example derives from *Precision Dippings Ltd* v *Precision Dippings Marketing Ltd and Others* (1985), where one company made a transfer of funds to another company within its group. This was a technical breach. However, the transfer still was still a breach within the 'knowing receipt' category, and the recipient company was liable as a constructive trustee for the funds it had received.

3.78 A crucial difference between the 'knowing receipt' and 'knowing assistance' and is that for 'knowing receipt' liability is dependant upon misapplied trust or company funds or assets being received by the person sought to be made liable as a constructive trustee. In contrast, as we have previously seen above, 'knowing assistance' requires an act of assistance.

3.79 This third element of the *actus reus* for 'knowing receipt' (required actions), will now be looked at.

3.80 In *Agip (Africa) Ltd* v *Jackson* (1990) Millett J, as he then was, made some important observations about what constituted a receipt. Such comments were (*obiter*) not strictly necessary for him to make, since the case did not involve a receipt of funds. Millett J was of the view that receipt meant receiving for one's own benefit. This is also the approach in New Zealand: *Westpac Banking Corporation* v *Savin* (1985).

3.81 This is a matter of importance for bankers. A bank will normally receive funds as agent for its customer, and will transfer them on the instructions of the customer. In such a situation, the bank could not be rendered liable as a constructive trustee under the 'knowing receipt' category, since it has not received funds for its own benefit. If the bank were to use customer's monies to set off against another account, this would constitute receipt for the bank's own benefit.

3.82 In contrast, if a bank engages in exchange transactions, then it can be rendered liable under the 'knowing receipt' category, since it is regarded at law as having received funds for its own benefit: *Polly Peck International* v *Nadir and Others (No. 2)* (1992).

3.83 We have also looked at the Guinness plc and Saunders litigation in Unit 10, as regards fiduciary duties. It should be remembered that in the High Court, the claim against Mr Ward, a former director, was originally brought against him under the category of 'knowing receipt'.

3.84 This claim succeeded in the High Court before Browne-Wilkinson J, as he then was, on the basis that Ward had sought to pocket £5.2m of Guinness's monies by placing them into his own bank account in his own name in Switzerland. Clearly this was a receipt of misapplied company funds for the benefit of Mr Ward, and he was held liable as a constructive trustee under the 'knowing receipt' category: *Guinness plc* v *Saunders and Another* (1988).

3.85 Turning to the fourth element, namely, the required knowledge with which the actions of the stranger sought to be rendered liable as a constructive trustee must be carried out.

3.86 The stanger must have knowledge of the following:

- first, of the trust or fiduciary relationship
- second, of the misapplication by which there is a breach of trust or fiduciary relationship
- third, of the receipt.

3.87 In order to establish liability under the 'knowing receipt' category, it is necessary for a plaintiff to prove knowledge on the part of the defendant of these three factors. This was established by the High Court decision of *Lipkin Gorman v Karpnale Ltd and Lloyds Bank plc* (1987).

3.88 The requirement of knowledge on the part of the defendant is entirely consistent with the claim of 'knowing receipt' being personal. A defendant is rendered personally liable because of his knowledge.

3.89 Some of the cases have suggested that the recipient must also act with a 'want of probity', and that knowledge is not sufficient unless the recipient satisfies this additional requirement.

3.90 The difficult issue is the required degree of knowledge. It is this that has proved problematic. The courts have taken various approaches. Some of the recent conflicting decisions will now be considered.

3.91 In *El Ajou v Dollar Land Holdings* (1993), Millett J, as he then was, appeared to be of the view that the appropriate standard was that the stranger knew or ought to have known. The requisite knowledge was subjective or objective.

3.92 In *Eagle Trust plc v SBC Securities Ltd and Others (No. 2)* (1996), Mary Arden J, was of the view that the appropriate standard was subjective, i.e., actual, wilful or reckless knowledge on the part of the stranger sought to be rendered liable as a constructive trustee.

3.93 In *Hillsdown Holdings plc v Pensions Ombudsman and Others* (1997), Knox J was of the view that some degree of knowledge was required for the 'knowing receipt' category.

3.94 Hillsdown Holdings plc, H, an employer, instigated a breach of trust by persuading the pension fund trustees to incorrectly transfer a pension fund surplus to it. This was an interference with the discretions of the pension fund trustees, and encouraging the trustees to break their duties of good faith to H's employees. The position as regards pension fund trusts and pension fund surpluses have been previously considered in Units 4, 9, 10 and 11.

3.95 As a consequence of this conduct, H could not assert that it did not know that what it was doing was inducing a breach of trust.

3.96 The surplus was actually transferred to H. Knox J recognised that this was an unjust enrichment, although he felt it inappropriate and unecessary to rule on this matter. The concept of unjust enrichment has been previously discussed in Units 1 and 12.

3.97 In *Royal Brunei Airlines Sdn Bhd* v *Tan* (1995), the Privy Council did suggest that because the 'knowing receipt' form of liability is receipt based, then restitutionary principles would apply to it. This would mean a fundamental review of the 'knowing receipt' category by the House of Lords, when a 'knowing receipt' claim comes before it in the future.

3.98 It should be pointed out that an unjust enrichment claim does not require knowledge to be shown at all. Such a claim is a strict liability dependant upon receipt. For this reason the distinguished academic and law commissioner, Charles Harpum: The Basis of Equitable Liability: Knowing Assistance and Knowing Receipt *The Frontiers of Liability* Vol 1 (ed. P B H Birks) 1994, Chapter 1, Part 1, considered that the recognition of unjust enrichment would radically change the 'knowing receipt' category.

3.99 In practical terms it would seem absurd for a plaintiff to bring a claim for 'knowing receipt' where knowledge on the part of the recipient defendant has to be shown. It is established after *Lipkin Gorman (a firm)* v *Karpnale Ltd* (1991) that a restitutionary claim is a strict form of liability (strict liability) where no knowledge needs to be shown. This would suggest that there should no longer be any need for a plaintiff to use the 'knowing receipt' category.

3.100 However, claims continue to be litigated under the 'knowing receipt' category. There are some possible reasons for this:

● first, that if a plaintiff is pleading (arguing for) a 'dishonest assistance' claim then it is relatively easy to plead a 'knowing receipt' claim as well, and such claims fit together

● second, a 'knowing receipt' claim can be readily pleaded with a tracing claim in equity, since both claims require receipt

● third, where funds are misapplied, an injunction will often be wanted and at the interlocutory (pre-trial) stage, the court will not be likely to investigate the knowledge of the defendant sought to be rendered liable as a constructive trustee.

Defences

3.101 In the same way that there are a number of recongnised defences for breach of trust – previously considered in Unit 12 – there are also a number of defences to claims for both 'dishonest assistance' and also 'knowing receipt'. The defences that are available are similar to those which are usually available to equitable claims.

3.102 The first defence effectively amounts to contributory negligence on the part of the defendant.

3.103 This defence was established in the High Court decision of *Lipkin Gorman* v *Karpnale Ltd and Lloyds Bank plc* (1987) in relation to the claims of 'dishonest assistance' brought against Lloyds Bank (which subsequently failed in the Court of Appeal since the claim was not drafted properly), and the claim of 'knowing receipt' brought against the Playboy Club (which failed since the club did not know or have any grounds to know of the stealing by a Mr Cass from his firm, Lipkin Gorman's client account). The decision of the House of Lords did not deal with either the 'knowing assistance' or 'knowing receipt' categories of constructive trust. It has been previously been discussed in Unit 12 in relation to tracing and restitutionary claims.

3.104 In the High Court, Alliot J, was of the opinion that this defence would, in principle, have been available, since Lipkin Gorman had delayed in making investigations of Mr Cass, their partner who controlled the client's account and could withdraw funds from this account on his signature alone. The defence would give rise to a 100% bar from the point in time when Lipkin Gorman should have made investigations. The defence is not available until after that point in time.

3.105 Another available defence is that of estoppel by acquiescence, confirmed by Staughton J, as he then was, in *Limpgrange Ltd* v *Bank of Credit and Commerce International S.A.* (1986). An example is where a bank, B, is about to make a transfer to A. C knows about this proposed transfer, but in no way objects to, or seeks to stop or discourage, the payment from being made by B. If C seeks to bring a claim for 'dishonest assistance' against B, B would be able to raise this defence. C would be estopped from bringing a claim by their conduct, in allowing the transfer to be made.

3.106 In *Limgrange Ltd* v *Bank of Credit and Commerce International SA* (1986) Staughton J also confirmed that a bank or other individual would have a further defence of set-off.

3.107 There is also a statutory defence under the Trustee Act 1925, section 61, that the defendant has acted honestly and reasonably, and that it would be fair to excuse the defendant from liability. This defence has been previously considered in Unit 12.

3.108 The reason is that the Trustee Act 1925, section 68(17) enables this defence to be raised to a claim of constructive trust.

3.109 Finally, the court can give directions as to what a third party should do with funds or assets which it has in its possession, or is about to receive: *Finers and Others* v *Miro* (1991). This would minimise the risk of that third party being rendered liable as a constructive trustee. Such direction, by the court, includes placing of funds into a separated and earmarked account: *Polly Peck International plc* v *Nadir and Others (No. 2)* (1992).

3.110 It is important to emphasise that if a trustee is unsure of what course to take, or if the law is uncertain, an application can be made to the court for directions. We have seen in Unit 4 in relation to trustee discretions, that this discretion can be surrendered to the court: *Marley* v *Mutual Security Merchant Bank and Trust Co Ltd* (1991). Similarly, in Unit 10 we have seen that where the trustees had a conflct of duty and interest, the court was able to give a ruling about a proposed distribution by the trustees, and whether this could be carried out: *Re Drexel Burnham Lambert U.K. Pension Plan* (1995).

Summary

Now that you have completed this Unit, you should understand:

☐ **trusts to evade creditors**

☐ **secret trusts**

☐ **constructive trusts.**

Self-assessment questions

1   Is a trust which seeks to to evade the rights of creditors valid?

2   What is a secret trust?

3   What types of secret trust are there?

4   What is a constructive trust?

5   What distinction may be made between resulting and constructive trusts in the context of couples who are married or live together?

6   What is the constructive trust of 'dishonest assistance'?

7   What is the constructive trust of 'knowing receipt'?

8   Susan, who is 70 years of age, wishes to make provision for her various relatives. She wishes to leave her 10,000 shares in Blue Chip plc on trust for them. She tells her brother, David, that she wishes him to decide which of their relatives shall benefit from these 10,000 shares in Blue Chip plc on her death, and that he is to do what is right in relation to these shares. He agrees to this in June 1997. In July 1997 she executes her will. The relevant clause regarding her shares in Blue Chip plc is as follows:

'I leave my shares in Blue Chip plc to my brother David on the trusts previously communicated to him'.

In August 1997 she dies. Advise David.

(The answers are given in the Appendix)

Caselist for Chapter 16 Miscellaneous

Tribe v *Tribe* [1996] Ch 107.

The Insolvency Act 1986.

Re Kayford (In Liquidation) [1975] 1 WLR 279.

The Trustee Act 1925, sections 32, 33, 61, 68(17).

Professor Jill Martin. Protective Trusts. *Hanbury and Martin Modern Equity* (Fifteenth ed. Jill E Martin) 1997, Chapter 7. Sweet and Maxwell.

The Family Law Reform Act 1987, section 1.

The Inheritance Tax Act 1984, section 88.

N G Jones. *Trusts For Secrecy: The Case of John Dudley, Duke of Northumberland* (1995) CLJ 545.

Thynn v *Thynn* [1684] 1 Vern 296.

Re Young, Young v *Young* [1951] Ch 344.

Law of Property Act 1925, sections 53(1)(b), 53(2).

Ottaway v *Norman* [1972] Ch 698.

Moss v *Cooper* [1861] 1 John & H 352.

Re Boyes, Boyes v *Carritt* [1884] 26 ChD 531.

Re Keen, Evershed v *Griffiths* [1937] Ch 236.

Blackwell v *Blackwell* [1929] AC 318.

Re Bateman's Will Trusts, Brierley v *Perry* [1970] 1 WLR 1463.

Re Spence (deceased), Quick v *Ackner* [1949] WN 237.

Re Cooper, Le Neve Foster v *National Provincial Bank Ltd* [1939] Ch 811.

Re Rees, Williams v *Hopkins* [1949] Ch 541.

Secret Trusts And Mutual Wills. *Constructive Trusts* (Third ed. A J Oakley) 1997, Chapter 5. Sweet and Maxwell.

Westdeutsche Landesbank Girozentrale v *Islington London Borough Council* [1996] AC 669.

Lloyds Bank plc v *Carrick and Another* [1996] 4 All ER 630.

The Law of Property Act 1925, section 105.

Re Jones (deceased) Jones v *Midland Bank Trust Co Ltd and Others: The Times* April 29th 1997.

Re Goodchild (decd) [1997] 3 All ER 63.

Phipps v *Boardman* [1965] Ch 992 (Court of Appeal).

Agip (Africa) Ltd v *Jackson* [1990] Ch 265 (High Court).

Royal Brunei Airlines Sdn Bhd v *Tan* [1995] 2 AC 378.

Baden Delvaux and Lecuit v *Société Générale* [1983] BCLC 325.

Charles Harpum: *Accessory Liability for Procuring or Assisting a Breach of Trust* (1995) LQR 545.

Simon Gardner: *Knowing Assistance And Knowing Receipt: Taking Stock* (1996) LQR 56.

Professor Peter Birks: *Accessory Liability* (1996) LMCLQ1

Anthony Oakley: Constructive Trusts imposed as a Result of a Disposition of Trust Property in Breach of Trust. *Constructive Trusts* (Third ed. A J Oakley) 1997, Chapter 4. Sweet and Maxwell.

Brinks Ltd (formerly Brink's-Mat Ltd) v *Abu-Saleh & Others* [1996] CLC 133.

Anthony Oakley: The Liberalising of Remedies for Breach of Trust. *Trends in Contemporary Trust Law.* (ed. A J Oakley) 1996, Chapter 10. Clarendon Press Oxford.

John Stevens: Deliminating the Scope of Accessory Liability (1996) *The Conveyancer* 447.

Cigna Life Insurance New Zealand Ltd v *Westpac Securities Ltd* [1996] 1 NZLR 80.

The unreported High Court decision *H.R.* v *J.A.P.T.* of Lindsay J. of March 19th 1997.

David Pollard: Liability of Directors of a Corporate Trustee (1997) TruLI 48.

Smith New Court Securities Ltd v *Scrimgeour Vickers (Asset Management) Ltd* [1996] 4 All ER 769.

Rolled Steel Products (Holdings) v *British Steel Corp and Others* [1986] Ch 246.

Precision Dippings Ltd v *Precision Dippings Marketing Ltd and Others* [1985] BCLC 385.

Westpac Banking Corporation v *Savin* [1985] 2 NZLR 41.

Polly Peck International v *Nadir and Others (No. 2)* [1992] 4 All ER 769.

Guinness plc v *Saunders and Another* [1988] BCLC 43 (High Court).

Lipkin Gorman v *Karpnale Ltd and Lloyds Bank plc* [1987] 1 WLR 987 (High Court) [1989] 1 WLR 1340 (Court of Appeal) [1991] 2 AC 548 (House of Lords).

El Ajou v *Dollar Land Holdings* [1993] 3 All ER 717 (High Court).

Eagle Trust plc v *SBC Securities Ltd and Others (No. 2)* [1996] 1 BCLC 121.

Hillsdown Holdings plc v *Pensions Ombudsman and others* [1997] 1 All ER 862.

Charles Harpum: The Basis of Equitable Liability: Knowing Assistance and Knowing Receipt. *The Frontiers of Liability Vol 1* (ed. P B H Birks) 1994, Chapter 1, Part 1. Oxford University Press.

Limpgrange Ltd v *Bank of Credit and Commerce International S.A.* [1986] FLR 36.

Finers and Others v *Miro* [1991] 1 WLR 35.

Marley v *Mutual Security Merchant Bank and Trust Co Ltd* [1991] 3 All ER 198.

Re Drexel Burnham Lambert U.K. Pension Plan [1995] 1 WLR 32.

APPENDIX

Answers

1

Introduction

Self-assessment questions

1. For a summary of the facts, please refer to paragraphs 1.2 to 1.5 of Unit 1.

2. It was held that Milligan could still claim her equitable interest in the house, despite the fraud that she and Tinsley had committed against the DSS. The monies used to purchase her interest in the house came from her joint business earnings with Milligan, and not the monies obtained from the DSS. The House of Lords adopted the common law rule: can you bring your claim without relying on the illegality? Since Milligan had not used DSS monies to purchase her interest in the property, she could bring her claim for an equitable interest (share) in the property. She was therefore held to be entitled to an equitable interest, and since her contributions were equal to Tinsley's, she was entitled to a half share in the property.

3. The case is of significance since the House of Lords followed the approach at common law rather than in equity in determining the scope of an equitable interest. They preferred the common law rule and felt free to apply it rather than the rule in equity. Whether this means that they will do this in all cases where there are analogous but different rules at common law and in equity, is unclear at present.

4. This question specifically directs the candidate to write a critical account of the decision in *Tinsley* v *Milligan*. The candidate should briefly go through some of the points in questions 1, 2, and 3 above.

   The criticisms of the case have been dealt with in some detail in Unit 1. These criticisms should be the focus for the answer to this question and should be as follows:

   First, because of the illegality by the plaintiff, the courts have established a somewhat rigid rule which does not require them to look at the substance of the matter.

   Second (and this follows on from the first criticism above), the extent and immorality of the illegality is not investigated by the courts.

   Third, the situation should be considered from the perspective of whether the defendant would be 'unjustly enriched' if the plaintiff claimant could not recover his or her interest owing to an irrelevant illegality. If the answer to this question is simply a matter of looking at the particular facts, then this criticism is a different way of making the point that the rule in *Tinsley* v *Milligan* (1994) is an over-rigid one.

5.   The situation may be seen as analogous to that in *Tinsley* v *Milligan* (1994), in that the ownership of a property has been changed in order to get round certain statutory provisions. A candidate could make a distinction between the two situations on the basis that one was to defraud the DSS, which was a criminal offence. The exact provisions of the legislation in Artania are not known but it is likely that a criminal offence has been committed.

A fundamental distinction is that concerning the relationship of the parties. In *Tinsley* v *Milligan* (1994) the two female lovers would in equity be regarded as 'strangers'.

In equity all relationships except husband and wife and parent and child are regarded as being ones where the parties are 'strangers'.

This has the important consequence that for all relationships where the parties are strangers (as in *Tinsley* v *Milligan* (1994)) where property is transferred into the name of another, then the relationship of trust is created. The recipient will obtain only the legal title and the transferor will keep the equitable title. As a consequence, in *Tinsley* v *Milligan* (1994), Milligan's equitable title was automatically created and she did not need to adduce any evidence to establish it. This meant she could bring her claim for an equitable interest without needing to mention the illegality involving the DSS.

However, the particular problem as between Jane and her children is distinguishable from *Tinsley* v *Milligan* (1994) in that the parties are not strangers and the presumption between them would be one of gift. The presumption of gift is a starting point and can be rebutted by contrary evidence. However, because of the illegality Jane would not be able to bring forward evidence of the intended true position.

This is what happened in the Australian case of *Nelson* v *Nelson* (1995) where Mrs Nelson could not recover a property transferred into her children's names in order to avoid the Defence Service Homes Act 1918. This case is discussed in detail in the chapter by Derek Davies in his book. On this basis, Kay and Larry would be entitled to a half share each in relation to 'Bleak Cottage'. As a consequence of the illegality Jane would not be able to rebut the presumption that she intended a joint gift of the cottage to her children. It has been suggested that this rule of presumption of gift as between mother and child is now dated and should be reformed. See Alan Dowling, 'The Presumption of Advancement between Mother and Child' [1996] *Conv* 274.

However, the presumption of gift is a presumption for transfers made by a parent to a child; it does not apply to a transfer by a child (minor) to his or her parents. In such a situation the transfer will be regarded as creating a trust in favour of the child. The recipient parent will not receive a gift. A trust is automatically established so that the child would be entitled to the equitable interest, and would not have to adduce evidence of the illegality in order to establish this equitable interest.

If this principle were applied in relation to the flat put into the name of Jane, the children would automatically have their equitable interest of a third each created in their favour. They would not have to adduce any evidence to establish their interest, and the court would not investigate the underlying illegal purpose. This was the approach in *Tinsley* v *Milligan* (1994) as regards the two female lovers (who were regarded in equity as 'strangers'), and it is suggested that this approach would be followed as regards the purchase of the flat in the name of Jane.

It is possible that the courts may not follow this approach in relation to the flat on the basis that the children in this problem are not minors. However, it is suggested that this would not make any difference to the proposed solution put forward in the paragraph above.

A good answer should of course end with a conclusion. One way of concluding is to summarise what has been said previously.

It is also possible to argue that in both of the above situations, Kay and Larry gain at Jane's expense. It may be that the court would regard this as an appropriate instance of unjust enrichment by Kay and Larry and modify the position. The fact of unjust enrichment in situations of illegality has been recognised in England: *Taylor* v *Bhail* (1996). This case is discussed in a casenote by Francis Rose. This casenote has been previously dealt with in Unit 1.

2

Basic Concepts

Self-assessment questions

1. The equitable interest is that to which a beneficiary is entitled. It is the right to receive income or capital or both, or some other benefit, from the trust. The legal interest is the technical interest: the trustee is the legal owner. The trustee administers the trust in accordance with the terms of the trust. The hallmark of a trust is the split legal and equitable ownership.

2. After a trust has been created the settlor has no rights in relation to that trust. His former legal interest, which is now part of the trust property, will have passed to the trustee. His former equitable interest is now held on trust for the beneficiary. The settlor cannot reclaim the property once it has been transferred to the trustee.

3. A trust may be created by the settlor (a) declaring himself trustee in trust for the beneficiary; or (b) transferring the property to the trustee, having previously agreed with the trustee that he is willing to hold the property on trust.

4. A trust of an already existing equitable interest can be created by the existing beneficiary, who owns the equitable interest, declaring himself trustee for the new beneficiary. The trustee then becomes the trustee for the new beneficiary.

5. An existing trust will be terminated when the beneficiary calls for the legal interest. This, combined with the equitable interest the beneficiary already owns, will give him an absolute right to the property. The beneficiary becomes the owner of the property previously held in trust. The trusteeship comes to an end, and the trustee will have no duties to perform.

6. The quote from *Milroy* v *Lord* (1862) is an accurate statement of the law. The quote represents exactly the principle that was applied in the case itself. If a gift is intended the courts will not give effect to it by holding that a declaration of trust was made. If the gift is ineffective it will fail. The same thing happened in *Jones* v *Lock* (1865) discussed in paragraph 5.2 of Unit 2. The same approach was taken in *Richards* v *Delbridge* (1874) discussed in paragraph 5.5 of Unit 2.

   In the recent case of *Paul* v *Constance* (1977) discussed in paragraphs 2.1 and 5.7 of Unit 2, a different approach was taken. The court did hold that words that might have been words of gift did succeed as a valid declaration of trust in relation to a bank account. One possible way of distinguishing this case is to argue that a gift was not intended. Albert Constance merely wanted to benefit Doreen Grace Paul, but did not know how to give effect to this wish. The courts merely carried out his wishes. This wish could be best effected through the creation of a trust.

7.   A major issue in this problem is whether Jack has made a declaration of trust to Jill in his conversation with her in the park. It is established from *Paul v Constance* that formal words of trust do not have to be used in order to create a trust. See paragraph 5.11 of Unit 2. He does identify a specific share – that they are each to have half. His words are even more specific than in *Paul v Constance*.

There is a further complicating factor to this problem. The property that is subject to the trust is land. Land is subject to certain formalities which will be discussed in Unit 5. For current purposes (in answering this problem) it is important to mention that section 53(1)(b) of the Law of Property Act 1925 provides that in order to create a valid declaration of trust of land or of any interest in land there is a formality concerning writing that must be complied with: the declaration must be manifested and proved by some writing. The conversation is the park would necessarily fall foul of this requirement.

Jill would be able to argue that a constructive trust has been created. This type of constructive trust will be discussed in Unit 7. A similar case in which a resulting trust was argued and succeeded was *Hammond v Mitchell* (1991) which is discussed in Unit 7. In a casual conversation the male cohabitee told the female cohabitee that the house would be divided equally between them and that he would always look after her and their son.

The court reasoned that this conversation showed an intention that she was to have an interest in the house. Although not clear enough for an express trust it did amount to an informal understanding. The male cohabitee could not then act contrary to such an arrangement. The court would impose a constructive trust to protect the female cohabitee. Since it was clear that a half share was intended, the court awarded the female cohabitee a half share. The facts of this case are similar to the facts of the problem, and an appropriate comparison should be drawn.

A further point is that section 53(2) of the Law of Property Act 1925 exempts constructive trusts from the formal requirement of writing. Jill would be likely to establish a constructive trust in her favour. She would also be likely to be awarded a half share. This constructive trust would not have to be in writing by virtue of section 53(2).

Note: In *Paul v Constance* the property that was sought to be made the subject of a trust was a bank balance. Section 53(1)(b) only requires declarations of trust of land to be in writing. Also, the focus of the court's attention will be the conversation between the parties when it comes to decide how much to award the female cohabitee. In contrast, with a constructive trust, the court is able to look at a wider range of factors including the whole relationship, and does not necessarily have to focus just on any conversations between the parties when deciding how much to award the female cohabitee.

8.   Under the *Saunders v Vautier* (1841) rule the complete class of beneficiaries is able to end a trust. However, the beneficiaries cannot use this rule to

manage the trust. It is up to the trustee to make decisions that affect the trust. This approach is confirmed in *Re Brockbank* (1948), in which it was held that the beneficiaries could not direct the trustee as regards the appointment of a replacement trustee. This has now been expressly reversed by sections 19 to 21 of the Trusts of Land and Appointment of Trustees Act 1996.

In addition this act allows the trustees to delegate carrying out the trust to the beneficiaries under section 9. This clearly would not have been allowed before the act as a consequence of the decision in *Re Brockbank* (1948), in which it was held that the beneficiaries could not direct the trustee as regards the appointment of a replacement trustee. This has now been expressly reversed by sections 19 to 21 of the Trusts of Land and Appointment of Trustees Act 1996.

This act also requires trustees to consult with beneficiaries in exercising their powers in relation to a trust of land by section 11(1) of the act. This type of consultation could not have been mandatory before the act as a consequence of the decision in *Re Brockbank* (1948).

Lastly, where trustees divide up the land held in trust the consent of each of the affected beneficiaries is required by section 7(3) of the act. Again, before the introduction of the act as a consequence of the decision in *Re Brockbank* (1948), the trustees would not have needed the consent of the beneficiaries.

It is apparent that the act has significantly altered the position.

Note: this outlines the points to be made in an answer to this question. The detail is contained in paragraphs 5.13 to 5.32 of Unit 2.

3

Classification of Trusts

Self-assessment questions

1. An express trust is one where the terms have been expressly stated. Where the terms of the trust are formally recorded in a trust document, this will be an express trust.

2. The presumed resulting trust is an example of one based on parties' intentions. The parties will not have recorded their agreement properly or totally. It will come into existence where the parties have both contributed to the purchase price of some property. There is an implied understanding that both are to have a share in the equitable interest in the property.

   On the other hand, an automatic resulting trust comes about irrespective of intention. They may not have thought about what will happen to the equitable interest. Where the parties are 'strangers' (i.e. not husband and wife or parent and child), equity will adopt the presumption of trust.

3. A constructive trust is remedial: it is imposed by the courts as a remedy: *Chase Manhatten Bank NA* v *Israel-British Bank (London) Ltd* (1981). It is normally imposed to remedy inequitable, unconscionable, improper or unjust conduct. It is imposed irrespective of intention. A common situation where constructive trusts are imposed is with cohabitees.

4. A private trust is for private individuals or organisations which will benefit under the trust. Barring certain exceptional categories of purpose trusts, and charitable trusts, an express private trust must be for identified individuals.

5. There are four categories of charitable trust: for the relief of poverty, the advancement of education and of religion, and for other purposes beneficial to the community. There is considerable case law regarding what falls within these four categories.

6. The *Quistclose* trust is a resulting trust. If one person transfers monies or property for a particular purpose then that will create an express trust. If that purpose cannot be carried out then a secondary resulting trust will arise.

   This trust is named after a leading House of Lords case, *Barclays Bank Ltd* v *Quistclose Investments Ltd* (1970) that confirmed this principle. This principle is discussed in paragraphs 1.9 to 1.24, in particular paragraph 1.15.

   Lord Browne-Wilkinson in *Westdutsche Landesbank Girozentrale* v *Islington London Borough Council* (1996) regarded the *Quistclose* trust as being an automatic type of trust that arises through operation of law and not because of the intentions of the parties.

7. The monies that the licensees make (less the commission owing to Barks and Fencers) is beneficially owned by those licensees. It may be put into an account of Barks and Fencers but it does not belong to the store. These monies are held on trust by the store for the benefit of the licensees.

Such a trust may be created expressly such as in the leading case of *Re Kayford* (1975) where the account was called a trust account. Such a trust is therefore an express trust. This decision has been applied in a number of cases. It is briefly dealt with in Unit 3, paragraph 4.24.

A trust may be imposed even if a separate trust account is not set up. Where an agent receives the principal's property or monies, the courts will be keen to infer a trust. See *Neste Oy v Lloyds Bank* (1983) applied in *Re Fleet Disposals Services Ltd* (1995). On our facts the store is an agent which receives the monies that belong to its principal, the licensees. This points to the creation of a trust.

On the other hand if the recipient is free to deal with the funds as he or she pleases and does not have to open up a separate account then the relationship with the provider of the funds will merely be a contractual one: *Re Holiday Promotions (Europe) Ltd* (1996). If the recipient is obliged to use those funds in a particular way, then an express trust will be created as in *R v Clowes (No. 2)* (1994). On our facts the store is obliged to use the funds to repay the licensees and for this reason it is suggested that a trust is created.

The next issue is the effect of this trust upon the bank. It is clearly established that if the bank has actual knowledge of the trust then it cannot set off the two accounts. This was the position in *Barclays Bank Ltd v Quistclose Investments Ltd* (1970), and also *Re Marwalt plc* (1992) where the bank was told by letter that it was dealing with an account created to receive funds held on trust for another. In both cases the court held that the bank was unable to exercise any rights of set-off in relation to these trust accounts.

There is less authority upon the issue of constructive notice, that is to say where the bank ought to be aware of the position because of the surrounding circumstances. An important authority is *Neste Oy v Lloyds Bank plc* (1993). Bingham J made specific mention of a sixth and last payment put into a bank account.

The judge concluded that the bank did not know all the facts but it did know that the company, whose account was maintained at the bank, was about to cease trading. The judge concluded that had the bank made further enquiries it would have found out that this account was subject to a trust. It is suggested that this is the clearest authority on the point and does confirm that constructive knowledge would be sufficient.

Applying this to the facts, the issue is whether the Sloppy Bank plc is put on enquiry (becomes aware that monies in the account of the store might not be owned by the store so that the bank should make further enquiries). If cash is being deposited then this would not of itself put the bank on enquiry: *Lipkin Gorman v Karpnale Ltd* (1987 High Court). If the monies are put into a separate account, it is doubtful whether this would in itself put the bank on enquiry. The account would have to be named or identified in a particular way.

If the bank is not put on enquiry then it should be able to exercise its rights to set off the overdrawn account against the account in surplus even though it contains monies that are in fact held in trust for the licensees.

8.   The express trust is substantive because it is based upon a particular statement or trust document. The constructive trust is imposed as a remedy by the courts.

In addition a constructive trust may be imposed over an express trust. The categories of 'knowing assistance' and 'knowing receipt' (which will be discussed in Unit 16 on constructive trusts) will be imposed against a third party who dishonestly assists in the misapplication or improper receipt of trust funds.

In the area of trusts and cohabitees there is an important distinction between resulting and constructive trusts which has been highlighted in Unit 3, paragraph 1.6 to 1.8, and 1.12 to 1.14. In essence the resulting trust is imposed because of the common intention of both (all) the parties. In contrast, the constructive trust is imposed because one party seeks to deny the intention of the other party.

Particular pieces of legislation recognise these different categories of trust. If either a constructive or resulting trust arises then for both of these trusts writing is not required under both section 53(2) of the Law of Property Act 1925, and section 2(5) of the Law of Property (Miscellaneous Provisions) Act 1925. These provisions will be considered in detail in Unit 5. They have been mentioned briefly in paragraph 1.32. of Unit 3.

Specifically, in the context of *Westdeutsche Landesbank Girozentrale* v *Islington London Borough Council* (1996), Lord Browne-Wilkinson makes a distinction between the resulting and the constructive trust in the context of a thief who steals money or property from another. The conscience of the thief is affected. The consequence is that the thief holds the property taken on a constructive trust for the owner. Lord Browne-Wilkinson makes clear that such a trust is not a resulting trust. This is dealt with in paragraphs 4.13 to 4.14 of Unit 3.

9.   The answer to this question is contained in paragraphs 4.1 to 4.20 of Unit 3. In particular this case establishes: first, that a resulting trust will not be established where there is a void contract; second, that the presumption of resulting trust applies where property is transferred to a stranger (this point has been dealt with when considering *Tinsley* v *Milligan* (1994) in Unit 1); third, that there were two types of resulting trusts – presumed resulting trusts and automatic resulting trusts; fourth, that a constructive trust will be imposed where the conscience of the recipient is affected; fifth, that in the future, where appropriate, consideration should be given to developing a 'remedial constructive trust'.

Exam-style question

This question falls within Syllabus sections 3.1(a) Public and Private Trusts, 5.2(f) Three Certainties and also 14 Charities. It was a two-part question in the Spring 1995 paper. The answer in the Examiner's Report is as follows.

(a) Charitable trusts are enforced by the Attorney-General and supervised by the Charity Commissioners. Private trusts, on the other hand, are enforced by the beneficiaries. Private trusts must have clear objects, i.e. identity of beneficiaries, whereas charitable trusts may be deliberately vaguer in this respect. If a charitable trust fails, the funds may be held cy-près for some other scheme so long as there is a general charitable intent. On the other hand, if a private trust fails there will usually be a resulting trust in favour of the settlor or of his estate.

Charities are usually exempt from taxes except for the initial vesting; charitable trusts are not subject to the perpetuity rules that apply to private trusts. With a charitable trust, the trustees are not limited to four in number and the majority may bind the minority (re Whiteley (1910)).

(b) Many candidates felt that the trusts here would fail because of the lack of clear objects. This criterion does not really apply to a charitable trust and indeed, discretionary charitable trusts (such as a grant-making charitable trust) are very common but many candidates seemed to be unfamiliar with this concept.

To be valid a charitable trust must be exclusively charitable, although its objects may be vague. The problem in this example is that 'deserving' does not necessarily mean the same as 'charitable'. There have been cases in which such an expression has been construed conjunctively, i.e. the cause must be both charitable and deserving. Thus, the bequest will be valid as a charitable trust. It is a matter of the construction of the individual document concerned – e.g. in *Attorney-General of Bahamas* v *Royal Trust Company* (1986) the expression 'education and welfare' was construed disjunctively, i.e. as meaning education *or* welfare, and was thus held not to create a charitable trust because welfare was not wholly and exclusively charitable.

If the gift is not charitable it will probably fail for uncertainty of objects (*Morice* v *Bishop of Durham* (1805)). Trustees cannot take beneficially and the gift will probably fall back into the residue of the estate.

4

Trusts and Powers

Self-assessment questions

1. A bare power is where someone has both legal and equitable ownership in some property. That person is the absolute owner and is therefore able to do what he wishes with the property. He may, at his absolute discretion, transfer part or all of that property to another person. Where a bare power over some property is granted to an individual it will normally be granted with a 'gift in default'. That is, if the donee of the power does not exercise the power, as he is free to do, then that property will be taken by the individual or group that is to take in default of its exercise.

2. In *McPhail* v *Doulton* (1971), Lord Wilberforce made an important distinction between a discretionary trust and a power put into a trust. The particular clause he was asked to interpret used the word 'shall', and this was ruled to mean that the trustee must carry out his duties. Therefore, a trust had been created. In contrast, with a bare power the individual would not be under any obligation.

3. With a discretionary trust no particular beneficiary can point to any particular interest he has. This is in marked contrast to a 'fixed' trust, where the particular share of each beneficiary is exactly quantified.

4. The trustee has a duty to select from the whole class of beneficiaries, and distribute the income and/or capital among the chosen beneficiaries in accordance with the terms of the trust.

5. Where a bare power has been given instead to a trustee to exercise under a trust, the power becomes a fiduciary power. In this situation the trustee is not under a duty to distribute the income (or capital). However, the trustee must consider on a regular basis whether to distribute the income or the capital. The trustee must consider whether and how he ought to exercise this fiduciary power.

6. There are several problems which arise as a result of the decision of the House of Lords in *McPhail* v *Doulton* (1971). These problems are discussed in paragraphs 6.1 to 6.21.

   In particular, the test of conceptual certainty may lead to the invalidity of discretionary trusts.

   The requirement of administrative workability may lead to invalidity for trusts with a wide class: *R* v *District Auditor, ex parte. West Yorkshire Metropolitan County Council* (1995).

Furthermore, the test of certainty of objects put forward by Lord Wilberforce in *McPhail* v *Doulton* (1971) is a test for validity. The trustees may still be in considerable difficulties in determining to whom income and capital should be distributed.

When the test of Lord Wilberforce in *McPhail* v *Doulton* (1971) was considered by the Court of Appeal in *Re Baden Deed Trusts (No. 2)* (1973), various interpretations (discussed in the text) were put forward as to what Lord Wilberforce meant.

An important interpretation was put forward by Megaw LJ, who regarded Lord Wilberforce's test as requiring that the trustees must be able to tell whether a substantial number of individuals fall within the class as described by the trust.

Since different interpretations are possible, it is clear that uncertainties in the legal position remain.

7. The first point is whether the first part of the clause creates a trust or a power. There are arguments which go both ways. In favour of a trust is the fact that it is given to trustees to exercise. However, a power may also be given to trustees. Another reason in favour of a power is the second part of the clause, which may be considered to be a gift in default. This would then point to the first part of the clause being a power.

Perhaps the crucial aspect is the importance of the word 'should'. In *McPhail* v *Doulton* (1971) Lord Wilberforce considered that the word 'shall' was a crucial matter in pointing to a trust. An important distinction can be drawn between the two words.

However, Lord Wilberforce in *McPhail* v *Doulton* (1971) made the point that the test for certainty of objects was the same for both powers and trusts. The test for both is whether it can be said with certainty whether any given individual is a member of the class.

In order for this test to be satisfied each (and all) of the various classes must be conceptually certain. Applying this to the facts:

The class of 'heterosexual pilots' is conceptually certain. However, evidential difficulties would present problems. As a matter of practice, how would the trustees tell? It is established that such difficulties do not invalidate that class.

Further, in considering the word 'dependant' in *Re Baden's Deed Trusts (No. 2)* (1972) Brightman J in the High Court considered that the degree of dependence was irrelevant. This approach was followed by Sachs LJ in the Court of Appeal in *Re Baden Deed Trusts (No. 2)* (1973). This approach would make it more likely that the class of 'heterosexual pilots' would be considered to be conceptually certain, since the degree of hetrosexuality could be ignored.

Although 'employees' were considered to be conceptually certain in *Re Baden's Deed Trusts (No. 2)* (1993), this word is not used by John. The word 'serving' is possibly equivalent to this. However, because of its tense, it appears to cover only current pilots, rather than pilots who have been employed previously.

The RAF would have a ready list of its service personnel. This would mean that the class would be considered to be administratively workable, even though it is a very large class numerically.

However, it is possible that the courts could consider this class to be capricious (not sensible) or contrary to public policy. It is difficult to predict their approach, though, in general, the courts try to give effect to a settlor's intentions.

It is established that both 'relatives' and 'dependants' are conceptually certain classes: *Re Baden Deed Trusts (No. 2) (1973)*.

There is no doctrine of severance (cutting out the invalid parts) for a private trust (*Re Leek* (1969)) so that if the class of 'hetrosexual pilots' was considered conceptually uncertain, the whole of this part of the clause would be invalid. If this were due to the use of 'heterosexual', the question then is whether John has set up an alternative trust by the second part of the clause.

One possibility is that this second part is a gift in default (meaning that the trustees were under no duty to distribute under the first part of the clause). This is unlikely for two reasons. First, the second part does not use words of gift. Second, the first part of the clause uses the word 'should' rather than 'may', so that this imposes some degree of obligation. If this creates a trust, then the second part of the clause cannot be a gift in default.

It is likely that the second part of the clause constitutes an alternative trust.

The question is whether the various classes of beneficiaries are conceptually certain. There is no problem with 'relatives' of John. This would be conceptually certain.

In *Re Barlow's Will Trust* (1979) the court considered that there were problems with the class of 'friends' and that it would not fulfil the test put forward by Lord Wilberforce in *McPhail* v *Doulton* (1971). The difficulties might be worsened by the use of the word 'good' to make the class 'good friends'.

It is possible that this could be held to make this class more certain since it would no longer include mere acquaintances. However, does 'good' mean close friends, or friends with whom John spent a considerable amount of time, or long-standing friendships? It is probable that the class is rendered more uncertain by use of the term 'good'.

The fact that the trustees are under the further duties to distribute to persons within the various classes who are 'deserving', may make the position more uncertain. It is unclear on what criteria the trustees should exercise their discretion. If the phrase merely confirms the position that the trustees have discretion, then it still does not resolve any uncertainty.

In the light of the uncertainties discussed above, the trustees should be advised to seek the assistance of the courts as to whether the trust is valid. If the trust is held valid the trustees should put proposals to the courts as to how they will exercise their duties to distribute funds, and request the courts to sanction these proposals.

Exam-style question

This question falls within Syllabus sections 4.3 and 4.4 – Powers of Appointment. It was a complete question in the Spring 1996 paper. The answer in the Examiner's Report is as follows:

(a)   This is a special power of appointment and it needs to be specifically exercised; it is only general powers which may be exercised by the residuary clause in the will of the appointor – Wills Act 1837. Thus, the child will take George's estate only if Adrian specifically refers to the special power in his will. Otherwise, the capital will pass to the named charity.

(b)   The power of appointment will have been exercised by Adrian within the original perpetuity period (he himself is the life in being). However, the suggested manner of exercising the power could take the ultimate vesting date way beyond Adrian's life plus 21 years. This could invalidate the gift, but section 3 of the Perpetuities and Accumulations Act 1964 allows us to 'wait and see'. This could mean that the gift is valid if Adrian's son ultimately fails to survive his father by 21 years.

(c)   A power of this nature must be exercised for the benefit of those intended to benefit. Adrian appears to be intending to exercise the power in such a way as to benefit from it himself and, as he was not intended to benefit in this way, it would be fraud on the power and the trustees would be in breach of trust if they acted on it. They would be liable to the persons who might otherwise have been benefited from the trust (e.g. any other children or the charity) – *re Brook* (1968).

5

Validity of Trusts

Self-assessment questions

1. Section 53(1)(a) of the Law and Property Act 1925 provides that no interest in land may be created or disposed of except in writing. In addition, section 53(1)(b) provides that a declaration of trust of land must be manifested and proved by some writing. Section 2(1) of the Law of Property (Miscellaneous Provisions) Act 1989 provides that a contract for the sale or other disposition of an interest in land can be made only in writing.

2. Section 53(1)(c) of the Law of Property Act 1925 provides that to transfer (dispose) any separated equitable interest to another person, that transfer must only be in writing.

3. Section 53(2) of the Law and Property Act 1925 provides that the other sections in section 53 (which require a written document or statement) will not affect the creation or operation of resulting or constructive trusts. Thus an oral contract which creates a constructive trust will not fall foul of the other sections, 53(1)(a), 53(1)(b) and 53(1)(c). (This is discussed in detail in paragraphs 2.8 to 2.15 of Unit 10.)

4. The three certainties are essential to create a valid trust: there must be clear intention to create a trust; it must be certain who the beneficiaries (the objects) are; and it must be certain what property is to be held under that trust.

5. The recent cases (discussed in the main text) have required the property that is subject to a trust obligation to be sufficiently identified.

6. One way in which this trust might be rendered invalid is through the doctrine of conceptual uncertainty (discussed in Unit 4). There have been problems of uncertainty where a particular religion is used: *Clayton v Ramsden* (1943).

    The other way in which this trust would be rendered invalid is public policy. The approach of the English courts derives from a House of Lords decision *Blathwayt v Baron Cawley* (1976) and is as follows:

    First, although they may consider such clauses to be reprehensible, their Lordships accept that there is a policy in English law allowing settlors freedom of action.

    Second, they accept that if this trust had been set up during the lifetime of Bert (inter vivos), it would be perfectly valid. They feel that there should not be a distinction between inter vivos trusts, and trusts arising on death (made by will). This is a further reason for their validity.

Third, it is not contrary to public policy for a settlor to have a forfeiture clause based upon religion in the way that Bert has provided by his will, *Re Lysaght (dec'd)* (1966).

Fourth, public policy was based on either specific rules of case law, or particular sections of statutes which show a clear policy.

Fifth, that public policy was not static and did adapt itself to meet changing circumstances.

Blathwayt v *Baron Cawley* (1976) involved a clause in which a beneficiary would loose his equitable interest if he practised the Catholic religion. This case could be distinguished from this problem involving Bert's will because the exclusion will happen if a beneficiary marries a person of a particular religion or colour, rather than practising or not practising a particular religion. A further distinction is that this problem involves exclusion on the grounds of colour.

In *Blathwayt* v *Baron Cawley* (1976), the House of Lords was of the view that a relevant factor was the time when the will was made. In that case, the will was executed (made) in 1936. The House of Lords accepted that public policy had changed since that date, and that it might be unfair to apply current rules of public policy to a will made a considerable time ago. It is relevant that in our problem, Bert's will was executed in 1950.

Blathwayt v *Baron Cawley* (1976) was decided before the introduction of the Race Relations Act 1976. It is now arguable that there is a policy against discrimination, and that this general category of public policy could be affected by the introduction of this important piece of legislation. However, the Race Relations Act 1976 does not cover express private trusts.

In Canada, where they have specific legislation protecting individual and human rights, it has been held that a clause in a charitable educational trust discriminating against black, Catholic and female students was contrary to public policy: *Re Leonard Foundation Trust; Canada Trust Company* v *Ontario Human Rights Commission; Royal Ontario Museum et al (Intervenors)* (1991) August TruLI).

If any parts of the clause were held to be contrary to public policy, then the whole clause would be invalid. There is no doctrine of severence in English law to allow the deletion of the offending parts of an express trust: *Re Leek* (1969).

Exam-style questions

1   This question falls within Syllabus sections 5.2(f) Three Certainties and 4 Trusts and Powers. It was one of three parts in the Spring 1995 paper. The answer in the Examiner's Report is as follows:

For the validity of a trust to be established, it is necessary to have the three certainties set out in *Knight* v *Knight* (1840). These are words, subject matter and objects. As for words, 'trusting' may not be as strong as 'on trust for'. The latter would certainly indicate a trust but the more informal words may indicate only a reliance on the donee to carry out the bequest. Thus, the words are probably only precatory.

As for the subject matter, 'residuary estate' is clear but the extent of the gift is unclear because of Anne's ability to choose whatever she wants. As for the objects of the proposed trust, are the beneficiaries clear? This is a discretionary trust and, following *McPhail* v *Doulton* (1970), one needs to be able to say whether a particular individual is included. Following *Re Baden* (1973) 'relatives' may be certain enough but 'friends' may well be too vague (*Re Barlow* (1979) is a little different in that, in that case, it was probably sufficient for the friends to show their status in order to claim). In the current context, a trust is unlikely to have been created.

2   This question falls within Syllabus sections 5.2(a) Inter Vivos Trusts of Land. It was one of three parts in the Spring 1995 paper. The answer in the Examiner's Report is as follows:

The three certainties are here satisfied but section 53 of the Law of Property Act 1925 requires a declaration of trust of land to be in writing. Thus, the declaration itself may not be sufficient but the subsequent letter should be.

6

Constitution of Trusts

Self-assessment questions

1. A trust will be constituted (validly created) when the property is transferred by the settlor to the trustee.

2. No, for reasons given in Unit 6 of this book.

3. No, for reasons given in Unit 6 of this book.

4. The same rules of marriage settlements apply to commercial trusts. The rules of enforceability of marriage settlements are described in detail in Unit 6.

    Since the monies are not transferred, the trust is not constituted.

    The employees are 'volunteers' (that is they have not given any consideration) as regards Robin. In addition, they are not parties to the agreement with Robin. They have no rights to bring contractual claims: *Cannon* v *Hartley* (1949).

    As the employees are 'volunteers' they cannot require the trustees to sue on their behalf. The trustees would be directed not to sue to compel performance of Robin's promise: *Re Kay* (1939). The position of trustees is also dealt with in Unit 6.

    There are statements in the cases which suggest that the trustees would be able to obtain substantial damages on behalf of the employee beneficiaries: *Re Cavendish Browne's Settlement Trusts* (1916). Further, such damages have been awarded where the purported settlor is under a moral obligation to the beneficiary: *Williamson* v *Codrington* (1750). It could be argued that Robin owes his employees such an obligation as chairperson of their company.

    However, any damages awarded would go on resulting trust back to Robin. For that reason, it is suggested that the court would not award them.

    Although Robin agrees to transfer a sum of money, there is nothing in the facts to suggest that he intended to create a completely constituted trust of the promise: *Fletcher* v *Fletcher* (1844).

    The above approach is confirmed by *MacJordan Construction Ltd* v *Brookmount Erostin Ltd* (1992), where an employer agreed to transfer a sum of money to the contractor, to be put into trust for that contractor. This was not carried out. In particular, the employer had not made financial provision for the transfer. Subsequently, the employer went into liquidation. It was held that the contractor was unable to enforce this promise.

5.   As a matter of construction, Sara and Tara fall within both clauses 1 and 2 as 'legitimate' and 'illegitimate' children.

There is also the problem of uncertainty of subject matter in relation to clause 1. The words 'cottage in the country' might be considered uncertain as both 'cottage' and 'country' are somewhat vague. However, if there is only one such cottage owned by David then uncertainty will not invalidate the clause: *Boyce* v *Boyce* (1849).

Additionally, a declaration of a trust of land must be made in writing: section 53(1)(b) of the Law of Property Act 1925. The question does not specifically make clear whether writing has been used, but it appears (from the quotes) that this is so.

Section 12 of the Trusts of Land and Appointment of Trustees Act 1996 gives a beneficiary the right to occupy land. By section 13 of this act, trustees may not unreasonably exclude a beneficiary's right to occupy land held in trust. For a discussion of this act, see Unit 7.

On the assumption of validity of clause 1, the issue is whether Sara and Tara are able to enforce the promise of David to transfer his cottage.

It is established that both legitimate children by a former marriage and illegitimate children are not able to enforce this promise since both categories are regarded as volunteers: *Attorney-General* v *Jacobs-Smith* (1895). Neither category falls within the marriage consideration. Only children of his second marriage, which is about to take place in the near future, will be within the marriage consideration, *Attorney-General* v *Jacobs-Smith* (1895).

It is possible for Sara and Tara to argue that they are objects of interest as regards their father David, and that they give him actual consideration.

As we have seen in Unit 6, while this originally represented the rule in equity it has been overtaken by the common law rule which did not regard love and affection as consideration.

Sara and Tara would be volunteers who would be unable to obtain specific performance of David's promise. This approach would also be the approach in relation to clause 2.

Since the promise by David involves the transfer of money, it is possible to argue, on the basis of *Fletcher* v *Fletcher* (1844), that there is a completely constituted trust of the promise.

If and when David has children from his future second marriage, such children are within the marriage consideration and are able to enforce his promise: *Attorney-General* v *Jacobs-Smith* (1895).

The interests of such children under both clause 1 and clause 2 are closely intertwined – it would be difficult, because of the way each clause is drafted, for a trustee to give to one beneficiary and not the other. The court will enforce the whole clause as a whole unit: *Attorney-General* v *Jacobs-Smith* (1895).

This is confirmed by the approach in *Re D'Angibau* (1880) where the court stated that where it enforces a trust it will enforce it in its entirety.

Any children of David, born to David and his partner after his second marriage, are deemed to give consideration, and would be able to obtain specific performance of his obligation to transfer the property and the monies to the trustees, *Attorney-General* v *Jacobs-Smith* (1895). The trustees would sue for specific performance on behalf of such children. Once such children obtained specific performance, the property and monies would then be transferred to the trustees.

At such point the trustees would obtain the legal title to the property and monies. The trust would be constituted for all beneficiaries: *Re Ralli's Will Trusts* (1964). This would mean that both Sara and Tara would be entitled to occupy the cottage and receive a share of the monies held in trust.

Discretionary trusts, and the duties of trustees, have been previously considered in Unit 4.

6. The rule in *Strong* v *Bird* (1874) is said to have derived from that case. It states that, where the title is transferred to a trustee, the trust will be constituted. It does not matter in what way the trustee obtains legal title. However, an illegal method – such as theft of the intended trust property by the trustee – would not count. If the trustee obtains legal title through subsequently being the executor of the settlor's estate, then the trust will be constituted.

Exam-style questions

1 This question falls within Syllabus sections 6.1/6.2/2.2/5.2(b). It was one of three parts of a question in the Spring 1995 paper. The answer in the Examiner's Report is as follows:

If it can be shown that Joseph had declared himself a trustee it may be effective, as a trust of personalty can be created by words alone. As the ring is still in his possession, the trust will have been fully constituted since he himself would be the trustee; but, following *Milroy* v *Lord* (1862), has there been effective delivery? Did he intend a present gift? If so, it is probably valid. Or was it a future gift, in which case it was probably not a valid trust. As there is no evidence of his keeping the ring as trustee it is probable that there is an ineffective gift and an ineffective trust.

2 This question falls within 6.2 Imperfect Gifts. It was a two-part question in the Autumn 1995 paper. The answer in the Examiner's Report is as follows:

The donor must effectively transfer assets in order to complete a gift or to make a trust, e.g. formal conveyance or actual handing over of assets concerned. Otherwise, he must declare himself trustee of the funds and the usual three certainties come into play. Either method would mean that the donor must have deprived himself of beneficial title to the assets concerned. The standard authority here is the case of *Milroy* v *Lord* (1862). If there is no consideration, the courts will not enforce a mere promise. Marriage settlements are an exception (as regards the parties to the marriage and any issue). Vesting in the donee or trustee may be accidental as in *Strong* v *Bird* (1874). Another example here is *donatio mortis causa*.

7

Trusts of Land

Self-assessment questions

1. Trusts of land may be held as any other trust, i.e. the land is simply held on trust. This is provided by the Trusts of Land and Appointment of Trustees Act 1996. This Act is briefly discussed in Unit 7 of this book.

2. A trust for sale will arise whenever there is co-ownership of land. Where there are two equitable owners, who have equitable interests under a resulting or a constructive trust, then a trust for sale will arise.

3. There is co-ownership of land where there are two equitable owners. The circumstances giving rise to joint equitable ownership are discussed in Unit 7 of this book.

4. A presumed resulting trust of land (property) will arise either where there are joint contributions to the purchase of that land, or where there is a common intention between the parties that there shall be joint ownership. The circumstances that give rise to this trust are discussed in paragraphs 3.1 to 3.7 of Unit 7. The same principles apply where the asset is not land.

5. A constructive trust of land will arise where two factors are both satisfied. First, that there is an arrangement between the parties that they are both to share the equitable ownership of that land. In effect, this means that there is a common intention between the parties that there shall be joint ownership. Second, that one party carries out acts of detriment (such as financial help, looking after the parties' children, assistance in the family business) because of that arrangement. The circumstances that give rise to this trust are discussed in paragraphs 4.1 to 4.16 of Unit 7. The same principles apply where the asset is not land.

6. Traditionally, the financial contributions would be the basis for assessing a party's share under a presumed resulting trust. In *Midland Bank plc* v *Cooke* (1995) the Court of Appeal decided that all the relevant factors would be taken into account in assessing a party's share. Such factors include not only financial contributions but also: any relevant discussions between the parties; contributions to the improvement of the property; looking after children; help and assistance in their business. It remains unclear whether this approach will be followed. In *Drake* v *Whipp* (1995) a different Court of Appeal followed the traditional approach and took into account only financial contributions in assessing a party's share. In the particular case the plaintiff was awarded a one-third share based upon her (Drake's) financial contribution. The court accepted that she might have been awarded a greater amount, that of a half-

share, had she argued for a constructive trust where a broader approach is taken. See the answer to question 7 below. The case of *Midland Bank plc* v *Cooke* (1995) is discussed in Unit 7.

7. The standard and continuing approach to assessing a party's share under a constructive trust is to look at all the relevant factors and not merely financial contributions: *Grant* v *Edwards* (1986). This approach was followed by the High Court in *Hammond* v *Mitchell* (1991). These factors are described in Unit 7 and have been listed in the answer to question 6 above.

8. Where cohabitees or a husband and wife purchase a property, the court asssumes that joint ownership is intended. Each will usually acquire an equitable interest under a presumed resulting or constructive trust. In contrast where a property is bought with assistance of a relative, the position is usually one of a loan or gift on the part of that relative. In particular, where the family member of the relative is an adult it will be presumed (i.e. the starting point will be) that a loan is intended. It will be presumed that there is no intention to create a trust (resulting trust): *Sekhorn* v *Alissa* (1989). The relevant principles and case law are discussed in detail in paragraphs 6.1 to 6.19 of Unit 7.

9. These provisions are outlined in paragraph 7.4 of Unit 7. There is a discussion of particular provisions of the Trusts of Land and Appointment of Trustees Act 1996 in Units 2 and 9.

Exam-style question

This question falls within Syllabus section 7 Trusts of Land and also 9.2(c) Trustees of Settled Land. It was a complete question in the Autumn 1995 paper. The answer in the Examiner's Report is as follows:

(a) In the absence of any binding trust for sale both properties appear to be settled land. Accordingly, the bank must transfer the legal title into the name of the life tenant, if she calls for it, rather than leave it in their own name. Many candidates recognised that the second property was settled land but few realised that this applied to the first property also.

(b) As it is settled land, Martha is entitled to exercise her power of sale. The subsequent provisions in the will appear to restrict her rights and are therefore made void by section 106 of the Settled Land Act 1925. Martha may sell the property but the proceeds of the sale must be paid to the trustee who must reinvest them at the direction of Martha who has the power to direct reinvestment of whole or part in the purchase of a new property. Any surplus would be vested in the name of the trustees so as to provide an income for Martha for life.

(c) The powers of repairing and improving the land are in the hands of the life tenant who should use income for routine repairs, although there are limits on her obligation to the trust to do so. Improvements may be paid for from capital but the trustee may require reimbursement from income by instalments – the Settled Land Act has schedules setting out the details of these requirements. If capital needs to be raised, the life tenant has power to mortgage the land. N.B. the tenant for life may be the landlord of property when it is leased and, in this event, the burden of the cost of repairs may have been passed to the tenant under the tenancy agreement. The tenant for life will then need to enforce these repairing covenants.

(d)   There is no statutory power to advance from capital monies held under the Settled Land Act since section 32 of the Trustee Act 1925 applies only to the proceeds of a trust for sale. If the will contains an express power to advance, any advance would have to be considered on its own merits.

[Note: this question was set before the Trusts of Land and Appointment of Trustees Act 1996.]

8

The Beneficiary Principle

Self-assessment questions

1. Effectively, a beneficiary of a trust has a proprietary right binding on third parties, that is good against the whole world. The exception to this is when the beneficiary loses his equitable interest at the hands of a *bona fide* purchaser for value.

2. This case is dealt with in paragraphs 1.7 to 1.12 of Unit 8 of this booklet.

3. The beneficiary principle is that, in order to create a valid express trust, the beneficiaries must satisfy the certainty of objects test. (This has been dealt with in Unit 5). With a trust for a purpose (a purpose trust), there must be some ascertainable beneficiaries who could seek to enforce the trust. The rule of certainty of objects is more relaxed when it comes to such a trust.

4. A bequest (gift) to an unincorporated association may take effect in one of three ways.

   ● The bequest must be held on trust for the association; if clear words such as 'trust' are used, the court will reach this conclusion. An example is *Re Denley*, discussed in Unit 8 of this booklet.

   ● As a gift to the association subject to the contractual rights of the members of the association. An example is Re Lipinski, discussed in Unit 8 of this booklet.

   ● As a gift to the association. An example is *Re Prevost*, discussed in Unit 8 of this booklet.

5. Brian's first wish for planting trees would appear to be a purpose trust. This would be invalid since there are no beneficiaries who are able to enforce the trust: *Re Astor's Settlement Trusts* (1952). The situation given in the problem can be distinguished from *Re Boyes* (1884) discussed in Unit 8 of this book.

   In *Re Boyes* (1884), the trees were to be planted on a particular piece of land which was settled land held by a particular tenant for life (refer to Trusts of Land and Appointment of Trustees Act 1996 discussed in Unit 7 of this book). The sum held on trust in this case was significantly greater than could be spent on planting trees. In these particular circumstances, the court held that all the monies would be held on trust absolutely for the tenant for life. See also, *Re Osoba* (1979) discussed in Unit 8 which supports the approach of: *Re Boyes* (1884). On our facts, there is no particular beneficiary who owns the land and the money could not be held on trust for a particular person.

There are also problems of uncertainty, i.e., which parks were intended, and how wide the geographical location was to be. Brian should be advised to change his plans.

Brian's second objective in leaving funds to maintain and improve the buildings of a particular club, are similar to the case of Re *Lipinski's Will Trusts* (1976). The fact that words of trust are used would impose a trust to carry out this objective. However, it might cause problems with perpetuity since the monies could be held on trust indefinitely. (See generally Unit 5 on the rules relating to perpetuity) For this reason the objective should be limited to a period of time within the perpetuity period. A suggested addition to the clause would be 'so far as the law allows': *re Dean* (1889).

Brian might leave the funds to the club for the general purposes of the club as an addition to its general funds: *Leahy* v *Attorney General of New South Wales* (1959), or alternatively, subject to the contractual rights of its members: *re Recher's Will Trusts* (1972). He could do either of these by using clear words of gift and deleting any trust obligation.

If the club's buildings are of significant historical importance, then there is the suggestion that the gift might be allowed as a purpose trust, even without ascertainable beneficiaries, *Glasgow Trades House* v *I.R.C.* (1970). However, the club is an incorporated association with members and so would not need to rely on this decision.

Brian's last wish to promote and further fox-hunting, would probably be valid as being an exceptional private purpose trust which was upheld in *Re Thompson* (1934). In that case the funds not used for this purpose would go to Trinity Hall Cambridge. The college had the right (*locus standi*) to complain to the court if the friend of the testator, who was to administer the trust, failed to carry it out properly. This was possibly a reason why Clauson J validated the trust. In our facts, there is no gift in remainder, and it is possible to distinguish *Re Thompson* (1934) for this reason.

Finally, the problem gives us separate clauses with separate amounts left for each purpose. This is a sensible approach to drafting Brian's objectives as there is no doctrine of severence in English law in relation to an express private trust: *re Leek* (1969). The consequence is that if the clauses are not drafted separately and one clause is invalid, then all clauses will be invalidated.

6.   There are three main issues: first, how the £5,000 raised from members and the public is held; second, whether the club is able to dissolve itself; third, how the assets of the club are held for its members.

   i)   The £5,000
   Firstly, that the donation is held on resulting trust for the donor. In *Re Gilligham Bus Disaster Fund* (1958) it was held that donations made for a specific purpose were held on resulting trust for the donors where the purpose of the donation could not be carried out. On our facts, the purpose cannot be carried out for two reasons: first, insufficient funds were raised, since they amounted to only half the cost of building a swimming pool; second, the club had decided to dissolve itself. (Resulting trusts through

failure to carry out the purpose for which monies have been provided have been previously discussed in Unit 5.)

Secondly, if the terms of the donation were that a club member or member of the public were to receive a particular benefit through the donation, such as being able to use the swimming pool when completed, then there would be a contractual relationship between the club and that person: *Re Gillingham Bus Disaster Fund* (1958).

A third possibility is that this £5,000, which is now surplus to the needs of the club, becomes the property of the club. This was the view of the High court in *Re Bucks Constabulary Widows' and Orphans' Fund Friendly Society (No2)* (1979). This would mean that an outright gift had been made by the donor to the club, and would exclude the operation of a resulting trust (discussed above). In *Re West Sussex Constabulary's Widows, Children and Benevolent 1930 Fund Trusts* (1971) a similar conclusion was reached by the court in relation to donations made by members of the public. The court regarded the donors as having intended to make an outright gift and part with their money. This decision, and approach, have recently been approved by Scott J in *Davis v Richards and Wallington Industries Ltd* (1990) and also by Lord Browne-Wilkinson in *Westdeutsche Landesbank Girozentrale v Islington London Borough Council* (1996).

ii) Dissolution of the club
If the rules of the club so provide, the club is able to dissolve itself: *re William Denby and Son Ltd Sick and Benevolent Fund* (1971).

iii) Distribution of the club's assets
On dissolution of the club, its assets are to be distributed to the members, *Re Bucks Constabulary Widows' and Orphans' Fund Friendly Society (No2)* (1979).

In *Re Hobourn Aero Components Ltd's Air Raid Distress Fund* (1946) distribution was ordered of a surplus fund in proportion to contributions to the fund by the employees. It is possible to distinguish this case from our facts since it does not concern a club.

The above approach was not followed in *Re GKN Bolts and Nuts (Automotive Division) Birmingham Works, Sports and Social Club* (1982). In this case, the court had to consider the basis of distribution where there was nothing in the rules of the club about distribution.

The court considered that distribution should be on the basis of equality, so that each member had one share in the proceeds of sale of club assets. The length of membership, and the amount of subscription paid were ignored. This is a similar case to our facts and would be likely to be followed and applied by a court to solving the facts of our problem.

An ex-member of the club who had left or died would not be entitled to any distribution. That member's interest became that of the continuing members, *Re Sick and Funeral Society of St. John Sunday School, Golcar* (1973).

The court in *Re Sick and Funeral Society of St. John Sunday School, Golcar* (1973) also took the approach that differences in the contributions of members were to be disregarded in determining the distribution of club assets. The court allowed distribution on the basis of a full share for adults and a half share for children. It is possible that a similar approach would be taken in relation to the Middlesex and Healthy Hearts Club if it has adult and junior members.

The court would carefully consider the rules of the club to ascertain whether they throw any light upon distribution, *Re Sick and Funeral Socieity of St. John Sunday School, Golcar* (1973), though we have been told that there is no rule of the Middlesex and Healthy Hearts Club which directly deals with distrbution.

Finally, in so far as the trustees or the committee of the club are involved in spending substantially additional time in distribution and sale of the club's assets, they are entitled to suitable remuneration for this: *Foster* v *Spencer* (1996). This is dealt with in detail in Unit 10 of this book.

9

Trusteeship

Self-assessment questions

1. The rules with regard to the appointment, retirement and removal of trustees are discussed in detail in Unit 9. First, there is the inherent jurisdiction to remove and appoint trustees. The cases of *Chellaram v Chellaram* (1985), *Letterstedt v Broers* (1884), *McPhail v Doulton* (1971), *Mettoy Pension Trustees Ltd v Evans* (1990), *Richard v The Hon A B Mackay* (1987) discussed in Unit 9 merit full consideration.

   Second, there is statutory jurisdiction under the Trustee Act 1925, discussed in Unit 9.

   Third, there is the particular statutory jurisdiction under the Trusts of Land and Appointment of Trustees Act 1996 regarding mentally incapacitated trustees, discussed in Unit 9. It should be pointed out that new rights are given to beneficiaries to direct the appointment of a new trustee(s) to replace a mentally incapacitated trustee.

   Fourth, the Pensions Act 1995 provides for the prohibition and suspension of trustees of an occupational pension scheme, and the appointment of replacement trustees. This is also discussed in Unit 9.

2. The position of custodian trustees is discussed in Unit 9. The central act is the Public Trustee Act 1906.

3. A bare trust is where a trustee holds the trust property on trust for a single beneficiary. In this situation the sole beneficiary, who is entitled to all the equitable interest, can call for the legal interest from the trustee. This ends the trust and gives the beneficiary absolute ownership.

4. The position and powers of a trust corporation are discussed in Unit 9.

5. A trustee is distinguished from a personal representative in Unit 9.

Exam-style questions

1. This question falls within Syllabus Section 9.1, Appointment, Retirement and Removal of Trustees. It was a three-part question in the Spring 1995 paper. The answer in the Examiner's Report is as follows.

   It is difficult to remove trustees against their will and beneficiaries can only do it by bringing court action if all else fails. The court may remove the trustees under section 41 of the Trustee Act 1925 but such actions are rare and the court would need strong evidence of wrong-doing, for which there are in any case other remedies. If the trustees can be persuaded to retire, section 36 of the Trustee Act may be used and the power of appointing falls on the person nominated (if any) or the surviving or continuing trustee. Many trust documents nominate a person as empowered to appoint new trustees but this power rarely extends to removing the trustee. The appointment of a new trustee must be in writing and preferably by deed.

Section 40 of the Trustee Act 1925 provides for the automatic vesting of trust property in new trustees when a deed is used. This will probably cover the land held in this trust. Stocks and shares will have to be transferred by standard transfer forms and other assets may need their own specific forms.

2   This question falls within Syllabus section 9.2, Different Types of Trustee. It is a complete question in the Autumn 1995 paper. The answer in the Examiner's Report is as follows.

   a)   A judicial trustee is appointed by the court to act as executor or trustee under the Judicial Trustees Act 1896 and this is now governed by 1983 rules. Any 'fit and proper person' may be appointed but it is usually a professional. He must produce annual accounts to the court and is usually appointed where there are great differences or disputes between beneficiaries and the trustee.

   b)   A custodian trustee may be either the public trustee or a trust corporation which never dies and which keeps the trust assets in its name, whereas the daily management of the trust remains in the hands of managing trustees on whose directions the custodian acts. He is not obliged to concur in any proposed breaches of trust. He receives and pays out all capital transactions but he may allow income to be received direct by the managing trustees. The office is usually required by unit trusts and private pension schemes. The appointment is usually contained in the original deed and is made by the original settlor.

   c)   The office of public trustee was established by a 1906 Act and is a trust corporation appointed by the Lord Chancellor. He acts in accordance with various statutory rules. He may carry out an audit of other trusts at the request of the beneficiaries. He may act only in English trusts and certain charitable trusts may not be handled. Recently, he has taken over responsibility for Court of Protection cases and the appointment of Receivers. He looks after funds held in court. He also registers and supervises enduring powers of attorney.

   d)   Such a trustee is appointed by the issuing company and is essential if the company is quoted on the London Stock Exchange. He holds the relative security, checks its value and checks that the company is observing the rules of the issue. If the loan is unsecured, he needs to ensure that the company remains able to repay. His primary duty is to the stockholders.

3   This question falls within Syllabus section 9.2(b), Custodian Trustees. It was a two part question in the Spring 1995 paper. The answer in the Examiner's Report is as follows.

Custodian trustees were set up by section 4 of the Public Trustee Act 1906 and have to be distinguished from managing trustees. The custodian holds all assets in his own name and acts on the proper instructions of the managing trustees but is not obliged to concur in any breach of trust. All receipts and payments should pass through it although it should allow income to be paid direct to the managing trustees. Among the advantages are the continuity of legal title and the fact that the custodian's independence helps to prevent any dishonesty. Among the disadvantages are the fact that a custodian can be removed only by the court and that it inevitably charges fees (although its statutory authority to charge may be seen by the bank as an advantage).

4   This question falls within Syllabus Section 9.1, Appointment, Retirement and Removal of Trustees. It was a complete question in the Spring 1996 paper. The answer in the Examiner's Report is as follows.

a)   There may be express authority in the deed but, otherwise, the matter is governed by Sections 36 and 41 of the 1925 Trustee Act. Under Section 36 a trustee may be removed by the appointment of a new trustee by the empowered party, i.e. the person appointed by the deed or by the continuing trustee. The circumstances in which this may be done include when he stays outside the UK for a continuous period of 12 months, he refuses to act, he is incapable or unfit, or he is an infant. Under Section 41 the Court may remove a trustee, usually as part of the appointment of a new trustee, and this is usually at the instigation of the beneficiaries of the trust, when Section 36 cannot be used without some difficulty.

b)   i)   The person given the power by the deed is the person to make this decision. If nobody, then the bank as continuing trustee will make the appointment under Section 36 after Elizabeth has been outside the UK for 12 months. If there are difficulties, e.g. Elizabeth's reluctance, the court may appoint under Section 41 and all matters would then be dealt with by the court.

ii)   If the appointment is under Section 36, it must be in writing although no particular form is required. A formal deed is necessary if it is desired to take advantage of the vesting provisions of Section 40 Trustee Act 1925.

iii)   If a formal deed is used Section 40 will operate to transfer freeholds and certain leaseholds. Otherwise, a separate deed is required, as it also will be in the case of leaseholds where the landlord's consent to an assignment is required. Bearer securities will pass by delivery or by giving notice to the relative custodian. As for stocks and shares, the usual transfer forms will be required.

10

Duties of Trustees

Self-assessment questions

1. A fiduciary owes particular duties of trust, loyalty and confidence to the other person for whom he acts. A trustee is a fiduciary, and owes these duties to his beneficiary. A company director is also a fiduciary and owes these duties to his company. Another class of persons who are fiduciaries are partners in a partnership, who owe fiduciary duties to each other. In some circumstances, an agent will owe fiduciary duties to his principal, in addition to the contractual relationship between them.

2. No. A fiduciary must not place himself in a position where there is a conflict of duty and interest.

3. There are some exceptions to this (strict) rule, that a fiduciary must not place himself in a position where there is a conflict of duty and interest. First, these include the further rule that, at the discretion of the court, the fiduciary may receive remuneration for his services. Second, the fiduciary may ask the court to exercise its discretion in place of that of the fiduciary.

4. The general duty that a trustee owes to a beneficiary is the same duty that a fiduciary owes to the other person for whom he acts. Trustees' general duties are considered in Parts 6 and 7 of Unit 10. Their duties in relation to investment of trust funds are considered in Unit 11.

5. This is dealt with at the end of Unit 15 on the Duties of Trustees.

Exam-style questions

1   This question falls with Syllabus Section 10, Duties of Trustees. It was a three part question in the Spring 1995 paper. The other two parts of this question appear in the Unit 14 questions. The answer in the Examiner's Report is as follows.

The basic rule is that a trustee cannot profit from his office. Any profit made should be accounted for to the trust. Appointment of a trustee as director of a company in which the trust is invested is not always wrong, as it may be to the advantage of the trust that the trustee can exercise greater control: *Bartlett* v *Barclays Bank Trust Company*. The trustee may be able to justify higher remuneration for the greater control that he is thus exercising: *Boardman* v *Phipps* (1966). Much may depend on whether the trustee used the trust holding to secure his appointment as a director – he may have been appointed without having to use those votes. The present trustees can be compelled to produce accounts to the beneficiaries.

2   This question falls within Syllabus Section 10, Duties of Trustees. It was a complete question in the Spring 1996 paper. The answer in the Examiner's Report is as follows.

a)   The personal views of the trustee should not enter into the matter and trustees should go for the best financial returns, as recommended by the professional adviser advising on the investments concerned: *Cowan* v. *Scargill*. In practice, it may well be possible to compromise by finding a similar investment that lacks moral objections.

b)   Assuming that Muriel is old enough: *Saunders* v. *Vautier* (1841) seems to apply and the trust may be brought to an end, preferably by deed. There is no need to bring in the Variation of Trusts Act 1958. It must be noted that Muriel would have to release her power of appointment in favour of any husband who survives her. This was a point that no candidate picked up although some referred to the existence of the power as being irrelevant. If the trust were brought to an end in this way there would be a capital gains tax liability on a deemed disposal by the trustee.

c)   The trust for sale is the primary duty: the power to postpone is subordinate and the exercise of that power requires unanimity. Where agreement is lacking, the trust for sale must prevail.

d)   The trustees must obtain the best price: *Buttle* v. *Saunders* (1950). The best price is not necessarily the highest. The earlier acceptance of an offer is not legally binding until contracts have been exchanged.

e)   Beneficiaries have a general right to see the trust documents but this does not extend to files or notes giving reasons for the way in which trustees exercise any discretions: *Londonderry's settlement* (1964).

[Note: this question was set before the Trusts of Land and Appointment of Trustees Act 1996 came into force.]

3   This question falls within Syllabus Section 10, Duties of Trustees. It was a two part question in the Autumn 1995 paper. The answer in the Examiner's Report is as follows.

Delegation may only be carried out where there is an express or implied power to do so. Agents may be employed for certain tasks, e.g. solicitors, accountants or other professionals: section 23 Trustee Act 1925 but this does not extend to the actual making of decisions and exercising of discretions. A trustee is not responsible if the agent is employed in good faith. It is often the case that investment advice has to be sought – e.g. section 8 Trustee Act 1925 and Trustee Investments Act 1961. Trustees may delegate in certain circumstances for up to one year (section 25 of the Trustee Act 1925 and Powers of Attorney Act 1971) whereas an enduring power of attorney delegates all the donor's powers, including any trusteeships. Section 29 of the Trustee Act 1925 allows for the delegation of land management to a life tenant.

11

Powers of Trustees in Specific Circumstances

Self-assessment questions

1. These are described in Part 1, and analysed in Part 2 of Unit 11.

2. These are described in Part 1, and analysed in Part 3 of Unit 11.

3. These are described in Parts 4, 5, 6, 7 and 8 of Unit 11.

4. The duties of trustees investing in land should be read in the light of the Trusts of Land and Appointment of Trustees Act 1996. The effect of this act is described in Unit 11 of this book. See Unit 11, where the investment powers of trustees of land are described in the light of the relevant provisions of the the Trusts of Land and Appointment of Trustees Act 1996.

Exam-style questions

1 This question falls within Syllabus section 11.3, Investment of Trust Funds. It was a complete question in the Autumn 1995 paper. The answer in the Examiner's Report is as follows.

a) This saying dates from *Re Whiteley* (1886). In *Cowan* v *Scargill* (1985), it was said that the duty of the trustees to the beneficiaries was paramount and that they should seek the best return in the light of their powers. They should ignore their own views and interests, a point also made in the recent case involving the Bishop of Oxford. In the *Nestlé* v *National Westminster Bank* case, the judge in the lower court made a wide-ranging review of these matters. Rather than speak in the traditional way of holding the scales between the different beneficiaries, he preferred to speak merely of the trustee acting fairly towards all the beneficiaries. This applies especially to life interest trusts where all trustees need to provide a fair level of income for the income beneficiaries and seek some capital growth for the longer term capital beneficiaries. Nevertheless. the trustees are not insurers and even a paid trustee cannot be expected to guarantee any level of growth. The trustee should be judged by the absence of proven default. Generally, a professional trustee is expected to provide a higher standard of care – see *Bartlett* v *Barclays Bank Trust Company* (1980).

b) Is the proposed investment authorised by the trust instrument? Is a non-income producing asset really an investment for this purpose? The investment is possibly a breach of trust as regards the income beneficiaries and also insofar as it may involve the payment of commission to the co-trustee. Proper advice would be required on the risk involved unless the co-trustee is to be regarded as sufficiently expert in this field. It would seem that 25% of the value of the trust would be too high, anyway, for a single investment and in breach of the trustees' duty to diversify their investments: Trustee Investments Act 1961.

c) No such general power exists under either the Trustee Investments Act 1961 or the Trustee Act 1925, the latter of which does, however, permit investment in certain mortgages. Section 28 of the Law of Property Act 1925 enables trustees to invest in land if they already own other land but this power ceases as soon as they cease to hold any land. Where trustees have Settled Land Act powers (e.g. when they are not vested in the life tenant) they may invest in land.

[Note: this part of this question was set before the Trusts of Land and Appointment of Trustees Act 1996.]

2　This question falls within Syllabus Sections 11.1, Maintenance and 11.2 Advancement. It was a six part question in the Autumn 1995 paper. The answer in the Examiner's Report is as follows.

a) As the gift carries the intermediate income, section 31 of the Trustee Act 1925 applies and the payment of school fees is generally considered as a proper use of such discretion, subject to enquiry as to other sources of income.

b) The surplus income is accumulated while the beneficiary is under the age of 18 and added to the capital. The trustee should consider making discretionary payments of income for the child since this may have taxation benefits for him.

c) After his 18th birthday, whether he leaves school or not, section 31 provides for the beneficiary to receive the income arising as to right. He is not, however, entitled to any past accumulations of income until the capital vests at age 25.

d) Section 32 of the Trustee Act 1925 apparently applies. Payment would be for setting him up in a career and this is a proper use of this power (the *Pilkington* case). The power should only be used in the light of circumstances relevant at the time and not now in advance.

e) In the absence of any express power to advance funds, section 32 of the Trustee Act 1925 is the only possible power, but does it apply? *IRC* v *Bernstein* (1961) indicates that direction to accumulate implied a need to keep the capital intact and thereby excluded section 32. The purchase of a partnership might otherwise have been a good reason for an advance.

3　This question falls within Syllabus section 11.3, Investment of Trust Funds. It was a complete question in the Spring 1996 paper. The answer in the Examiner's Report is as follows.

a) The Trustee Investments Act 1961 will apply. If there is a power to postpone or to retain, ordinary shares may be held in the special range. Otherwise, they must be in the wider range which initially cannot be more than one half of the value of the trust. The shares concerned must be fully paid-up shares of UK quoted companies with paid-up capital of £1 million and dividends must have been paid in each of the last five years. Proper advice by a person reasonably believed to be qualified to give such advice is required and the trustees are under a duty to diversify the investments concerned.

It should be noted that the question asked candidates to describe the powers available to invest in ordinary shares. A number of candidates took the opportunity to set out at some length the investments permitted in the narrower range, but they did not gain any marks for having done this since it was not part of the question.

(b) Investment in land is not directly authorised by the Trustee Investments Act 1961 or by the Trustee Act 1925. If land is already held, Section 28 of the Law of Property Act 1925 gives trustees the powers of a Settled Land Act life tenant to use sale proceeds to buy other land. Such a power expires when the last land is sold. If such a power is held, the trustees may only invest, an expression which presupposes some kind of return. Thus, they cannot buy for occupation by a beneficiary – *re Power*. In a settled land trust, there is no power for the trustees as such to invest in land so long as the life tenant is capable, since powers of investment are vested in the Settled Land Act life tenant. Otherwise, trustees have certain powers of investment in mortgages of land.

[N.B. The Trusts of Land and Appointment of Trustees Act 1996 will modify this answer now that this Act is in force.]

4   This question falls within Syllabus Sections 11.1, Maintenance, 11.2, Advancement and 15, Outline of Taxation Aspects of Trusts. It was a complete question in the Spring 1996 paper. The answer in the Examiner's Report is as follows.

a)   Both Sections 31 and 32 of the Trustee Act 1925 will apply. Section 31 applies to income and all of it may be used for the maintenance, education or benefit of the child at the discretion of the trustees. This includes past accumulations and the trustees must have regard to other sources of income, e.g. her parents, who are primarily responsible for her. The discretion must be reviewed from time to time. There is little point in paying school fees for a year or so only – it is best to ensure that there is likely to be enough for a longish period.

Section 32 applies to capital, of which up to one half of the child's presumptive share may be advanced for the advancement or benefit of the child and capital could be used if income is insufficient.

As for tax, the net income released may have additional rate tax vouched on it to the child. The parent may be able to recover some for the child, in which case the trustees will have to have regard to it when further payments are requested. A surprising number of candidates felt that any income released in this way for the benefit of the child would become income of the parents for tax purposes, but this would only apply if the parent were the settlor which cannot have been the case here.

If capital is released assets may have to be sold and this may bring about a capital gains tax liability at the additional rate.

b) Section 32 will apply since under Section 31 all the income is already being paid to John. The trustees must consider carefully whether it is desirable to make so much capital available at one time. They need to be satisfied of his intentions and that the money will be properly used. It may be appropriate to recommend that John take independent advice about having so much money spent in this way. Otherwise, this sort of 'setting up' in life is an ideal use of Section 32. The trustees must have regard to *Re Pauling* (1963) and ensure that the money is used for the designated purpose. In this connection, they may consider paying the supplier direct.

c) On her 18th birthday her income interest will vest, i.e. she will receive income as of right, but there will be an apportionment of income on the 18th birthday: *re Joel* 1966.

The trustees should consider making a discretionary payment of income before the 18th birthday so that they may vouch to the beneficiary some of the higher rate tax that will have been paid over the years. The benefit of this will otherwise be lost.

This subsection was the least well answered of this question.

d) The use of Section 31 is still possible, although a surprising number of candidates seemed to think that investment in investment properties would not have produced any income. However, Section 32 will become difficult if there is no cash readily available. The trustee would then need to consider a sale of one or more of the properties and this may not be easy, since he has probably rejected this course of action previously for other reasons. The trustee has certain powers to mortgage the properties but is unlikely to want to use such powers just for the purpose of making a small advance of capital.

5 This question falls within Syllabus section 11.3, Investment of Trust Funds. It was a complete question in the Spring 1995 paper. The answer in the Examiner's Report is as follows.

In the absence of any specific investment powers, the Trustee Investments Act 1961 will have to be followed. The trust fund will therefore have to be divided into two ranges and one half invested in the narrower range and one half in the wider range. The narrower range includes some National Savings products, gilt edged securities, loan stocks, mortgages and building society deposits.

The wider range covers building society shares and ordinary shares in UK companies which have £1 million of capital, have paid dividends in each of the last five years and are quoted on a recognised Stock Exchange.

Mortgages are allowed (section 8, Trustee Act 1925) but are not nowadays usually recommended. They must be on freehold or leasehold land with at least sixty years unexpired. They can be of up to two-thirds of the value as recommended by a valuer. The purchase of land is not authorised.

Advice is required from a competent person. A trust company normally has such a person. There is a need to diversify investments and to keep them under review. The trustee needs to act fairly as between different classes of beneficiaries (the *Nestlé* case).

As for the specific comments:

i) such an investment would not be authorised

ii) it might be possible to grant a mortgage but the trust has no responsibility to him and the trustees are unlikely to favour such a course of action

iii) this would almost certainly involve committing too much of the fund to one investment and would thus not be in keeping with the duty to diversify investments

iv) the nephew has no status in the trust and there is no reason at all for the trustees to consult him

v) nevertheless, the trustees must act fairly as between the beneficiaries

vi) this cannot be done directly because of the trustees' limited powers. They can go some way towards achieving this objective by choosing investments with some foreign content but which are otherwise authorised.

12

Breach of Trust

Self-assessment questions

1. If a trustee acts contrary to the terms of the trust instrument, then he or she will act in breach of trust.

    If a trustee distributes either income or capital in a way not provided for in the trust instrument, then the trustee will act in breach of trust. Trustees' statutory duties in relation to the distribution of income and capital are considered in Unit 11. A trustee is not allowed to be in a position of conflict between duties owed to himself or herself, and the duties owed to the trust. Trustees must act in good faith. In particular see Unit 10. A trustee is not allowed to make a secret profit. Trustees are allowed to delegate their duties, but must do so with care, and exercise appopriate supervision. Trustees must act as prudent people engaged in business. In particular they must exercise appropriate care in relation to making investments. These duties are considered in section 2 of Unit 12. There are various additional statutory duties, in particular under the Trustee Act 1925, The Trustee Investments Act 1961, The Pensions Act 1995, The Trusts of Land and Appointment of Trustees Act 1996. The trustees' duties in relation to these statutes are considered in Unit 11. The duties imposed by the Trusts of Land and Appointment of Trustees Act 1996 are considered in Units 2,7 and 11. Trustees' duties in relation to pension fund schemes and pension fund surpluses are considered in Units 4, 9, and 11.

2. There are a number of defences. First, the breach did not cause the loss to the trust fund. Causation questions are now relevant in this area. This is discussed in section 1 of Unit 12. Second, a trustee is able to exclude liability for breach, if appropriate wording is used. This has been confirmed by *Armitage* v *Nurse* (1997). Third, The Trustee Act 1925 section 61 grants a trustee relief from liability if the trustee is shown to have acted honestly and reasonably, and that it would be fair to grant relief from liability. Fourth, one particular defence of set-off is put forward in *Bartlett* v *Barclays Bank Trust Co Ltd* (1980). The trustees were held to be in breach of trust by making two speculative investments. One made a gain, and the other a loss. It was held that set-off was available. Fifth, there is also the defence of delay. Normally, a claim for breach of trust must be brought within 6 years of that breach. Sixth, there is a further defence of acquiescence in that breach. If the beneficiaries know, consent and acquiesce in that breach, then they will be unable to bring a claim for breach of trust. This defence was considered in Unit 10.

3. The damages that are awarded for breach of trust are broadly the same as would be awarded for breach of contract or the commission of a tort, such as negligence. This is confirmed in *Target Holdings* v *Redferns (a firm)* (1996). In particular, this means that the plaintiff, the beneficiary, is to be restored to the position he or she would have been in had the breach not occurred. The damages awarded are to be assessed at the date of trial.

4. Common law tracing is dealt with in detail in sections 7 and 8 of Unit 12.

5. Currently as the law stands, where funds are mixed then common law tracing is not available, *Agip* v *Jackson* (1991) and *Jones* v *Jones* (1996). This is dealt with in section 8 of Unit 12.

6. Equitable tracing is dealt with in detail in sections 7 and 8 of Unit 12.

7. Two important and related points should be made by way of introduction. First, the company is insolvent, and this means that a proprietary claim is necessary. Only tracing in equity gives such a proprietary right. Second, the two funds, and also the company's monies have been 'mixed' together. It is established that there is no tracing at common law in such a situation, *Agip (Africa)* v *Jackson* (1991), and *Jones* v *Jones* (1996). For these reasons, this answer will focus on equitable tracing claims.

Broadly, there are two central questions or issues in relation to an equitable tracing claim. (i) Is tracing available? (ii) How much is recoverable?

(i) Availability of tracing

If the funds have been placed into a special earmarked account, then this would create an express trust for the benefit of investors, *R* v *Clowes (No2)* (1994). This would enable a tracing claim to be brought.

Alternatively, it might be possible to argue that Harlow Clouds International plc is acting as an agent for the investors and owes them fiduciary duties, *El Ajou* v *Dollar Land Holdings plc* (1993).

That company can be considered either to have stolen the investors' funds, in which case equitable tracing is available, *Westdeutsche Landesbank Girozentrale* v *Islington London Borough Council* (1996). Alternatively, the company can be considered to have obtained those funds by deception, in which case equitable tracing is available, *A.G. for Hong Kong* v *Reid* (1994).

(ii) Amount recoverable

There is some similarity between the problem and the facts of *Barlow Clowes International* v *Vaughan* (1992). The Court of Appeal apportioned pro rata (proportionate equality) the amounts that remained with Barlow Clowes between the various investors. The time of deposit was irrelevant. Applying this principle to our facts, the City Minwell pension fund would obtain 40/60ths (2/3rds) of £10 million, and the Westshire local authority would obtain 20/60ths (1/3rd) of £10 million.

Specific issues raised in the question:

(a)   Gambling at the casino

The issue is whether the investors are able to recover the funds lost by gambling at the casino. The casino would have two defences available to it in relation to a tracing action brought in equity by the investors. First, that it is a bona fide purchaser for value without notice. This concept was dealt with in Units 1 and 8. Purchase is wider than mere buying and includes the exchange of currencies, *Polly Peck International plc v Nadir (No 2)* (1992). Since cash is exchanged for chips, this would give the casino a defence provided the casino had no notice of the fraud.

In this regard, notice includes actual or constructive notice. In relation to the gambling of Cass at the Playboy Club, in *Lipkin Gorman* v *Karpnale Ltd* (1987), the High Court was of the view that a casino did not have to make enquiries about its customers who gambled large amounts of money. Cass, who gambled a couple of hundred thousand pounds in a few months, was considered to be a relatively ordinary punter.

Second, the casino would have a defence of change of position in relation to any winnings paid out. This defence was confirmed in the House of Lords in *Lipkin Gorman (a firm)* v *Karpnale Ltd* (1991) and has been discussed in sections 7 and 8 of Unit 12.

(b)   The donation to a charitable organisation

The recipient charity is an 'innocent volunteer'. It is not a buyer, having received a gift, and cannot be a bona fide purchaser for value without notice. It has no knowledge of the fraudulent activities of Harlow Clouds International plc, and cannot be a 'knowing recipient'. This will be dealt with in Unit 16. In principle, a tracing claim in equity can be brought against an innocent volunteer.

The factual situation in the problem bears some similarity with that in *Re Diplock* (1948). In this case, one of the charities which had received monies in error from the executors and trustees who were administering the estate of Diplock, invested those monies in land. In particular, the monies were used to alter and improve certain buildings owned by the charities. Some of the monies to do this were the charity's own monies, and some were monies incorrectly transferred to the charity by the executors and trustees. The Court of Appeal in *Re Diplock* (1948) were of the view that there could be no tracing since it would be difficult to ascertain the amount of the 'charge' that would operate over this asset. The charge is the method that equity invokes in this situation.

In addition, the charity would also have a defence of change of position. In *Lipkin Gorman (a firm)* v *Karpnale Ltd* (1991) the House of Lords confirmed the requirements that were necessary for this defence to operate.

First, the charity has altered its position. If the charity spent monies (whatever their source) on improvement or alteration of its buildings which it otherwise would not have done, then that would be altering its position.

Second, the charity must have altered its position in good faith. The charity is entitled to assume that the donation to it is proper, *Re Diplock* (1948). It would seem that this requirement is satified.

The charity would be able to successfully raise this defence.

(c)   The yacht

Equity will trace into an asset or its proceeds, *Lake* v *Bayliss* (1974). Where an asset is destroyed or dissipated then no claim is available, *Re Diplock* (1948). Since there are no insurance monies, the tracing claim could not operate in this situation since there is no asset.

13

Variation of Trusts

Self-assessment questions

1. This is dealt with in Section 1 of Unit 13.

2. It enables a court to grant new powers to trustees. This is discussed in Section 3 of Unit 13.

3. This is dealt with in Section 4 of Unit 13. The variation of a trust of land is dealt with in Section 5 of Unit 13.

4. This is dealt with in Section 6 of Unit 13.

5. This is dealt with in Section 6 of Unit 13.

6. A beneficiary who has an equitable interest in a trust of land may call for that equitable interest from the trustee, provided that the trust instrument does not expressly or implicitly stop the beneficiary from doing so. (See Sections 6 and 8 of the Trusts of Land and Appointment of Trustees Act 1996.) This act is discussed in Unit 13.

Exam-style question

This question falls within Syllabus section 13 Variation of Trusts. It was a complete question in the Spring 1995 paper. The answer in the Examiner's Report is as follows.

The question involved a discussion of the principles involved in exporting trusts. A number of candidates saw the vesting age as being 30 and allowed themselves to be side-tracked into unnecessary discussions of perpetuities. In fact there are no perpetuity problems here because of the 'wait and see' rule.

The first point to consider is whether or not the export of the trust is permitted by the deed. If so, there should not be any technical problem but one needs to consider whether it is worthwhile. If the export is not permitted then it is probably permissible to appoint an offshore trustee, although the UK Courts frown on this practice since they thereby lose jurisdiction. The appointment of the offshore trustee may therefore be voidable at the instigation of the beneficiaries.

One needs to bear in mind the difference between appointing non-resident trustees of an existing trust and the setting up of a fresh trust into which the assets of the first trust are transferred, the first trust having somehow been brought to an end.

The former can usually be arranged where the new country has a similar concept of trusts. The latter is usually more difficult to achieve.

It is desirable for the beneficiaries to agree and it may be appropriate to use the Variation of Trusts Act 1958 to obtain Court approval on behalf of (a) minors and those otherwise incapable of consenting, (b) future members of a class or (c) persons unborn. Thus, the Court cannot agree on behalf of Jane but may for the two minors and any future children born before the class closes. Generally, proposals may not go ahead if all agreements are not forthcoming.

The Court must be satisfied that the proposal is for the benefit of the party concerned and in this connection one should contrast *Re Weston* with *Re Seale*. The Weston case was concerned with a re-settlement although, in the present case, the settlement may probably remain as it is.

One needs to be careful of taxation matters, in particular capital gains tax which may be charged on the exit of the trust from the UK. Thereafter, beneficiaries resident here may be liable for capital gains tax on payments received by them arising from gains made offshore. This needs careful consideration in order to see the likely effect, bearing in mind the mix of investments involved and the current and likely future gains.

An offshore company is not a UK Trust Corporation and an extra trustee may be required. The existing trustee may require an indemnity from the new trustees.

14

An Outline of the Law of Charities

Self-assessment questions

1. A charitable trust is one falling within one or more of the following categories:

   - The relief of poverty.

   - The advancement of education.

   - The advancement of religion.

   - Other purposes beneficial to the community.

2. This broadly means what it says. In addition, it must be shown for each category that it is for the 'public benefit'. The reduction of poverty is regarded by the law as a noble and beneficial thing of general benefit to the community. Even if the class of beneficiaries (who are to have their poverty reduced or alleviated) is small, it will be assumed that this will be of general benefit to the community. This category is discussed in Unit 14.

3. Again, this broadly means what it says. There may be problems if the class of beneficiaries who are to receive the education is a small one. Where the trust was to provide education to children of employees of a particular company, it was held that the trust was not a charitable trust since it lacked the necessary 'public benefit', *Oppenheim* v *Tobacco Securities Trust Co Ltd* (1951). This category is discussed in Unit 14.

4. This too broadly means what it says. If the class of beneficiaries is solely a group of nuns in a convent, the trust will not be a charitable one, since it will lack the necessary 'public benefit', *Gilmour* v *Coates* (1949). This category is discussed in Unit 14.

5. Once more, this broadly means what it says. For this category, the class of beneficiaries must be a wide one. A trust for a particular religious group in a particular area will not satisfy the 'public benefit' test, *Inland Revenue Commissioners* v *Baddeley* (1955). This category is discussed in Unit 14.

6. It is a doctrine which allows monies or property left by will for one charitable purpose which can no longer be carried out, to be applied for a modified purpose. It is discussed in Unit 14.

7. The major provisions of the Charities Act 1993 are discussed in Sections 2 and 3 of Unit 14.

Exam-style question

This question falls within Syllabus section 14 An Outline of the Law of Charities. It was a complete question in the Autumn 1995 paper. The answer in the Examiner's Report is as follows.

(a) The modern law on charities stems from Pemsel's case (1891). Much depends on the precise construction of each document. The rules are not fixed and the protection of the environment was not something that would have entered the minds of those considering these matters until recent years. Nevertheless, the protection of the environment may well come within the category of 'purposes beneficial to the community'. This usually means within the UK but can be extended where there is an indirect benefit to the UK. Rainforests contain rare animals and animal charities are usually permitted on grounds of moral benefit arising from kindness to them (*Re Wedgwood* (1915)). The word 'encourage' may cause difficulty since it does not necessarily mean that funds would have to be used exclusively and expressly for the purpose concerned. If the gift were to be considered political it might well be invalid since charities are not permitted to campaign for changes in the law as it is not clear that that is beneficial and the Attorney-General may have difficulty in enforcing such a provision. Charities are permitted to put forward reasoned recommendations but the borderlines here can be rather vague. There is a tendency to allow charitable status for well-meaning trusts unless there is good reason not to.

(b) Pemsel's case covers advancement of religion which is the purpose of a vicar and churchwardens. But is all parish work under this heading? There are two contrasting cases – *Re Simpson* (1946) concerned with vicar's work in a parish. This was held to be valid. The other case is *Farley* v *Westminster Bank* (1939) where there was a gift 'for parish work'. This was held to be too wide although there is a feeling that the case is much stricter than other charitable cases.

(c) Sport is not itself within the definition of a charity (*Re Nottage* (1895)) but it may be if it is part of a wider purpose such as education. Is snooker educational? It is probably not, but chess, for example, has been held to be (*Re Dupree*). The Recreational Charities Act 1958 now provides for the provision of recreational facilities to be charitable if they are in the interests of social welfare. Do young bank clerks need such facilities? Such provision for young clerks (as opposed to clerks generally) may be valid in view of their probable relative poverty. Both aspects need to be valid for charitable status to be assured.

15

An Outline of the Taxation Aspects of Trusts

Self-assessment questions

1 Tax avoidance is where a potential taxpayer arranges his affairs so as to minimise, or totally avoid, the effects of taxation. Such an approach is legitimate. However, where there is a circular, artificial and pre-ordained scheme to avoid taxation, then the various steps in that scheme will be disregarded.

   A particular scheme to avoid income tax, which then resulted in litigation between the Inland Revenue and a taxpayer, is considered in section 2 of Unit 15, and another scheme to avoid inheritance tax, which then resulted in litigation between the Inland Revenue and certain beneficiaries, is described in section 5 of Unit 15.

2 This is discussed in section 3 of Unit 15.

3 Vandervell had failed to describe which beneficiaries would beneifit under an option regarding shares which were previously his. As a consequence, the shares were held on an automatic resulting trust for him. Resulting trusts have been considered in Unit 3.

   Since he had an interest in those shares he was liable to income tax.

   The Vandervell litigation is considered in detail in section 3 of Unit 15.

4 This is discussed in section 4 of Unit 15.

5 This is discussed in section 5 of Unit 15.

Exam-style questions

1 This question falls within Syllabus section 15 An Outline of Taxation Aspects of Trusts. It was a complete question in the Spring 1995 paper. The answer in the Examiner's Report is as follows.

   This was the second least popular question but the average mark was the highest. Even so, some candidates wasted time and effort in attempting to describe the characteristics of the three types of trust involved, whereas the question clearly asked for a description of the taxation implications involved.

   (a) Inheritance tax is chargeable on the making of the trust at the settlor's lifetime rate. Thereafter, it is chargeable every ten years or on any exit.

Capital gains tax is charged on the deemed disposal on the making of the trust but this may be held over. Thereafter, it is chargeable at 35% both on actual disposals and on any deemed disposals, although it may be held over on the latter. As for income tax, the trustees are charged at 35% and this may be vouched to the beneficiary concerned when any payment is made and the beneficiary may be able to recover some of the tax according to his own circumstances.

(b) Inheritance tax is not chargeable on the making of a trust since this constitutes a potentially exempt transfer. Future withdrawals are free of tax although this may change if the trust changes its status at some time in the future. Capital gains tax is chargeable on the making of the settlement if chargeable assets are transferred into it. There is no hold-over. Subsequently, the trustees are charged at 35% in the lifetime of the trust or when a beneficiary becomes absolutely entitled. Again, the latter gain may be held over in some circumstances. As for income tax, this is charged at 35% and may be vouched at this rate on any payment to beneficiaries.

(c) As for inheritance tax, the making of such a trust is a potentially exempt transfer by the settlor. Any transfers out of the trust during the lifetime of the life tenant are a potentially exempt transfer by him. On his death there is a charge to tax on aggregated values. Capital gains tax may be chargeable on the making of the trust but there is no hold-over. In the lifetime of the trust, gains are chargeable at 25% but there is no charge when the life tenant dies. As for income tax, this is charged at the basic rate only and vouched as such to the life tenant.

2 This question falls within Syllabus section 15 An Outline of Taxation Aspects of Trusts. It was a two-part question in the Autumn 1995 paper. The answer in the Examiner's Report is as follows.

(i) For Inheritance Tax purposes, the advance is a potentially exempt transfer (PET) by Megan. Two years' allowances may be available as well as marriage allowance. Capital Gains Tax may be chargeable on any actual disposals made to raise the required cash. This liability will fall on Dai since, as possible ultimate remainderman, he has retained an interest in the trust. No trustee allowance is thus available and the liability will be charged at Dai's highest rate. He may pass it back to the trustees for payment.

(ii) There is no immediate tax liability but Capital Gains Tax will in future fall on the trustees and be charged at the trust rate.

(iii) Inheritance Tax is chargeable on the whole of the remaining trust and there will be aggregation with Megan's own chargeable estate. The 1989 PET will also be chargeable (in chronological order). There would not be any tapering relief as only two years have expired since the PET was made but agricultural relief at the full 100% will apparently be available. For Capital Gains Tax purposes. there will be a revaluation but no charge.

(iv) Inheritance Tax will again be chargeable on the whole of the remaining trust and there will be aggregation with the whole of Blodwyn's chargeable estate. As a similar charge had been made only three years previously there will be some quick succession relief. Agricultural relief at 50% appears to be available but there is no business property relief as the conditions are not satisfied (neither the trust not the life tenant appears to have any interest in the business being transacted on the land). For Capital Gains Tax purposes, there will again be a revaluation but no charge.

16

Miscellaneous

Self-assessment Questions

1. No. It would be a trust which was invalid due to illegality (see Unit 1). It would also be a transaction at undervalue, contrary to section 423 of the Insolvency Act 1986. The position of the creditors will be as if no trust was in existence. Transactions at undervalue and preferences are considered in Unit 3.

2   This is dealt with in part 2 of Unit 16.

3   This is dealt with in part 2 of Unit 16.

4   A constructive trust is one imposed by the court to remedy inequitable, unconscionable, improper or fraudulent conduct. The various types of constructive trust are dealt with in part 3 of Unit 16.

5   In particular, the resulting trust is based upon the financial contribution of each party, in the light of their agreement. However, the constructive trust is based upon one party seeking (improperly) to deny that agreement. In such a situation, the courts will look at the acts of detriment carried out in reliance of the agreement, by the other (innocent) party. This distinction has been dealt with in Units 3, 7, and 16.

6   This type of constructive trust has been discussed in some detail in part 3 of Unit 16. However, it is not a true constructive trust since there is no receipt of trust property. The assister is made liable to account for all the loss caused to the trust or company.

7   This type of constructive trust is discussed in some detail in part 3 of Unit 16.

8. Susan is seeking to create a half secret trust by her will. There is communication by her, and acceptance by her brother David. We are told that 'he agrees to this'. With a half secret trust, communication must be prior to, or contemporaneous with, the execution of her will, *Re Keen* (1937). This requirement is satisfied. Further, the communication prior to the will is entirely consistent with the terms of the will. The secret trust cannot be invalidated for being inconsistent with the will as happened in *Re Keen* (1937) and *Re Bateman's Will Trusts* (1970). If there was a conflict between the terms of a will and the terms of a purported secret trust, the secret trust would be invalid. This situation does not arise on our facts.

It is also clear that there is the necessary intention to create a trust. The word 'trust' was used in the conversation between Susan and David. This would strongly suggest such intention to create a trust, *Re Snowden* (1979), which was a fully secret trust. These two cases can be distinguished since Susan clearly intends to create a trust, and intends to impose a binding obligation upon her brother. She has also executed a will which is entirely consistent with such an obligation.

There is no difficulty as to subject matter since Susan has clearly identified the trust property, namely her 10,000 shares in Blue Chip plc.

The problem is whether the test for certainty of objects is satisfied, since Susan has created a discretionary trust for her relatives. It is established from *McPhail v Doulton* (1971) discussed in Unit 4, that 'relatives' is conceptually certain, and satisfies the test of certainty of objects.

This test is as follows: can it be said with certainty whether any given individual is a member of the class. We know from *McPhail v Doulton* (1971) that 'relatives' does fulfil this test.

The direction for David 'to do what is right' in relation to these shares would enable David to distribute income or capital. However, the words might be considered to have a degree of uncertainty about them. The trust could be invalidated for this reason.

There is a further difficulty in that there is no perpetuity period limiting the length of this trust. The rules relating to perpetuities and accumulations have been considered in Unit 5. If there is no perpetuity clause at all, the half secret trust would be invalidated for this reason. The whole of the will would have to be looked at to know whether there is a perpetuity clause limiting the length of this half secret trust.

List of Cases

307

List of Statutes

Index